The Friendship wi

Facets of God the Holy Spirit
Volume Two: July through December

*"Let [the one] who boasts boast about this:
that [they] understand and know Me..."*
Jeremiah 9:24

*"But when He, the Spirit of truth, comes,
He will guide you into all truth."*
John 16:13

Compiled, updated, and edited
by
Bryan L. Herde

Available on Amazon

Published September 2024

Sovereign Grip Communications
www.sovereigngrip.com

Scripture taken from the HOLY BIBLE, NEW INTERNATIONAL VERSION Copyright© 1973, 1978, 1984 International Bible Society. Used by permission of Zondervan Bible Publishers.

Scripture taken from the Holy Bible, New Living Translation, copyright © 1996, 2004, 2007, 2013 by Tyndale House Foundation. Used by permission of Tyndale House Publishers, Inc., Carol Stream, Illinois 60188. All rights reserved. (NLTSE)

Scripture quotations taken from the AMPLIFIED BIBLE, Copyright ©1954, 1958, 1962, 1964, 1965, 1987 by the Lockman Foundation. Used by permission. (www.lockman.org)

Scripture quotations are from the ESV® Bible (The Holy Bible, English Standard Version®) copyright ©2001 by Crossway Bibles, a publishing ministry of Good News Publishers. Used by permission. All rights reserved.

His Facets

VOLUME ONE

Abiding	Abolishing	Absence
Abstinence	Administration	Advent
Anger	Anointing	Appearing
Assets	Authority	Baffling
Baptism	Beauty	Benefits
Better-ness	Breath	Call
Chains	Chastising	Cloud
Comforting	Coming	Communion
Companionship	Compelling	Condescension
Condition	Conflict	Conscience
Continuity	Controlling	Convicting
Convincing	Counseling	Courage
Creating	Danger	Desires
Diminishing	Discerning	Divinity
Doctrine	Dove	Driving
Dynamite	Earnest	Elevating
Establishing	Excavating	Expediency
Expelling	Extensiveness	Faith
Fellowship	Filling	Fire
Flood-Tide	Flowing	Freshness
Fruit	Genuineness	Gifts
Giving	Glorifying	Goodness
Gospel	Grace	Grief

Growing	Guaranteeing	Guiding
Healing	Heredity	Heroism
Holiness	Hope	Ideals
Identity	Illuminating	Increasing
Indwelling	Infinity	Influence
Inspiration	Interceding	Invigorating
Joy	Keeping	Knowing
Leading	Liberty	Life
Light	Loneliness	Love

VOLUME TWO

Love	Luxury	Mastering
Message	Method	Ministry
Mission	Missions	Mothering
Motivating	Name	Nature
Necessity	Newness	Oil
Outpouring	Patience	Peace
Penalizing	Pentecost	Place
Power	Practicality	Praying
Precedence	Preparing	Presence
Prohibiting	Promise	Prosperity
Qualifying	Quenching	Quickening
Rapture	Realization	Receiving
Recognizing	Redeeming	Regenerating
Rejection	Renewing	Requiring
Rest	Restraining	Retrospection
Revealing	Revival	Rock
Sacrifice	Sanctifying	Sealing
Searching	Seat	Secret
Separating	Settling	State
Strengthening	Striving	Supplicating
Sustaining	Sweetness	Sword

iv

Symbols	Teaching	Temple
Tongues	Trusting	Truth
Unforgiving	Unifying	Victory
Vision	Vulnerability	Waiting
Walking	Wellspring	Wind
Wisdom	Withering	Witnessing
Word	Working	Worship

Facets of God the Holy Spirit
Volume Two: Love through Worship

July 1: His Love - 4
by George Matheson
Excerpted from "The Love of the Spirit", *Voices of the Spirit*, published by A. C. Armstrong & Son, New York, New York in 1892

Who also declared unto us your love in the Spirit.
Colossians 1:8

"Love in the Spirit," what is that? It is the only thing worth having in human affection. It is the love of the inner person as distinguished from the love of the outer person. There is a love which is not spiritual; it rests on the beauty of the form, and with the beauty of the form it fades away. It comes to the Son of Man when He is feeding the multitude with bread, but it leaves Him alone under the shadow of the Cross. But spiritual love is impervious to shadow. It does not come because the leaves are green, and therefore it does not go when the leaves are dry and yellow. It pays its homage to the soul as a soul — sees its royalty amid rags, detects its greatness amid ruins. It will find the Son of Man in the dark and cold of the sepulcher and anoint Him there with myrrh and aloes. It will find the Apostle to the Gentiles [Paul] in the lowness and degradation of a Roman dungeon and will recognize in him a perfect beauty though his bodily presence were weak and his speech contemptible. Well might Paul revere that form of devotion which he calls "love in the Spirit."

"Love in the Spirit," be this, O Lord, my love for You. Let me love You for what You are, not for what You give. There are times in which You give nothing. There are seasons in which we tarry in the wilderness all night and have no bread. Why do You not always multiply the loaves? It is because You long to be loved "in the Spirit," loved for Yourself alone. Let me abide with You in the desert when there is no bread. I came to You when You were loading me with benefits; let me stay with You when You have taken Your benefits away. I came to You when the multitude cried "hosannah;" let me remain with You after they have shouted "crucify." I came to You when Your way was strewn with palm leaves; let me linger with You when Your brow is wreathed with thorns. Teach me to feel that the wilderness with You is better than the garden without You, that famine by Your side outweighs plenty where You are not near. Then shall I know the peace that passes understanding—the peace which the world cannot take away. The loss of Your gifts will not break my joy when I have learned to love You—to love You in the Spirit.

July 2: His Love - 5
by A. B. Simpson
Excerpted from "The Love of the Spirit", *When the Comforter Came*, published by The Alliance Press Company, New York, New York in 1911

I implore you by the love of the Spirit.
Romans 15:30

We say much of the Father's love and the wonderful love of Jesus, but do we fully realize and appreciate the love of the Spirit?

The very fact that the Holy Spirit has left the love and joy of Heaven and made His residence for nearly two thousand years in this uncongenial world, places His sacrifice alongside that of Jesus Christ in His incarnation and redemption. Indeed the sacrifice of the third Person of the Trinity has been a far longer one than that of the Son. If we would stop to realize what Heaven is and then how different this dark and sinful world must seem in comparison with that glorious abode we will be able to form some idea of the infinite humility of the Holy Spirit. Some realization of it is possible, if we look at the lives of missionaries who have gone forth from happy Christian homes and confined themselves for a whole lifetime among the brutal and degraded people of some heathen land. Far deeper was the descent of the Holy Spirit in coming from Heaven to earth and dwelling for all these ages in continual contact with the selfishness, wickedness, and uncleanness of this polluted world.

The love of the Spirit is seen in His union with the Lord Jesus Christ during His earthly ministry and His partnership with Him in all that He felt and said and did. All the Savior's works of benevolence were equally accomplished by the Holy Ghost who rested upon Him; all His greatest words were spoken at the impulse and through the anointing of the Holy Spirit. Do we admire and adore the love of Jesus in forgiving sinners, in comforting mourners, in healing sick and suffering men and women and in taking the little children in His arms? That was also the love of the Spirit. Do we love to remember His gentle and gracious promises, those immortal words of love and grace that never can be forgotten, and that no human language can ever parallel or approach? That was all spoken through the Spirit quite as much as by the lips of the Lord.

The love of the Spirit is seen in the grace with which He seeks and saves lost sinners. In the three parables of Luke chapter 15, the Holy Spirit is represented by the woman who had lost one piece of silver and with a woman's invincible patience and perseverance swept the house and sought diligently till she found it; so the Holy Spirit seeks the lost jewels of human souls in the dust and grime of sin, sparing no pains and counting no time too long until at last He finds and restores them. There are men and women in Heaven today who met all the approaches of Divine grace for nearly a whole lifetime with hardness of heart, indifference and even scorn, and who at last were won to God through His patient love.

July 3: His Love - 6
by A. B. Simpson

How we shall adore Him some day as He takes us back over our past and at every stage reminds us again, "Yes, I have loved you with an everlasting love, therefore with lovingkindness have I drawn you."

The Holy Spirit's love is manifested in His indwelling in human hearts. His making our bodies His temples, and His infinite and ceaseless tenderness and care in our spiritual life and training. What humility for the most glorious of beings to become incarnate in humble beggar, or some illiterate convert who has just accepted Christ in the slums of one of our cities. In such lowly habitations the Heavenly Comforter condescends to dwell for a lifetime, patiently teaching, cleansing and comforting. Like a true mother the Holy Spirit is always busy with His charge. Nothing is too trifling for His interest, nothing is too hard for His love and power. Truly we may say:

> Like a web of lovingkindness,
> All our life His mercy wove,
> Every thread and fiber telling,
> Of His everlasting love.

The love of the Spirit is suggested by the language used even when we offend Him. The Scriptures do not speak of the anger, but of the grief of this gentle Friend: "Grieve not the Holy Spirit of God, whereby you are sealed unto the day of redemption." How this ought to humble us and make us ashamed of our negligence and disobedience!

The Holy Spirit loves us with a jealous love. In James 4:9 we read, "The Holy Spirit that dwells within us loves us to jealousy." The Holy Spirit is grieved when Christians set their affections upon the world and allow anything to separate them from supreme devotion to the Lord Jesus. With such a loving Friend let us also be jealous for His supreme rights and endeavor so to live that He will find in us the satisfaction and the delight which we have found in Him.

July 4: His Luxury
by George Matheson
Excerpted from "The Luxuries of the Spirit", *Voices of the Spirit*, published by A. C. Armstrong & Son, New York, New York in 1892

Restore unto me the joy of Your salvation;
and uphold me with Your free Spirit.
Psalm 51:12

When a man commits sin and is forgiven, he finds the old peace but he does not at once find the old joy, he does not at once regain the old freedom. Jacob wrestles with the angel of his own conscience and prevails, but as he returns from the battlefield he limps upon his thigh. How should it be otherwise? The Divine Spirit like every other spirit is a habit of life, and a habit is only acquired by time. If my soul casts off its old habit today, it can easily put it on again tomorrow, but it must not expect it to fit so well as it did yesterday. David has slain Uriah, and his conscience has pursued him. He has struggled for pardon, he has wrestled for peace; he has conquered, but he has come back with the shrunk sinew. He has received the forgiveness, he has obtained the blessing, he has paid the exacted penalty, but he misses the old elasticity, he wants the former joy. He is afraid to put down the foot with the vigor of other years; the breaking of the habit has broken his confidence, and so it has broken his freedom. He has returned in safety from the midnight struggle, but he wants something more than safety: "Restore to me the joy of Your salvation and uphold me by Your free Spirit."

My Father, give me back the luxuries of Your Spirit—His freedom and joy. I am not content with mere pardon; I am not satisfied with bare redemption. I am not comforted with simple salvation; I want the joy of salvation. It is not enough that I am at peace with You, it is not enough that I am reconciled to You; I must be able to be glad in You. Only in perfect joy shall I find perfect freedom. I would not like to be always in tremor lest by any word I should offend You; prayer would die on the threshold of my heart if it were not winged by fearlessness. I shall never lose my fear until I have felt myself akin to You, and I shall never feel that kinship until Your Spirit has come. I shall never meet You face to face until Your will is my will, until I have realized that between You and me there exists an equality of soul. I tremble before You because I look up to You as a master; teach me to feel that I am not a servant but a son. I ask piteously for the crumbs that fall from Your table; make me to know that I have a right to the fatted calf and the best ring and the fairest robe. I am speaking of my religious duties; inspire me with a sense of my religious privileges, of the ease that comes from living on the lap of luxury. Your grace shall become my nature when I have reached the joy of Your salvation.

July 5: His Mastering
by George Matheson
Excerpted from "The Mastership of the Spirit", *Voices of the Spirit*, published by A. C. Armstrong & Son, New York, New York in 1892

Take heed therefore unto yourselves, and to all the flock, over which the Holy Ghost has made you overseers, to feed the Church of God, which He has purchased with His own blood.
Acts 20:28

To be made an overseer by the Holy Ghost is a very different thing from being made an overseer by the world. To be made an overseer by the world is to be made a master, but to be created overseer by the Spirit is to be made a servant. One would have expected the words to be "the Holy Ghost has made you overseers, therefore take care to rule." Instead of that it is the contrary: "the Holy Ghost has made you overseers, therefore take care to feed, to nourish, to minister." Divine power is not like any other power. Every other power lifts me above my brother, but Divine power puts me beneath my brother, it is the power of stooping. God Himself has purchased His conquest "with His blood." It is because the power of His Spirit is a power of sacrifice that the presence of His Spirit in me must be manifested in sacrifice. The Son of Man proclaimed Himself a king when before the judgment seat of Pilate He put on the martyr's crown; even so, the hour when the Spirit makes me overseer must also be that hour in which I feed the needs of others.

Spirit of Christ, give me the sign that You are in me. The sign that You are in me is the possession of Your power, and Your power is sacrifice. It is the sacrificial blood of love that makes You a Providence; let the same life make me an overseer. You rule in the armies of Heaven and among the inhabitants of the earth because You open Your hand to satisfy the desires of all that live; Your empire is built on ministry. Even such would I have my empire to be. I would have it founded on the seas and established on the floods. I would have it constructed on the power to toil with those who work, to bear with those who are burdened, to weep with those who weep. Help me to realize day by day that the possession of the keys of Your kingdom is the commission to feed Your sheep. Help me to learn hour by hour that the test of loving more than others love is the stooping to feed Your lambs. The measure of my power shall be the measure of my self-forgetfulness; I shall know that You have made me an overseer when in sacrifice I have shed my blood.

July 6: His Message
by George Matheson
Excerpted from "The First Message of the Spirit", *Voices of the Spirit*, published by A. C. Armstrong & Son, New York, New York in 1892

In whom, after you believed, you were sealed with the Holy Spirit of promise.
Ephesians 1:13

The first gift of life to my soul is a promise. It is so with natural life. Its earliest consciousness is neither of today nor of yesterday, but of tomorrow. Its vision is that of streets paved with gold, of suns that never set and of days that never rain; it begins its youth where Moses began his old age—on the summit of Mount Nebo. The Spirit of Divine life also begins with Mount Nebo; its first message to the heart is a vision of the promised land. Before it asks me to take one step of the journey it presents me with the grapes of Eshcol—the specimen fruits of the glory yet to be. It shows me the end at the beginning—shows it nearer than the reality. It conceals the intervening spaces—the brakes and briars between. It takes me out like Abraham below the stars and it says to my proud spirit, "So shall your seed be," but it does not tell me that between me and the stars there intervenes that terrible hill of Moriah with its great ordeal of faith and its mighty surrender of will. It says, "Surely I come quickly," but it conceals as yet that it "comes with clouds;" it hides the sword of crucifixion during the shepherd's song; it is the Spirit of promise.

O You blessed Spirit, I thank You for this first message to my soul. I thank You that Your first voice to me has been the voice not of warning but of promise. I thank You that my earliest vision has not been the cross of Calvary but the opened Heaven and the descending dove. The journey is too long and too arduous to be encountered without good cheer. I need a drink of joy before starting; I want a stimulus of the heart to help me on. I would faint by the way if I did not get bread before leaving. Therefore, O Spirit, I bless You that first of all there has come the rapturous vision, that You have shown me the crown of glory before the crown of thorns. The brightness of Your morning shall keep me all the day. It shall keep me through the cloud and the cold; it shall keep me amid the burden and the care; it shall keep me in the labor and the strife. It shall lift me up in the depression of the valley; it shall hold me erect in the monotony of the plain; it shall make me calm on the billows of the sea. I shall walk aloft through the storm when I hear Your morning song behind me, and the yoke of toil shall be easy when I remember Your promise in the dawn.

July 7: His Method - 1
by R. A. Torrey

Excerpted from "How God Guides", *The Voice of God in the Present Hour*, published by Fleming H. Revell Company, New York, New York in 1917

Nevertheless I am continually with you: You have held my right hand. You shall guide me with Your counsel, and afterward receive me to glory.
Psalm 73:23-24

There are no promises of God's Word more precious to the man who wishes to do His will, and who realizes the goodness of His will, than the promises of His guidance. What a cheering, gladdening, inspiring thought that contained in this text is that we may have the guidance of infinite wisdom and love at every turn of life and that we have it to the end of our earthly pilgrimage.

One: God Guides By His Word. First of all God guides by His Word. We read in Psalm 119:105, "Your Word is a lamp unto my feet, and a light unto my path," and in the 130th verse of this same Psalm we read, "The entrance of Your words gives light; it gives understanding unto the simple." God's own written Word is the chief instrument that God uses in our guidance. God led the children of Israel by a pillar of cloud by day and a pillar of fire by night. The written Word, the Bible, is our pillar of cloud and fire. As it leads we follow. One of the main purposes of the Bible, the Word of God, is practical guidance in the affairs of everyday life. All other leadings must be tested by the Word. Whatever promptings may come to us from any other source, whether it is by human counsel, or by the prompting of some invisible spirit, or in whatever way it may come, we must test the promptings, or the guidance or the counsel by the sure Word of God, "To the law and to the testimony; if they do not speak according to this Word, it is because there is no light in them" (Isaiah 8:20).

Whatever spirit or impulse may move us, whatever dream or vision may come to us, or whatever apparently providential opening we may have, all must be tested by the Word of God. If the impulse or leading, or prompting, or vision, or providential opening is not according to the Book, it is not of God. "The prophet that has a dream, let him tell a dream; and he that has My Word, let him speak My Word faithfully. What is the chaff to the wheat? says the Lord" (Jeremiah 23:28). If Christians would only study the Word they would not be misled as they so often are by seducing spirits, or by impulses of any kind, that are not of God but of Satan or of their own deceitful hearts. How often people have said to me that the Spirit was leading them to do this or that, when the thing that they were being led to do was in direct contradiction to God's Word.

July 8: His Method - 2
by R. A. Torrey

A man once called upon me to consult me about marrying a woman who he said was a beautiful Christian, and that they had deep sympathy in the work of God, and the Spirit of God was leading them to marry one another. "But," I said to the man, "you already have one wife." "Yes," he replied, "but you know we have not gotten on well together." "Yes, I said, I know that, and furthermore, I have had a conversation with her and believe it is your fault more than hers. But, however that may be, if you should put her away and marry this other woman, Jesus Christ says that you would be an adulterer." "Oh, but," he replied, "the Spirit of God is leading us to one another." Now whatever spirit may have been leading that man, it certainly was not the Spirit of God, for the Spirit of God cannot lead anyone to do that which is in direct contradiction to the Word of God. I replied to this man: "You are a liar and a blasphemer. How dare you attribute to the Spirit of God action that is directly contrary to the teaching of Jesus Christ?" Many, many times Christian people have promptings from various sources which they attribute to the Holy Spirit, but which are in plain and flat contradiction to the clear and definite teachings of God's Word. The truth is, many so neglect the Word that they are all in a maze regarding the impulses and leadings that come to them, as to where they are; whereas, if they studied the Word they would at once detect the real character of these leadings.

But the Word itself must be used in a right way if we are to find the leading of God from it. We have no right to seek guidance from the Word of God by using it in any fantastic way, as some do. For example, there is no justification whatever in the Word of God for trying to find out God's will by opening the Bible at random and putting our finger on some text without regard to its real meaning as made clear by the context. There is no justification whatever in the Bible for any such use of it. The Bible is not a talisman, or a fortune-telling book, it is not in any sense a magic book; it is a revelation from an infinitely wise God, made in a reasonable way, to reasonable beings, and we obtain God's guidance from the Bible by taking the verse of Scripture in which the guidance is found, in the connection in which it is found in the Bible, and interpreting it, led by the Holy Spirit, in its context as found in the Bible. Many have fallen into all kinds of fanaticism by using their Bible in this irrational and fantastic way.

Furthermore, the fact that some text of Scripture comes into your mind at some time when you are trying to discover God's will is not by any means proof positive that it is just the Scripture for you at that time. The devil can suggest Scripture. He did this in tempting our Lord (Matthew 4:6), and he does it today.

July 9: His Method - 3
by R. A. Torrey

Two: God Leads By His Spirit. God also leads us by His Spirit, i.e., by the direct leading of the Spirit in the individual heart. Beyond a question there is such a thing as an "inner light." We read in Acts 8:29: "And the Spirit said unto Philip, 'Go near and join yourself to this chariot.'" In a similar way we read in Acts 16:6-7, of the Apostle Paul and his companions: "And they went through the region of Phrygia and the region of Galatia, having been forbidden of the Holy Spirit to speak the word in Asia; and when they were come over against Mysia they tried to go into Bithynia; and the Spirit of Jesus did not allow them." In one of these passages we see the Spirit of God by His Holy Spirit giving direct personal guidance to Philip as to what he should do, and in the other passage we see the Spirit restraining Paul and his companions from doing something they would otherwise have done. There is no reason why God should not lead us as directly as He led Philip and Paul in their day, and those who walk near God can testify that He does so lead.

I was once walking on South Clark Street, Chicago, near the corner of Adams, a very busy corner. I had passed by hundreds of people as I walked. Suddenly I met a man, a perfect stranger, and it seemed to me as if the Spirit of God said to me, "Speak to that man." I stopped a moment and stepped into a doorway and asked God to show me if the guidance was really from Him. It became instantly clear that it was. I turned around and followed the man, who had reached the corner and was crossing from one side of Clark street to the other. I caught up to him in the middle of the street. Providentially, for a moment there was no traffic at that point. Even on that busy street, we were alone in the middle of the street. I laid my hand upon his shoulder as we crossed to the further sidewalk, and said to him, "Are you a Christian?" He replied, "That is a strange thing to ask a perfect stranger on the street." I said, "I know it is, and I do not ask every man that I meet on the street that question, but I believe God told me to ask you." He stopped and hung his head. He said, "This is very strange. I am a graduate of Amherst College, but I am a perfect wreck through drink here in Chicago, and only yesterday my cousin, who is a minister in this city, was speaking to me about my soul, and for you, a perfect stranger, to put this question to me here on this busy street!" I did not succeed in bringing the man to a decision there on the street, but shortly afterward he was led to a definite acceptance of Christ.

Furthermore, let me repeat again that we should bear in mind about the Spirit's guidance, that He will not lead us to do anything that is contrary to the Word of God. The Word of God is the Holy Spirit's Book, and He never contradicts His own teaching. Many people do things that are strictly forbidden in the Word of God, and justify themselves in so doing by saying the Spirit of God guides them to do it, but any spirit that guides us to do something that is contrary to the Holy Spirit's own Book cannot by any possibility be the Holy Spirit.

July 10: His Method - 4
by R. A. Torrey

But though it is oftentimes our privilege to be thus led by the Spirit of God, there is no justification whatever in the Word of God for our refusing to act until we are thus led. Remember this is not God's only method of guidance. Oftentimes we do not need this particular kind of guidance. Take the cases of Philip and of Paul to which we have referred. God did not guide Philip and Paul in this way in every step they took. Philip had done many things in coming down through Samaria to the desert where he met the treasurer of Queen Candace, and it was not until the chariot of the treasurer appeared that God led Philip directly by His Spirit. And so with Paul, Paul in the missionary work to which God had called him had followed his own best judgment as God enlightened it until the moment came when he needed the special guidance in the direct prohibition of the Holy Spirit of his going into a place where God would not have him go at that time. There is no need for our having the Spirit's direction to do that which the Spirit has already told us to do.

For example, some time ago in reasoning with one of the leaders of the Tongues Movement about the utterly unscriptural character of their assemblies, I called his attention to the fact that in the 14th chapter of 1st

Corinthians we have God's explicit command that not more than two, or at the most three, persons should be allowed to speak "in a tongue" in any one meeting, and that the two or three that did speak must not speak at the same time, but "in turn," and if there were no interpreter present, not even one should be allowed to speak in a tongue, that (while he might speak in private with himself in a tongue, even with no interpreter present) he must "keep silence in the church." I called his attention to the fact that in their assembly they disobeyed every one of these three things that God commanded. He defended himself and his companions by saying, "But we are led by the Spirit of God to do these things, and therefore are not subject to the Word." I called his attention to the fact that Word of God in this passage was given by the Holy Spirit for the specific purpose of guiding the assembly in its conduct, and that any spirit that led them to disobey these explicit commandments of the Holy Spirit Himself, given through His Apostle Paul and recorded in His Word, could not by any possibility be the Holy Spirit.

Here again we should always bear in mind that there are other spirits beside the Holy Spirit, and we should "try the spirits whether they are of God," and we should try them by the Word. One of the gravest mistakes that anyone can make in his Christian life is that of being so anxious for spirit guidance that he is willing to open his soul to any spirit who may come along and try to lead him. Further still, we should always bear in mind that there is absolutely no justification in the Word of God for supposing that the Holy Spirit leads up in strange and absurd ways, or to do strange and absurd things.

July 11: His Method - 5
by R. A. Torrey

For example, some have certain signs by which they discern, as they say, the Holy Spirit's guidance. For example, some look for a peculiar twitching of the face, or for some other physical impulse. With some the test is a shudder, or cold sensation down the back. When this comes they take is as clear evidence that the Holy Spirit is present. In a former day, and to a certain extent today, some judge the Spirit's presence by what they call "the jerks," that is, a peculiar jerking that takes possession of a person, which they suppose to be the work of the Holy Spirit. All this is absolutely unjustified by the Word of God and dishonoring to the Holy Spirit. We are told distinctly and emphatically in 2 Timothy 1:7 that the Holy Spirit is a Spirit "of power, and of love, and of a sound mind." The word translated "sound mind" really means sound sense, and, therefore, any spirit that leads us to do ridiculous things, cannot be the Holy Spirit. There are some who defend the most outrageous improprieties and even indecencies in public assemblies, saying that the Holy Spirit prompts them to these things. By this claim they fly directly in the face of God's own Word, which teaches us specifically in 1 Corinthians 14:32-33, that "The spirits of the prophets are subject to the prophets; for God is not a God of confusion, but of peace." And in the 40th verse we are told that "all things" in a Spirit-governed assembly should be done decently and in order. The word translated "decently" in this passage means a becoming (or respectable) way, and this certainly does not permit the disorders and immodesties, and confusions and indecencies and absurdities that occur in many assemblies that claim to be Spirit led, but which, tested by the Word of God, certainly are not led by the Holy Spirit.

Three: God Guides Us By Enlightening Our Judgment. In the third place God guides us by enlightening our judgment. We see an illustration of this in the case of the Apostle Paul in Acts 16:10. God had been guiding Paul by a direct impression produced in his heart by the Holy Spirit, keeping him from going to certain places where he would otherwise have gone. Then God gives to Paul in the night a vision, and, having received the vision, Paul, by his own enlightened judgment, concludes from it what God has called him to do. This is God's ordinary method of guidance. When His Word does not specifically tell us what to go to God for, we make sure that our wills are completely surrendered to Him, and that we realize our dependence upon Him for guidance, then God clears up our judgment and makes it clear to us what we should do. God's guidance is clear guidance, and we should not act until things are made perfectly plain. Many miss God's guidance by doing things too soon. Had they waited until God had enabled them to see clearly, under the illumination of His Holy Spirit, they would have avoided disastrous mistakes. The principle that "he who believes shall not make haste" (Isaiah 28:16) applies right here. On the other hand, when any duty is made clear we should do it at once.

July 12: His Method - 6
by R. A. Torrey

Four: God May Guide By Visions and Dreams. In Acts 16:9-10, we are told how God guided Paul by a vision, and there are other instances of such guidance not only before Pentecost, but after. God may so guide people today. However, that was not God's usual method of guiding men even in Bible times, and it is even less His usual way since the giving of the Word of God and the giving of the Holy Spirit. We do not need that mode of guidance as the Old Testament saints did, for we now have the complete Word and we also have the Spirit in a sense and in a fullness that the Old Testament saints did not. God does lead by dreams today. When I was a boy, sleeping in a room in our old home in Geneva, New York, I dreamed I was sleeping in that room and that my mother, who I dreamed was dead (though she was really living at the time) came and stood by my bed, with a face like an angel, and begged me to enter the ministry, and in my sleep I promised her that I would. In a few moments I awoke and found it all a dream, but I never could get away from that promise. I never had rest in my soul until I did give up my plans for life and promise God that I would preach. But the matter of dreams is one in which we should exercise the utmost care, and we should be very careful and prayerful and Scriptural in deciding that any dream is from Him. Only the other day a brilliant and highly educated woman called at my office to tell me some wonderful dreams that she had and what these dreams proved. Her interpretation of the dreams was most extraordinary and fantastic. But while dreams are a very uncertain method of guidance, it will not do for us to say that God never so guides, but it is the height of folly to seek God's guidance in that way, and especially to dictate that God shall guide in that way.

Five: God Does Not Guide By Casting Lots in This Dispensation. In Acts 1:24-26 we learn that the Apostles sought guidance in a choice of one to take the place of Judas, by the lot. This method of finding God's will was common in the Old Testament times, but it belongs entirely to the old dispensation. This is the last case on record. It was never used after Pentecost. We need today no such crude way of ascertaining the will of God, as we have the Word and the Spirit at our disposal. Neither should we seek signs. That belongs to the imperfect dispensation that is past, and even then it was a sign of unbelief.

Six: God Guides By His Providence. God has still another way of guiding us beside those already mentioned, and that is by His providences. He so shapes the events of our lives that it becomes clear that He would have us go in a certain direction or do a certain thing. For example, God puts an unsaved man directly in our way so that we are alone with him and thus have an opportunity for conversation with him. In such a case we need no vision to tell us, and we need no mighty impulse of the Holy Spirit to tell us, that we ought to speak to this man about his soul.

July 13: His Method - 7
by R. A. Torrey

We must, however, be very careful and very prayerful in interpreting "the leadings of providence." What some people call "the leading of providence" means no more than the easiest way. When Jonah was fleeing from God and went down to Joppa he found a ship just ready to start for Tarshish (Jonah 1:3). If he had been like many today he would have interpreted that as meaning it was God's will that he should go to Tarshish, as there was a ship just starting for Tarshish, instead of to Nineveh, to which city God had commanded him to go. In point of fact, Jonah did take the ship to Tarshish but he was under no illusion in the matter, he knew perfectly well that he was not going where God wanted him to go, and he got into trouble for it. Oftentimes people seek guidance by providence by asking God to shut up a certain way that is opening to them, if it is not His will that they should go that way. There is no justification whatever for doing that. God has given us our judgment and is ready to illuminate our judgment, and we have no right to act the part of children and to ask Him to shut up the way so we cannot possibly go that way if it is not His will. Some fancy that the easy way is necessarily God's way, but oftentimes the hard way is God's way. Our Lord Himself said, as recorded in Matthew 16:24, "If any man would come after Me, let him deny himself, and take up his cross and follow Me." That certainly is not the easy way. There are many who advise us to "follow the path of least resistance," but the path of least resistance is not always God's way by any means.

The main point in the whole matter of guidance is the absolute surrender of the will to God, the delighting in His will, and the being willing to do joyfully the very things we would not like to do naturally, the very things in connection with which there may be many disagreeable circumstances, because, for example, of association with, or even subordination to, those that we do not altogether like, or difficulties of other kinds, doing them joyfully, simply because it is the will of God, and the willingness to let God lead in any way He pleases, whether it is by His Word, or His Spirit, or by the enlightening of our judgment, or by His providence, or whatever way He will. If we will only completely distrust our own judgment and have absolute confidence in God's judgment and God's willingness to guide us, and are absolutely surrendered to His will, whatever it may be, and are willing to let God choose His way of guidance, and will go on step by step as He does guide us, and if we are daily studying His Word to know His will, and are listening for the still small voice of the Spirit, going step by step as He leads, He will guide us with His eye; He will guide us with His counsel to the end of our earthly pilgrimage, and afterwards receive us into glory.

July 14: His Ministry - 1
by Henry Robert Reynolds
Excerpted from "The Ministration of the Spirit", *Light and Peace Sermons and Addresses*, published by E. P. Dutton & Co., New York, New York in 1892

How shall the ministry of the Spirit not be rather glorious?
2 Corinthians 3:8

In order to understand the ministration of the Spirit, contrast the Spirit with that which is most often brought into comparison with it, namely, the body. We cannot understand what is meant by body, without answering the previous inquiry: What is spirit? Nor can we reply to this question without setting in our minds something about the body which it inhabits. If we see several things, or parts of things, united to each other by some secret bond, and serving some general purpose, we are accustomed to speak of them as a body, and of that secret intention or purpose as their uniting spirit. In the same way a crowd of persons in the street, an assembly of individuals embodying a common idea or intention, are constantly spoken of as bodies of men, and their common object is the spirit which activates them. This doubtlessly arises from our consciousness that we are ourselves compounds of many parts, organs, members, and passions, over the strange assemblage of which a presiding spirit rules. We have a body; we are spirits. The body is dependent on the spirit, not the spirit on the body; the body may perish while the spirit lives, the body may be still alive when the spirit is virtually dead.

Now, associations of men, when governed by strong principle, in view of great objects and ruled by those whose spirit is capable of being infused into all those around them, are such bodies; and even the bodies of these fellowships have a great work to do, for without their aid, however strong the spirit might be, it would evaporate and be lost to the world. Paul very frequently speaks of the Christian Church under this image. He says that it is the "body of Christ," and that it is inhabited by the Spirit of Christ. "There is," he says, "one body and one Spirit, even as you are called in one hope of your calling. "As the body is one and has many members, even so are you one body in Christ, and every one members one of another." The body of Christ has a great work to do. It has to hold as it were in sacred keeping the invisible Spirit of Jesus; it has to exhibit in its countenance His feelings, and in its conduct His will. It has to seek its food and support amid the circumstances and according to the laws of human life. It has, like every other "body" to take up and turn as it were into its own wonderful substance the proper kind of sustenance that is adapted to nourish it; it has to bring the knowledge, the science, the business, the politics, the poetry, and the reality of life under the same Divine influence, to submit it to the power of the same Spirit; and in fact all these functions of man as well as all classes of men are baptized into one body. Truly the body of so Divine a Spirit must be the most glorious association and the most powerful existence in the world.

July 15: His Ministry - 2
by Henry Robert Reynolds

Under the Old Testament dispensation a similar but inferior body grew up from childhood to maturity in the Holy Land; and the revelation of God made through it consisted to a great degree in the rules that were assigned to this body. The religion of Moses and Samuel and Ezra might with reverence and truthfulness be termed a ministry of the body. It consisted of innumerable regulations for the external management of the individual, the community, the priest, the king, the temple, and the State. Implicit obedience to these laws was grand and glorious until the prejudices of Israel led them to suppose that the body was of more consequence than the spirit, and the form more precious than the power. It must have been an awful and sublime spectacle to have witnessed the first revelation of the Divine law and the accompanying manifestation of the Divine presence. It was a grand education in the best days of the Hebrew theocracy to trace the government of the Heavenly King in His earthly kingdom; to witness the splendor of the ceremonial when the Lord in very deed dwelt with man upon the earth; when the temple in which He shone forth upon the eyes and hearts of men was fashioned after His own design; and when the body was fed by His own loving hand, clothed and adorned by His own absolute wisdom and unbounded resources. But just as this ministry to a body was glorious, the ministry of the Spirit exceeds it in glory; and directly that the body considers itself to be the chief end of existence, whether it is the body of a man, of an institution, or of a church, the spirit is impaired and hastens to its end. The man who sinks into such a condition becomes a morbid hypochondriac, a slave of his poor body; the institution thus perverted becomes obstructive to the end that called it into existence; and the churchy Hebrew or Christian, which in gorgeous ceremonial, antique rite, or prescriptive usage substitutes a care for the body in place of all the weightier matters of law and gospel, is unquestionably quenching the Spirit of God. When the Spirit works upon us as individuals, it transfigures our whole nature, and supplies us with abundant principles for every action; and while it convinces us of sin, of righteousness, and of judgment to come, it puts the Divine law in our inward parts, and will make us love holiness, do justly, and walk humbly with our God. It will eat out the evil desires of the flesh by filling us with holy passions. We shall then never be satisfied with the most careful attention to the most venerable rule or use, but shall be moved to live a Divine life.

In the childhood of the Divine life it is very important to strengthen the spirit by the nutrition and education of the body; and there are many things that minister to the process. But the ministry of the Spirit, direct communion with the living God—with the Fountain of all life, truth, wisdom, and purity—excels the dispensations of childhood, the prescriptions given to the infancy of our race. By forgetfulness of this, many a soul, many an institution, many a church has sunk into lethargy, ceremonialism, and formality.

July 16: His Ministry - 3
by Henry Robert Reynolds

Contrast the Spirit with the letter. The simplest illustration of this antithesis may be found in the nature of language. Take any word you please. Write it down. Look at it. Of what does it consist? Of a few strokes only, which in themselves are utterly meaningless. Pronounce the word. What is it? A sound or collection of sounds which have no meaning in themselves. All that you know, after you have looked or listened long, is that you and others agree to represent certain ideas and feelings by that word; but there is no necessary connection between the word and the meaning, for the same word may convey ideas and suggest thoughts that are altogether dissimilar to different people or nations. Illustrations of this are unnecessary, even though some may be unwilling to grant it, so soon as the word or letter has been used to represent for them some of the most precious or noble ideas. Thus, though the letter and the word have great value, they are transitory, accidental, liable to change; but the thing itself suggested, or the spirit conveyed by the letter, may have an undying worth, and be a permanent, eternal truth.

We speak of the letter and the spirit of a law or of a testament. The one may be observed, while the other is violated. It is quite possible to break the spirit and fulfill the letter of the law of our country, or to respect the spirit and reject the letter of it. It is very easy to fall in with the injunctions of a dying man, rigidly to obey the letter of his instructions, and to violate their spirit and set at nothing all his wishes.

Often has the letter of the Divine law been scrupulously kept, while its spirit has been irreverently trifled with; and very often the spirit of that law has been established, while the letter has been discarded and set at nothing. Thus a Divine Spirit penetrated and illumined the restrictions and rules of the Old Testament dispensation; the spirit of that covenant of God with man has been ministered afresh in the gospel of Jesus Christ, but the letter in which that spirit has been conveyed by Moses and by Christ has widely differed. At one time the nation and government of Israel were the form in which God's love for mankind and His providence over His whole Church were made known to the world; but now the holy nation, the distinct people, are not enclosed by the mountains around Jerusalem, are not fed with honey from the rock, nor cheered with the milk and wine of earthly prosperity; but they are found wherever hearts beat high with loyal childlike love for the Father and Ruler of the universe, and wherever the Son of God has been revealed to living faith. They are found in the general assembly and Church of the First-born. The spirit has been preserved, the letter has been changed.

July 17: His Ministry - 4
by Henry Robert Reynolds

Many are striving to bind down even the spirit of the gospel by prescribing rules for holy living, by special modes of expressing the Divine life, by logical inferences drawn from the revealing Word, by the experience which has been sanctified in the Church, by words and phrases of our holy gospel itself. It is nonetheless true here, also, that though the ministration of the letter is glorious, the ministration of the Spirit is rather more glorious.

Another contrast, and one which is still more frequently unfolded in the New Testament, is that between the Spirit and the flesh. This contrast, upon which the Apostle Paul enlarges at great length in the Epistle to the Romans and elsewhere, involves a far more profound view of human character and destiny.

It is clear that by "the flesh," Paul does not mean the mere physical system as opposed to the soul or to the spirit, but he refers to the fleshly nature of man. By the flesh he means the whole of our nature when left to itself, or, as he elsewhere expresses it, "the natural man." He means man such as he is when untouched by higher influences; man, when he is following the desires and is walking in the imaginations of his own heart. He means that which is born of the flesh and is flesh; the carnal mind, which is enmity against God and is not subject to the law of God. Paul and the other writers of the New Testament mean by "the flesh" the mere functions, tendencies, and impulses of the human being, in un-renewed and unregenerate humanity, not such as God had made it, but such as sin has left it. We know that the society of heathendom in Paul's day was so bad, and the light of truth and the working of the Holy Spirit were so new and so much restrained, that it was necessary that he should dip his pencil in the darkest shades to give a true outline of the corrupt state of man. But even in the present day the higher faculties of man reveal some of his worst characteristics; and poetry, science, philosophy, business, pleasure, when left to develop themselves without a Divine and controlling principle, reveal the lamentable anarchy of our nature and the miserable bondage of our will. It is with this flesh, this un-regenerated humanity, that Paul contrasts the ministration of the Spirit to the life of the spiritual man.

By the "Spirit" as opposed to the "flesh," Paul means the dwelling in us of the living Christ, the overpowering and overawing of both the lower and the more cultivated passions of the soul by Christlike and Heavenly longings. He means that expunging and renunciation of ungodliness and worldly lust, that strengthening of our inner man, that being rooted "and grounded in love," by which we both comprehend and "know that which passes knowledge." Paul by this phrase aims at nothing less than the completion of man after the completeness of Christ, the quickening of our whole spiritual being, and an alliance with God Himself.

July 18: His Ministry - 5
by W. K. Pendleton

Excerpted from "The Ministry of the Holy Spirit", *The Living Pulpit of the Christian Church*, published by R. W. Carroll & Co., Cincinnati, Ohio in 1869

"Nevertheless, I tell you the truth; it is expedient for you that I go away: for if I do not go away, the Comforter will not come unto you; but if I depart, I will send Him unto you. And when He is come, He will reprove the world of sin, and of righteousness, and of judgment: of sin, because they do not believe on Me; of righteousness, because I go to My Father, and you see Me no more; of judgment, because the prince of this world is judged."
John 16:7-11

When the Savior said to His apostles, "It is expedient for you that I go away," it must have been to them a declaration hard to understand. His presence had been so necessary to their confidence, and so full of comfort and of power, that they could not regard a separation with less than the gloomiest forebodings. They had hung upon His words with the fond and newly-awakened hopes of eternal life; they had forsaken all to follow Him; and now, to be left alone, what could it seem but the saddest and darkest disappointment? When "many of His disciples went back, and walked no more with Him," and He had asked them, with such poignant tenderness, "Will you also go away?" Peter, the prompt and impulsive Peter, had answered, "Lord, to whom shall we go? You have the words of eternal life." There was no light, no strength, no hope to them but in Christ, and how could it be expedient for them that He should go away? It was a saying hard to be understood, requiring, in fact, a fuller revelation of the Divine economy of redemption than He had yet made known to them.

Until that time, the central power of this economy had been in His sensible person, Martha, weeping over the death of Lazarus, says, "Lord, if You have been here, my brother had not died." Before Jairus' daughter is raised, Jesus goes to the house of her parents, stands over the bed, takes her by the hand, and says, "Daughter, arise."

The power of Christ to help was centered in His visible, tangible Person, and that was limited to time and place. True, in sending out the seventy, and healing the centurion's servant, we have instances of power exerted where He was not personally present. But even in these cases there was direct connection with His person by someone before the influence was imparted. Evidently these tangible limitations were not suited to the omnipresent needs of a spiritual kingdom. An omnipresent agent is needed for a universal kingdom. A spirit-presence must take the place of a tangible-presence. The heart must be filled where the eye cannot see; and Jesus must go away, so that the Paraclete, the Advocate and Comforter, may come.

July 19: His Ministry - 6
by W. K. Pendleton

Let us consider the difference. Suppose Jesus is today at Jerusalem, and seated on the throne of David, in the person He wore when He stood, eighteen centuries ago, arraigned as a criminal before the bar of Pilate. Around the throne there might be the radiance of glory, and in His presence fullness of joy. But what would He be to us, in this far distant land of the West? Between Him and our hearts an ocean-barrier rolls; the radiance of His countenance does not beam upon us, and His words come to us through the telegraph, chilled by the distance and void of the vital breath of the King. We cannot see Him, or hear Him. Like Moses, wrapped in the misty shroud of Mount Sinai, He is hidden from our view. What would be left us but, like the children of Israel, to turn to our own devices, and cry, "Up, make us gods which shall go before us." Peter returns to his nets, and the rest go with him.

On the other hand, enthrone Jesus in Heaven, invest Him with all power, and fill the earth with the presence of the Spirit—the Paraclete—the official Advocate and comforting Minister of His reign. Here is a power wide as the domain of His truth, breathing with ever-present influence through words of eternal life; working with the same energy that brooded over the primitive chaos, and molding into order, and form, and beauty, and conscious blessedness, the new spirit-world, a glorious regeneration of the wreck of the old.

Doubtlessly, the apostles felt disconsolate when the Savior said, "I go away;" but when, on the day of Pentecost, the Spirit came, and they were baptized in His power, and began to speak with tongues, and felt the mighty energy of truth burning for utterance, and saw its two-edged sharpness piercing the hearts of their enemies, they could say, "We are not left comfortless; the blessed Jesus has indeed gone away; but, being by the right hand of God exalted, and having received of the Father the promise of the Holy Spirit, He has shed forth this which you now see and hear." Truly did He say, "It is expedient for you that I go away," because, as He promised, He has sent the Comforter.

Thus, in one passage, the Savior very formally announces His purpose to devolve the advocacy of His cause upon the Holy Spirit, to replace His personal presence by the ministration of the Paraclete, and declares it to be expedient for His disciples that He should do so. There is to be a new administration of affairs, and a new ministry.

The Minister. He is called the Paraclete. The term, in its fullness, means a comforting helper. It is a name by which the Savior calls the Holy Spirit (John 14:26). In our passage He is presented to us as the successor of Christ in the administration of the economy of redemption. He proceeds from the Father, and is sent by the Son (John 15:26). He is, therefore, a distinct manifestation of God. That the Holy Spirit is a distinct, personal manifestation of God is evident.

July 20: His Ministry - 7
by W. K. Pendleton

He is called "the Paraclete," and "the Holy Spirit;" and the latter designation is expressly given as His name: "Baptizing them into the name of the Father, and of the Son, and of the Holy Spirit" (Matthew 28:19). The expression is literal, and the distinctness of the Three marked by a definiteness that could not be more sharply indicated by language. Our baptism brings us equally into relation to the Three as Persons, and presents the Three to us, at the same time, as also One in nature.

From the fact that both intelligence and determining will are ascribed to Him. "He is a Spirit of wisdom, of understanding, of counsel, and knowledge" (Isaiah 11:2). "He searches all things, even the deep things of God" (1 Corinthians 2:10). He is the Author of spiritual gifts; and the Apostle Paul declares that, in distributing these, "He distributes to every person as He wills" (1 Corinthians 12:11). These are not isolated passages, but the general drift of revelation, concerning the Holy Spirit, is to the same effect.

Not only does He have intelligence and free choice, but also accompanying power. He descends on the day of Pentecost, as a mighty rushing wind; He imparts the power of working miracles to the apostles, just as Christ had done; He raises up Christ from the dead; He strikes the hypocrites Ananias and Sapphira with death in the instant of their falsehood; and many other marvelous works are ascribed to Him, which present Him constantly before us, in the boldest and most striking aspects of personal grandeur and power.

Our passage speaks of Him as a Person, as one that can come, that may be sent, that can glorify the Son, and guide the disciples into all, or the whole truth. "He shall take of Mine," says the Savior, "and show it unto you" (John 16:15). Can an Agent like this be a mere influence? Can language like this be applicable to merely impersonal means, having no distinct energy of their own, and moving simply as they are moved by some other power? Surely words are meaningless, and all reality must be banished from the Scriptures, if these expressions are simply metaphors, shadows of shades, misty utterances about unknown phantoms, that vanish from our view when we attempt to fix them in thought, or give them, in our faith, "a local habitation and a name."

Paul says, "You are the temple of the living God; as God has said, 'I will dwell in them, and walk among them.'" This He accomplishes in the Person of the Holy Spirit. "Do you not know, that you are the temple of God, and that the Spirit of God dwells in you? For you are the temple of God." While, then, the Holy Spirit is personally distinct, He is, in nature, God; so that, when He fills the temple of the human heart, it is truly God who dwells in it.

July 21: His Ministry - 8
by W. K. Pendleton

Thus is this Minister of the new reign set before us; by His official and His essential name; by His omniscient intelligence and self-determining will; by His omnipotent power; by His glorious and official procession from the Father and the Son, and by His representative dignity as the personal manifestation of God in the new and spiritual kingdom. By all these, and many other tokens, He comes to us, our Comforter, Helper, Friend. He introduces Himself wondrously to us in the magnificent and overpowering scenes of Pentecost, and opens up the new empire over the hearts of men, with a grand exhibition of His power to perform the work for which He is sent.

To whom is He sent. This question need not detain us long; but it is important, in approaching it, to notice the different economies or dispensations of the Father, the Son, and the Holy Spirit. Before the fall, man enjoyed the full manifestation of God. The unveiled Majesty stood before him in the garden. He walked with God, as a son with a father.

His heart is open to God in all pure worship. He moves, a peer among the cherubim, and mingles his praises with theirs. The will of God thrills through his nature as his vital breath. He trembles with fullness of joy. "God is all in all" — omnipotent, immutable, immortal, infinite, eternal King." This is the dispensation of the Father. Man is without sin, and God is manifested only as life, light, and love.

The entrance of sin breaks this harmony. Man is banished from the garden of Eden. The dispensation of love gives place to the dispensation of law. Remedial grace holds the world in quarantine. God operates far off through His Son. He does not utterly abandon us, but out of the thick darkness He speaks in tones of thunder, and, at long intervals, by the "angel of the presence." He appears to Abraham, and speaks with Moses in the Mount of Sinai, adding the law, till He should come in full accomplishment of the promise (Galatians 3:19). Yet when, in the fullness of time, He is manifested in the flesh, His operation is transient, and mostly limited to His personal presence. Even His apostles do not comprehend Him. He speaks in parables, and holds the truth under a veil. Until sin is atoned for, and His work of redemption done, there can be no closer or more intimate relation to the sinner. God and man must be reconciled before the lost fellowship of Eden can be restored. This is His work, and it leads Him by the gate of death. He must glorify humanity in His own Person before He can sanctify it with His Holy Spirit. This is the remedial dispensation — the dispensation of the Son. Not until "it is finished" could the Holy Spirit be given. True the Spirit, as of the Divine essence, appears in every dispensation as an inseparable, cooperating Divine Agent. The glorification of the Son opens up a new era — the dispensation or economy of the Holy Spirit — a manifestation of the Spirit fuller and more permanent and intimate than had ever been enjoyed before.

July 22: His Mission - 1
by George Bowen
Excerpted from "On the Mission of the Spirit: Note F", taken from
The Spirit of Christ, written by Andrew Murray, published by
A. D. F. Randolph & Co., New York, New York in 1888

[Murray] Such is the title of a book from which I give some extracts, in which the thought is put with great clearness and force that many Christians are living on an pre-Pentecostal level, and that the promise of Christ to reveal His Power to the world by His presence among His people, made obvious through the Spirit, is still waiting for its fulfilment in our experience.

[Bowen] "I will love him and will manifest Myself to him" (John 14:21).

If we wish, therefore, to sound the depths of this promise, "I will manifest Myself to him," we must honor Christ and the Father and the Spirit by believing in the power of the Spirit. To have faith in Christ and not to have faith in the Spirit seems to be a great contradiction, yet we submit it for the judgment of candid inquirers if this contradiction is not strikingly exhibited in the case of almost all who profess to be followers of Christ. To know the Father we must know the Son; to know Christ we must know the Spirit. "He shall glorify Me," said Christ. Do you believe this? Is this your conception of Christ's glory, that it is a glory that the Spirit of God can enable you to behold?

When the omnipotent Spirit has been allowed by our faith to go to the full extent of His resources in the revelation of Christ, it will be time enough for us to turn away from Him to some more perfect way of bringing Christ near to us.

Now all these views of the glory of the present dispensation seem to vanish into night when we subject them to a comparison with the actual experiences of Christians in general. But we do them foul injustice in this way. We are rather to submit the experiences Christians to the test of Scripture. When we do so, does it not appear that the Church has fallen back into an ante-Pentecostal state? That it has slipped out of its own dispensation? There was a measure, a feeble measure, of spiritual influence enjoyed by the disciples before the death and resurrection of Christ, else they would not have been able to call Jesus Lord; but it was nothing in comparison with what they were before Pentecost. But it should be borne in mind that when truths have once been fully revealed and been made a part of orthodoxy, the holding of them does not necessarily imply an operation of the Spirit of God. We deceive ourselves, doubtlessly, in this way, imagining that, because we have the whole Scripture and are conversant with all its great truths, the Spirit of God is necessarily working in us. We need a baptism of the Spirit as much as the apostles did at the time of Christ's resurrection; we need that the unsearchable riches of Christ should be revealed to us more abundantly than they were to Isaiah in the temple.

July 23: His Mission - 2
by George Bowen

We profess to love Him. We profess, therefore—the inference is unavoidable—to desire to enjoy higher and more satisfactory manifestations of Him than have been yet permitted unto us. It follows, then, that we ought to feel very greatly the pressure of the obligation to seek the outpouring of the Holy Spirit. Blessed be God! the Holy Spirit is being poured out in many churches, and many Christians are at this very hour enjoying such views of Christ as fill them with a supernatural joy and love and strength. But we have not yet entered into the fulness of this glorious dispensation. If we love Christ, we will press deeper into it, believing that Omnipotence will find ways of revealing Himself in the spiritual world of which we have as yet no conception.

"Nevertheless I tell you the truth: it is expedient for you that I go away: for if I do not go away, the Comforter will not come unto you; but if I depart, I will send Him unto you" (John 16:7).

"And when He is come, He shall reprove the world of sin, and of righteousness, and of judgment" (John 16:8).

"When He." "He" in the original is emphatic. It might be rendered "that One." He it is who, coming, will convince mankind of sin. His very advent will revolutionize their ideas of sin, being a testimony from Heaven more striking than that of the voice from Heaven at the baptism of Jesus, to the fact that Jesus the crucified is none other than Christ the glorified. By the simple fact that the world has placed itself in opposition to Jesus, testimony for Jesus will be testimony against the world. Observe that the promise of the Spirit was unto the disciples: "I will send Him unto" and the change here intimated as to be accomplished in the sentiments of men generally was to be in consequence of the descent of the Spirit of God upon the disciples. The gospel is preached to convince people of sin, of righteousness, and of judgment. The disciples of Christ are in the world that they may make known the sin of humankind, the judgment of God, and the means of escaping that judgment by means of the righteousness of Christ. But here we are told that the work of introducing the new convictions on these subjects into the minds of men is to be accomplished by the Spirit of God. Accordingly the apostles speak of themselves as having preached the gospel with the Holy Ghost sent down from Heaven.

What is here promised, then, is such an outpouring of the Spirit of God as shall not only reveal itself in the consciousness of the disciples, but substantiate itself as an undeniable and wonderful fact to the understanding of the onlooking world. And such was the advent of the Spirit on the day of Pentecost.

July 24: His Mission - 3
by George Bowen

The Greek is wonderfully suitable in that it does not represent the Spirit of God as coming once for all, but as persistently coming. He it is who, coming, shall convince. He comes as the rain from heaven, that must still come and come again; as the wind, that must still blow and blow again. We are not to look back for our Pentecost. The Pentecost of the Acts is simply given to make the Church of Christ acquainted with the privileges belonging to this dispensation. It is only the first step in a ladder of Pentecosts by which the world and the kingdom of Christ are to be brought together. It is the specimen to accompany the promise, that we may be stirred up to plead the promise with the greatest fervency.

Oh, it were unpardonable if, in a day when God is doing so much to inspire us with lofty conceptions of the power of the Holy Spirit, we should still refuse to capture the glorious unlimited meaning of this promise. Consider it: We are to look at the work here assigned to the Holy Spirit, in order that we may obtain a just view of His power. Look abroad upon the earth, and see the nations, tribes, and tongues refusing to be convinced by all that God in His Providence has taught them during thousands of years; by all that missionaries are teaching them, at this eleventh hour, of sin, of righteousness, of judgment; form an estimate of the wickedness which envelopes the earth like a dense and deadly atmosphere, scarce allowing any of the rays of the Sun of Righteousness to penetrate it; then consider that the Spirit of God, for whose outpouring we are taught to pray, is pledged to rain conviction upon the world, and anticipate for a most wonderful and blessed end the final judgment by leading men to look to the righteousness of Christ, the Desire of all nations.

"These things I have spoken unto you in proverbs, but the time is coming when I shall no more speak unto you in proverbs, but I shall show you plainly of the Father" (John 16:25). When figures are made use of in speech, there is an outside meaning and an interior meaning. As the shell conceals and yet protects the kernel, so a truth conveyed topically may be unperceived at first. Afterward, when additional light is given, it becomes apparent, and the saying ceases to be a riddle. The gospel is full of parables that could very little be understood until Christ had suffered and entered into His glory. When the Spirit of God was poured out upon His disciples, the veil which had been over the words of Jesus disappeared, and the interior truths flashed forth upon them in all their luster. Christ Himself was such a proverb. Once His Divine glory had flashed forth upon their astonished gaze, and that was by way of anticipation, it very little dissipated the confusion of their minds. Nothing about Christ could produce its legitimate and full effect upon them until they had been brought out of the restricted and depressed valley of Judaism, and placed upon the elevated platform of the New Dispensation.

July 25: His Mission - 4
by George Bowen

The Spirit of God inundates the minds of men with truths which previously had no meaning to them. Now it appears to us that an observation of no little importance may here be made. Truths which the Holy Ghost has taught us may be retained in the mind by the mere natural power of memory. Are we not thus in danger of deceiving ourselves as to the measure of spiritual power enjoyed by us? We might have as scanty a measure of the Spirit's influence as the disciples had in the days preceding the death of Christ, and yet be immensely in advance of them in respect to the amount of our knowledge of the way of life. Is it not to be feared that in those portions of the Church which have not yet been visited by a true revival, Christians are to be compared with the first disciples, not as they were on the day of Pentecost, but as they were previously—compared, we mean, as regards the actual Divine influence enjoyed by them? Because they have the truth, they imagine they have the Spirit of truth. Perhaps the word of Christ to them is, "Tarry in Jerusalem until endued with power from on high." We are baffled, bewildered, confounded by our utter inability to convince men of sin, of righteousness, and of the judgment to come. Is it not that we fail to realize how absolute is our need of the mighty and evident advent of the Spirit? It is possible for Christ so to cause the Holy Spirit to be seen descending upon us that the world around shall discover, by this fact alone, the heavens opened and the Son of God standing at the right hand of God. Many in these days occupy no worthier position than that first inferior one of the apostles. The apostles were not absolutely without the influence of the Spirit during the time that Jesus dwelt among them, but these influences did little more than make the present darkness visible, and show them in the dim distance the light of the future. Without knowing it, there are thousands of Christians who have that feeble and vague measure of influence which belongs to a different dispensation from this, and shows them to be two thousand years behind their privileges.

We have said it, and without shame we say it again. They have of course knowledge such as the pre-Pentecostal Church did not have. It is the consciousness of this superior knowledge that tends to keep them ignorant of their spiritual destitution. Their position is appalling, for they are familiar with the inspiring promises, and have no faculty to catch a glimpse of the glorious things offered in these promises. They actually suppose that these promises have no more exalted interpretation than that which their own emotionless and inglorious experience affords. Blessed be God! we are not limited to one Pentecost under this dispensation. Let us only become aware of the abnormal state in which we are, and take knowledge of the lofty experiences to which God is inviting us. Pentecost was not so much a mountain summit as a mountain high path or plateau, along which the Church should have traveled to the New Jerusalem. Let us look steadfastly up above, and see among the clouds this highway of holiness, and prove the power of the Savior to bring us to it.

July 26: His Missions - 1
by Adoniram Judson (A. J.) Gordon

Excerpted from "The Holy Spirit's Present Help in Missions", *The Holy Spirit in Missions*, published by Fleming H. Revell Company, New York, New York in 1893

As imperatively as you will need the Holy Spirit *in* the work, not less imperatively do you need Him to equip you *for* the work. What we call sacred learning constantly tends to become secular, because of the absence of daily dependence upon the illuminating and sanctifying Spirit. I do not know that the study of Hebrew or of theology is any more Divine in itself than the study of mathematics. I go further and affirm what the history of the Church is constantly proving, that the pursuit of these studies without a humble and prayerful dependence on God may be absolutely injurious to one's Christian life.

Professor Johann T. Beck [German theologian, 1804-1878] of Tubingen uttered a bold but true remark when he said to his class one day: "Gentlemen, remember that without the illumination of the Spirit, theology is not only a cold stone, it is a deadly poison." You can verify this saying by asking and answering the question: From where comes the most subtle and dangerous form of unbelief which we are encountering at the present time? Does it not come from the theological chairs in Germany, in Holland, and elsewhere, which have been founded to instruct young men in the principles of our Divine religion?

The Holy Scriptures, literally inspired and doctrinally infallible — these are the foundations on which the Protestant Church has been taught to rest for her faith, for her life, for her hope. And who is it that is doing most to unsettle those foundations today? Not the illiterate layperson of our churches, whose misfortune is that they have never studied Hebrew or mastered theology; nor the brilliant and cultured opponents of Christianity — the skeptics and agnostics and theists; but the ones whose office is to teach Hebrew and theology, and to instruct our young people in the doctrines and principles of the gospel of Christ. And these are leading astray, I believe, principally because they suppose that the Bible can be understood by microscopic interpretation and by philosophical analysis, when the Book itself repeatedly declares the contrary. "For what man knows the things of a man, except the spirit of man which is in him?" asks the Apostle Paul; "even so the things of God knows no man, but the Spirit of God" [1 Corinthians 2:11]. There is a finer sense than the scientific; there is a more delicate touch than the interpretive. It is written, and cannot be altered: "The natural man receives not the things of the Spirit of God, for they are foolishness unto him; neither can he know them, because they are spiritually discerned" [1 Corinthians 2:14].

The Bible is burglar-proof against all unsanctified learning. It repeatedly suffers violence at the hands of scholars, and the violent seek to take it by force. But the Holy Spirit alone holds the key to it. He alone knows the combination of faith and study by which it can be unlocked and all its hidden treasures of wisdom and knowledge appropriated.

July 27: His Missions - 2
by Adoniram Judson (A. J.) Gordon

It was a very notable utterance that a French preacher expressed when he exclaimed, "My brethren, we have unlearned the Holy Spirit." Not to know is one thing; to not know that which we have once learned is quite another thing. If through a growing pride of culture we gradually outgrow that childlike trust in the guidance and illumination of the Spirit which we once enjoyed, what is our learning but a deplorable unlearning? To modify a famous phrase of Augustine, I would affirm that "the sufficiency of our learning is to discover that our learning is insufficient." The great teacher is now the Holy Ghost. He has come to take His place in the Church. Our glorified Lord entrusted us with His teaching, saying, "He that has an ear let him hear what the Spirit says unto the churches" [Revelation 2:17]. You are bound to give the highest respect to your theological instructors; but it is also your most solemn duty to have the Holy Spirit as your private Tutor—in your prayer closet, in your classroom, and ultimately in your ministry, to have Him for your personal Instructor; for He offers Himself to be that for you.

We talk much of the baptism of the Spirit, the anointing of the Spirit, and the infusing of the Spirit, meaning thereby something above and beyond what we received in conversion. I cannot emphasize too strongly the importance of this transaction. And yet I want to avoid perplexing you by causing you to strive after some stereotyped experience of the Spirit's anointing. I remember that it was a great discovery in my own study of redemption when I learned that justification comes not so much through Christ's doing some new thing for us, as by our realizing and taking hold, through faith, that which He has already done. So does the Holy Spirit. The promise of His coming and indwelling in the Church has been fulfilled: "If I go away, I will send you another Comforter" [John 16:7], Advocate, Helper, Teacher. If we consciously and believingly surrender to the Holy Spirit, and accept Him implicitly in all these roles, this is the infusing of power. Attach the train to the locomotive and immediately all the power and speed which belongs to the engine is linked to the cars; and so the energy of the Holy Ghost is ours in proportion as we surrender to Him and attach ourselves to Him.

An eminent teacher of theology, Principal [Handley] Moule of Cambridge, England, in his admirable work on the Holy Spirit, describes his own experience this way: "Never shall I forget the gain to conscious faith and peace which came to my own soul, not long after a first decisive and taking hold of the crucified Lord as the sinner's sacrifice of peace, from a more intelligent and conscious hold upon the living and most gracious personality of that Holy Spirit through whose mercy the soul had gotten that blessed view. It was a new development of insight into the love of God. It was a new contact, as it were, with the inner and eternal movements of redeeming goodness and power, a new discovery in Divine resources."

July 28: His Missions - 3
by Adoniram Judson (A. J.) Gordon

This "new discovery of Divine resources" is what I would instruct you to seek. "The promise of the Father" of which Jesus spoke has been fulfilled. The Holy Ghost has been given. And now the question which I would urge upon you is that which Paul put to certain Ephesian Christians: "Have you received the Holy Ghost since you believed?" [Acts 19:2]. Have you solemnly and definitely surrendered to His guidance? Have you consciously taken hold of Him as your supreme dependence for strength and service? If you have, you have discovered the secret of power, and that power will become more and more real to you every day you live. How imperatively do you need this infusing of the Spirit to equip you for your work as missionaries of the cross!

More than a hundred years ago a young missionary lay dying at thirty-eight years of age. David Brainerd, who passed away from earth at the house of Jonathan Edwards in Northampton, on October 9, 1747, was one of the holiest men and one of the most remarkable missionaries who has appeared in any age of the Church. One of his last recorded prayers was "for the influences of the Divine Spirit to descend on ministers in a special manner." His dying counsel to his brother, whom he desired to succeed him, was "to strive to obtain much of the grace of God's

Spirit in the heart," significantly adding, "When ministers feel the special gracious influences of the Holy Spirit in their hearts, it wonderfully assists them to come at the consciences of people, and, as it were, to handle them; whereas without these, whatever reason or oratory we may employ, we do but make use of stumps instead of hands." I know of nothing more nearly resembling Pentecost than the scenes which followed David Brainerd's preaching at Crossweeksung, New Jersey. Even he himself looked on with astonishment and awe at the power of the gospel on the hearts of the Indians [Native Americans]. But the secret is clear when we look from the field to the prayer closet and see him praying whole days for the anointing of the Holy Ghost to come upon him; and praying with such intensity that his garments were wet with the sweat of his intercession. What an example for us to set constantly before us! And now that he had been heard, he could grasp the hearts of these unresponsive Indians, not with the "stumps" of reason and logic, but with the invisible and irresistible fingers of the Holy Spirit. What an incalculable difference it makes when either we preach the gospel in the energy of the flesh or in the might of the Spirit!

Peter, who had witnessed the marvelous scenes of Pentecost, had only this single explanation of the results, when afterwards referring to them: "We have preached the gospel unto you with the Holy Ghost sent down from Heaven" [1 Peter 1:12]. It costs much to obtain the power of the Spirit: It costs self-surrender and being humbled and the yielding up of our most precious things to God; it costs the perseverance of long waiting, and the faith of strong trust.

July 29: His Missions - 4
by Adoniram Judson (A. J.) Gordon

When we are really in that power we shall find this difference: That whereas before it was hard for us to do the easiest things, now it is easy for us to do the hardest things.

James Hervey, the friend of [John] Wesley at Oxford, describes the change which took place in him through his anointing by the Spirit: That while his preaching was once like the firing of an arrow, all the speed and force thereof depending on the strength of his arm in bending the bow, now it was like the firing of a rifle-ball, the whole force depending on the powder, and needing only a finger-touch to set it off. O Holy Spirit, come upon us in Your fullness, and teach us this secret of the irresistible might of weakness—of doing great things for God through the energy of that Spirit by whom God does great things for us!

The missionary especially needs the indwelling of the Spirit to enable them to reproduce the life of Christ in the middle of the heathen. "Be not conformed to this world, but be transformed by the renewing of your minds" [Romans 12:2], is the great word of Paul. And this must be accomplished by inward transformation, and not by outward imitation. It is only the Spirit of the Lord within us that can reproduce the image of God set before us. This image, literally manifested, is the most powerful of all sermons for impressing the heathen.

An intelligent and respected Hindu, Surendra Nath Banerjya, in addressing a company of students not long ago in Calcutta, said: "What India needs for her regeneration is not simply sermons and speeches and Bible texts, but the presentation of a truly Christian life, the gentleness and meekness and forgiveness such as your Christ exhibited in His life and death." Undoubtedly this is true, and of the signs and wonders and gifts of the Holy Ghost which God has promised to accompany the preaching of His Word among the heathen, none is greater than this. I do not refer simply to an exhibition of the agreeable virtues of Jesus Christ, but to a literal conformity to His life of poverty and suffering and self-denial for the good of others.

The impression made by Christian Frederick Schwartz [German missionary, 1726-1798] upon the people of India is to this day spoken of by missionary historians with a kind of suppressed astonishment. Among the lower classes his influence was apostolic [like the influence of the Apostles]; with the upper classes it was almost imperial. Yet he did not win people from a palace. On the contrary, he lived in a single room just large enough to hold himself and his bed, existing on rice and vegetables cooked in native fashion, his entire support costing less than two hundred and fifty dollars annually. By this humbling to people of low status, he won people of all ranks as few others have ever done in the history of the Church.

July 30: His Missions - 5
by Adoniram Judson (A. J.) Gordon

A remarkable life lived in our own time — that of George Bowen [American missionary, 1816-1888] of Bombay — provides perhaps the nearest likeness to that of Schwartz. He repeated the Savior's self-denial without falling into the monk's austerity, so that Dr. William Hanna [1808-1882] of Scotland speaks of him as "one who exhibited a degree of self-sacrificing devotion to which there is perhaps no existing parallel in the whole field of missionary labor." The influence which he exerted and the reverence which he inspired were equal to his devotion. It will take many years to obliterate from India the memory of either.

Such also was William C. Burns [Scottish missionary, 1815-1868] of China. He traveled, like his Master, from city to city, accepting such hospitalities as the people might offer, content with the pilgrim's portion, the plainest food and clothing, and enduring for Christ's sake with the utmost meekness every indignity laid upon him. We are not surprised to find his biographer declaring that the impression of his words on the people of China was insignificant in comparison with that of his Christ-like life. So it always is. The person is greater than the sermon. Translators are always needed on heathen fields; but the greatest among them is the one who can translate the example of Jesus Christ into the dialect of daily life, into the universal speech of pain and poverty and suffering for the sake of others.

Anskar, a missionary to the Scandinavians in the ninth century, when asked by his heathen listeners whether he could perform miracles, replied with noble wisdom: "If God were indeed to grant that power to me, I would only ask that I might exhibit the miracle of a holy life." The evidential character of such a miracle is perhaps even greater than those formed on external nature; for it touches the heart by its brotherly appeal instead of staggering the intellect by its supernatural mystery. Surely it is a prayer worthy of being offered daily, that the Holy Spirit will work in us and exhibit through us the miracle of a Christ-like life.

We should make very practical for the actual, daily experience of missionary life all that we are saying concerning the power and blessing of the Holy Spirit. Why not rely upon this Divine Executor of missions with a hundred times more confidence than we extend to any person or to any group of people? Once at least are we implored by "the love of the Spirit" in the exhortations of Scripture. It is a comforting and uplifting expression. Our Almighty Helper has such affection towards those who are striving to fulfill their Lord's commission that He will be most ready in His assistance when they need Him most in their weakness.

July 31: His Missions - 6
by Adoniram Judson (A. J.) Gordon

The following glimpse into the inner life of a missionary church is more instructive and cheering than any formal exhortations which we can make about the importance of repeatedly seeking the filling of the Spirit. It is from a report by Dr. Griffith John [Welsh missionary, 1831-1912] of Hankow, China. He says:

> Feeling my lack of spiritual power, I spent the whole of Saturday in an earnest prayer for a baptism of the Holy Ghost. On the following morning I preached on the subject. At the close of the service I proposed that we should meet for an hour every day of the following week to pray for a baptism of the Holy Ghost. From fifty to seventy of the converts met day by day, and confessing their sins pleaded with tears for an outpouring of the Spirit of God. The native Church at Hankow received an impulse the force of which continues to this day. The Holy Ghost became a mighty reality to many. Where once other things were preached, Christ and His power became a living reality.

The Church is not merely a voluntary association of believers. It is the body of the Holy Ghost, the "habitation of God through the Spirit." Why, then, when it is faint or declining, should our immediate impulse not be to seek a renewal of the Spirit's indwelling life? Shall the exhausted missionaries in the tropics move to higher altitudes for the reinvigorating atmosphere, and not with far more eagerness seek to enter into the freer air of the Spirit, when their inward strength has become weakened? No, why not strive to make our communion with the Spirit so habitual that we shall never become exhausted? This is but the same exhortation in another form with which the Scripture presents us: "If we live in the Spirit, let us walk in the Spirit" [Galatians 5:25]. The Divine provision and intention is for His perpetual indwelling. "In the old dispensation, the Spirit worked upon believers, but He did not in His person dwell in believers. Engaged to the soul, the Spirit went often to see His betrothed, but was not yet one with her; the marriage was not consummated until Pentecost, after the glorification of Jesus Christ. Then was Christ's word fulfilled: He shall be in you…"[G. Tophel].

It is the indwelling of the Holy Spirit, given to Christ's servants for sustaining them in their labors and discouragements. The Holy Ghost is omnipresence [everywhere] in the great body of Christ; and omniscient [all-knowing] in His oversight of the vast work of that body in evangelizing the world. It is because the individual disciple can take in so little of the complete arrangement that he is so exposed to discouragement. The thwarting of well-planned missionary endeavors; the removal from the field of devoted laborers, and the death of others before their work has been fairly begun—these are circumstances which often perplex and confuse the thoughtful missionary.

August 1: His Missions - 7
by Adoniram Judson (A. J.) Gordon

Has He who commands His servants to go into all the world and preach the gospel to every creature no oversight of His work, no protection over His workers, that going in implicit obedience to His Word they are still without a guarantee of Divine preservation and support? Who knows the inner, unwritten, tearful book of questionings on this theme which has been written in many a missionary's heart! But the great brooding, over-watching Spirit abides in the Church to solve all these difficulties and to silence all these doubts. He alone sees the relationship of present loss to future gain; of suffering for Christ now to the glory that shall follow; and the final overbalance of present light afflictions by the "far more exceeding and eternal weight of glory" [2 Corinthians 4:17]. And knowing all, He alone can strengthen us to labor "in the kingdom and patience of Jesus Christ" [Revelation 1:9].

Of how many modern heroes of the gospel may it be said, as of the ancient ones, "These all died in the faith, not having received the promises, but having seen them afar off, and were persuaded by them, and embraced them" [Hebrews 11:13].

Allen Gardiner [British missionary, 1794-1851], upon his third heroic but futile attempt to plant the gospel in Tierra del Fuego [Argentina], dies of slow starvation; yet he writes as his last testimony: "I neither hunger nor thirst, though five days without food. Marvelous lovingkindness to me, a sinner!"

The young and accomplished Bishop John Coleridge Patteson [English missionary, 1827-1871], cruising among the New Hebrides and telling from island to island the story of Jesus, comes at last to Nukapu, where he tells to the natives on the shore the story of the martyrdom of Stephen; when, without warning, he is suddenly slain, and, like his Master, sent back with five ghastly wounds upon his person, inflicted by the hands of those to whom he had gone preaching peace. And yet they that looked upon his dead face declared that it seemed "as it had been the face of an angel."

That gifted young missionary martyr, Bishop James Hannington [English missionary, 1847-1885], dying at Uganda amid every degradation and cruelty which African savagery could inflict, is yet filled with such love and faith for his enemies that he said to his executioners: "Go tell [Chief] Mwanga that I die for Baganda, and that I have purchased the road to Uganda with my life." Such was his word to his enemies; and to his friends his farewell message was: "If this is the last chapter of my earthly history, then the next will be the first page of the Heavenly—no blots, no blemishes, no incoherence, but sweet conversation in the presence of the Lamb."

August 2: His Missions - 8
by Adoniram Judson (A. J.) Gordon

How long is the list of such untimely deaths on the missionary field! And how rich and moving the dying confessions gathered from there. "Though a thousand fall, let not Africa be forgotten!" is the last plea of the young and ardent Melville Cox [American missionary to Liberia, 1799-1833], falling on the field of the Dark Continent almost as soon as he had put his hand to the plow. And the lovely, sweet-faced boy, as he seems to us as we gaze upon his picture—Adam McAll—stricken down with fatal disease before his work on the Congo was barely begun, and yet breathing out as his dying prayer: "Lord, You know that I consecrated my life to preaching the gospel in Africa. If You do take me now instead of the work which I intended to give You, what is that to me? Your will be done."

And what shall we say of such untimely removals of the most devoted and useful servants from their work? We can say nothing; but the Holy Ghost witnesses: "Yes, says the Spirit, for they rest from their labors, and their works do follow them" [Revelation 13:14]. As sure as the ordinances of Heaven this is true. Adalbert [of Prague, 956-997], a missionary to the Wends of Prussia in the tenth century, went out singing to meet the infuriated savages, and crying in pleading tones: "For your salvation I am come, that forsaking your mute idols you may believe in the one true God, and believing in His name you may have eternal life." But like those noble bishops whom we have just mentioned, his message of love was met by the weapons of murder. Pierced by the lances of the pagans, he stretched forth both his hands, and saying, "Jesus, receive Thou me," he fell, with his face to the ground, in the form of a crucifix, thereby, as [Thomas] Carlyle [Scottish philosopher, 1795-1881] says, "signing that heathen country with the sign of the cross." The martyr's mortgage then placed upon the land has long since been redeemed, and the nation has become Christian. So it ever has been, so it ever will be, when time enough has elapsed for God to fulfill His far-reaching purposes. And it is the work of the Holy Ghost to inspire the long patience and the confident hope which grasps and rejoices in this completion.

The last word of the Spirit on the last page of Scripture is one with which we may fittingly close this lecture: "And the Spirit and the Bride say, Come" [Revelation 22:17]. Some commentators explain this as an advent-call rather than a gospel-call; as a response to the Lord's, "Surely I come quickly" [Revelation 22:20], which has just been heard, rather than a part of the evangelical invitation, "Whoever will, let him take" [Revelation 22:17]. If this is so, what a lovely ideal is presented here of the watchful and faithful missionary Church! With eyes turned heavenward, the Bride is ever calling to the Bridegroom, "Even so, come, Lord Jesus" [Revelation 22:20], the Holy Spirit, the Friend of the Bridegroom, inspiring and sustaining this cry throughout the ages.

August 3: His Mothering
by A. B. Simpson
Excerpted from "The Motherhood of God", *When the Comforter Came*, published by The Alliance Press Company, New York, New York in 1911

"As one whom his mother comforts so will I comfort you and you shall be comforted in Jerusalem."
Isaiah 66:13

The tendency of the human heart to look for something in God answering to womanly tenderness and maternal love is illustrated by the strong hold which Mariolatry or the worship of the Virgin has always had upon the Roman Catholic mind. The ignorant and superstitious feel that in a woman's sympathy they can look for something which not even the love of Jesus Himself fully satisfies. They do not understand that the heart of Christ is not only the heart of a man but has in it also all the tenderness and gentleness of woman. Jesus was not a man in the rigid sense of manhood as distinct from womanhood, but, as the Son of Man, the complete Head of humanity, He combined in Himself the nature both of man and woman even as the first man Adam had the woman within his own being before she was separately formed from his very body.

Back even in the Old Testament we find God revealing Himself under the sweet figure of motherhood. "As one whom his mother comforts so will I comfort you." And this aspect of His blessed character finds its perfect manifestation in the Holy Ghost, our Mother God. So that we have in the Divine Trinity not only a Father, and a Brother and a Husband, but also One who meets all the heart's longing for motherhood. The beautiful figure which the Lord Jesus used in John 14:18, "I will not leave you orphans," covers this suggestion of motherhood. The Comforter as our spiritual Mother is the author of our being and gives us our new and Heavenly birth. We are born of the Holy Spirit, our very life comes to us through the quickening life of the Holy Ghost.

As our Heavenly Mother, the Comforter assumes our nurture, training, teaching, and the whole direction of our life. All this is in accordance with the Master's words in the fourteenth chapter of John, in explaining the mission of the Spirit: "He shall guide you into all truth," "He shall teach you all things and bring all things to your remembrance," "I have many things to say unto you but you cannot bear them now, howbeit, when He, the Spirit of truth is come, He will guide you into all truth." The special feature of the Spirit's teaching and guiding is its considerate gentleness and patience. He does not force upon us truths for which we are not yet prepared but leads us tenderly and teaches us, as He Himself has expressed it in the Old Testament, "line upon line, precept upon precept, here a little and there a little" [Isaiah 28:10].

And so the Holy Spirit loves us with such enduring love that He would rather cause us pain than let us miss our way.

August 4: His Motivating
by George Matheson
Excerpted from "The Motive of the Spirit", *Voices of the Spirit*,
published by A. C. Armstrong & Son, New York, New York in 1892

Walk in the Spirit, and you shall not fulfill the lust of the flesh.
Galatians 5:16

It is of no use to attempt the weaning from one joy except through another joy. The lusts of the flesh are pleasures; it is a shame that we need to say so, but it is true. How then shall we be cured of these pleasures? Paul says that we can only be cured of them on the principle of homoeopathy — by creating a like desire in the higher parts of our nature. The lust of the flesh can be counteracted only by a longing of the spirit. How different are God's methods from mine; I am always seeking to heal badness by restrictions; I would keep my brother from evil by tying his hands. I forget that mere prohibition makes the heart beat quicker; the tree is never so dear to me as when a voice says "You shall not eat." It is a fearful thing when the unclean spirit has gone out and the clean spirit has not yet come in; my house then is left unto me desolate. Who shall remove the desolation? Who shall lift me out of these dry places where I wander and where I protest against my bereavement? Nothing can do it but a new love — no pains, no chains, no threats, no prisons; my restraint will be just the place of my torment from which I shall cry for water to cool my tongue. If I would forget the past, father Abraham, or some other ministering spirit must bring me a drink of a purer water, whereof they that taste shall never thirst again. If I would quench the lusts of the flesh I must walk in the Spirit.

Spirit of love, You can set me free; You can quench the thirst of my lower soul. I cannot keep my heart from evil by merely ceasing to think; if the door of thought is unguarded the unclean spirit will return. I want something to fill the vacancy; I want You. My eye has long been gazing on impurity and it will not be cured by being sent into darkness; lift upon it the light of Your countenance and it shall be safe. My ear has long been listening to discord, and it will not be healed by being draped in silence; let it hear Your voice upon the waters and it shall have melody evermore. My hand has been long raised in wrath against my brother, and it will not be redeemed by being put in chains; let it be compelled to bear Your cross and it will hurt no living thing. Come, You Fire of Heaven, and extinguish the fire of Hell. Your love can burn up all contrary loves. You are the only fire by which the bush of life is not consumed. The lust of the flesh weakens me, wearies me. But Your burning makes me stronger day by day. It consumes my care but it preserves me. It destroys my selfishness but it magnifies myself. Like the three men in the fiery furnace, I feel that a fourth power is added to me when, O Spirit, I walk in You.

August 5: His Name - 1
by David James Burrell

Excerpted from "The Holy Ghost", *The Wonderful Teacher and What He Taught*, published by Fleming H. Revell Company, New York, New York in 1902

Jesus was a revolutionist. His purpose was not to stir up a temporary furor, as agitators had frequently done before His day; nor was it even to produce a lasting impression in favor of certain new and improved forms of thinking and living, as reformers ever want to do. He came to establish a kingdom, and there must be a tearing down before there could be a building up. The kingdom of righteousness could only be established on the ruins of the kingdom of evil. The world must be turned upside down, in order to be right side up.

All history is to be interpreted in the light of this purpose. The progress of events thus far may be divided into three dispensations. The first was the dispensation of the Father, beginning with "The seed of the woman shall bruise the serpent's head" [Genesis 3:15]. It was an economy of law and ordinances, of dreams and prophecies, of angel's visits and theophanies; through all of which "the one eternal purpose" ran. It closed with the quenching of the lights of the sanctuary, the voice of Malachi crying in the gathering gloom, "The Sun of Righteousness shall arise with healing in His wings!"

The second dispensation was that of the Son. It began with the angel's song, "Glory to God in the highest" [Luke 2:14] and continued for a brief period of thirty years. Thirty wonderful years of Immanuel! Their story is written in the simple monograph, "He went about doing good." This dispensation also closed in darkness; the darkness which enshrouded the cross, out of which issued the cry, "It is finished!"

The third dispensation, in which we are now living, is that of the Holy Ghost. It began on the day of Pentecost and will continue until "the restitution of all things" in the setting up of the Messianic throne.

It must not be supposed, however, that these dispensations are exclusive. The oneness of the Godhead is such that whichever Person may be the official Head of affairs, the others are truly present. Thus, while the Father was Administrator or Executive of the Old Economy, the Son and the Holy Ghost are also referred to as cooperating. In the dispensation of the Son, likewise, the presence and participation of the Father and the Spirit are plainly noted. Jesus was on such terms of intimacy with the Father that He was said to be "in His bosom" (John 1:18). He was officially set apart by the Spirit to His priestly work (Luke 4:18; Acts 10:38) and endued by Him without measure (John 3:34); insomuch that He was thus directed (Luke 4:14), invigorated (Matthew 12:28) and controlled (Luke 4:1). In like manner under the present dispensation of the Spirit, the other Persons of the Godhead are with us. We pray to the Father and He hears us. And the promise of Jesus is fulfilled: "Lo, I am with you always."

August 6: His Name - 2
by David James Burrell

It thus appears that the three Persons of the Godhead are sympathetically and cooperatively concerned in the progress of the kingdom; a fact illustrated at the baptism of Jesus, where, as He stands in the water, the Father speaks from Heaven, "This is My beloved Son" and the Holy Ghost descends like a dove upon Him (Matthew 3:16-17).

But at the close of the ministry of Jesus, He, with the concurrence of the Father, formally delivered up the executive office to the Holy Ghost (John 14:16; also 16:7). Wherefore, while the Son is said to have been "sent by the Father," the Holy Spirit is said to "proceed from the Father and the Son."

The official title of the Holy Spirit, in this executive capacity is The Paraclete. The term does not allow adequate translation. It means literally one who is called to stand by, or one who answers an appeal. Comforter (*con-fors*) had a like meaning at the time when the King James Version [KJV] was made, but is now used in a much more restricted sense. The Paraclete or Comforter is an Advocate, a Counselor, a Champion, a Knight-errant hastening to the cry of the oppressed; in brief, a universal Helper. He is to preside over the affairs of the Kingdom until it shall extend from the river unto the ends of the earth. He stands by God's people in all emergencies (Mark 13:11), arguing down opposition (Luke 21:15), silencing objections, making an end of persecution, advancing the royal standards till rival thrones and dynasties shall totter to their fall and Christ shall come to be King over all and blessed forever.

The official work of the Spirit was indicated by Christ as follows: "And when He is come, He will reprove (convict) the world of sin, of righteousness and of judgment: of sin, because they believe not on Me; of righteousness, because I go unto My Father, and you shall see Me no more; of judgment, because the prince of this world is judged" (John 16:8-11). He is to convict the world of sin by showing its exceeding sinfulness. We see sin's most flagrant manifestations, such as theft, perjury and adultery, and are repelled by them. But the essence of sin, namely its antagonism toward God, is of little or no consequence to the average man. This is made to appear in its true light in the rejection of Christ, as He said, "because they believe not on Me." The Spirit convicts the world in respect of righteousness, also by making known its true character. Here again the natural comprehension is perverted. We see the outward forms of morality and are attracted by them. In fact, however, all such righteousness are as filthy rags. The only true righteousness is that which is by faith in Jesus Christ; the fine linen, clean and white, with which He shall clothe His people on the Great Day. And this also the Spirit alone reveals to us.

August 7: His Name - 3
by David James Burrell

The Holy Ghost is called the Spirit of Life. At the creation He is said to have "moved upon the face of the waters," bringing life out of death, order and organization out of chaos (Genesis 1:2). The life communicated to man in the beginning was from Him as the Breath or Spirit of God (Genesis 2:7).

And this is true particularly in the spiritual province. In the Lord's conversation with Nicodemus He ascribed the work of regeneration to the Spirit. Here is the great miracle which is being accomplished every day. The wonder will never cease. "The wind blows where it wills; and you hear the sound thereof, but cannot tell from where it comes and where it goes; so is every one that is born of the Spirit" (John 3:8). Our Lord came into the world to give life, and to give it more abundantly; and this life is communicated by the Spirit to the children of men. It is by the power of the Holy Spirit that we are brought into such vital union with Jesus as to be mystically one with Him (parable of the Vine, John 15). One who is born again is born of the Spirit; and whoever is born of the Spirit can say, "I no longer live, but Christ lives in me"; and "My life is hidden with Christ in God."

He is also the Spirit of Truth (John 14:17). It is through Him that the revelation of truth is made to us; by inspiration on the one hand and interpretation on the other. It must be remembered that Jesus, in His teaching, expressly disavowed any purpose of completing the canon of revealed truth; He only "began to teach" (Acts 1:1). He expressly said that there were some things which His disciples were as yet not able to bear (John 16:12-14); but, breathing upon His apostles the influence of the Spirit, He qualified them to complete the outline, to elaborate and codify the sum total of revealed truth.

We have no means of knowing the method of inspiration, only so far as this: "Holy men of God spoke as they were moved by the Holy Ghost" (2 Peter 1:21). It is evident that this gift of inspiration must have been wholly different from what we call "genius;" the latter, as the word indicates, being something born within a man, while the former, as the word also indicates, is something from without breathed in. The writers of Scripture, under the control of the Spirit, are "moved," that is, borne onward, or directed as to what they should write; and are furthermore restrained so that what they write is truth vouched for by the Spirit of God.

It is not enough, however, that the truth shall be impressed upon the written or printed page; it must be made clear to men. There is a double veil, over the Word and over the heart, to be removed (2 Corinthians 3:12-16). It is the function of the Holy Spirit to anoint the eyes with eye salve that men may see, for spiritual things can only be discerned by the Spirit of God (1 Corinthians 2:13).

August 8: His Name - 4
by David James Burrell

The Comforter is called the Holy Spirit, or the Spirit of Holiness. This is not because He is holier than the other Persons of the Godhead, but because it is His official function to make men holy. This is done negatively in justification; and positively in sanctification.

It is the part of the Holy Ghost to apply the redemption purchased by Christ (John 16:14). We are inclined by Him to accept Christ as our Redeemer, and declared by Him to be purged of sin. Our faith is the hyssop branch by which the atoning blood is sprinkled on our hearts, and His is the hand that wields it.

Then begins our sanctification, or growth in holiness. There is nothing magical nor mysterious about this. The process is indicated by our Lord in His priestly prayer, "Sanctify them by Your truth, Your Word is truth" (John 17:17). The Scriptures are the means used by the Spirit for our increase in spiritual stature. A child that would advance to a vigorous maturity must eat at the table provided for it. The Spirit spreads our table; here are truths, precepts, promises, warnings, admonitions, incentives to duty, all the rich food of God. And the word of the Spirit is, "Eat and drink abundantly, O well beloved!" There is truth outside of the Scriptures; but here is the official, authoritative table spread for us. The Christian who neglects his Bible to feed on dreams and visions must expect to lament, "O, my leanness! my leanness!"' But he who shows himself in sympathetic accord with the Master's prayer, "Sanctify them by Your Word," becomes partaker of the Divine nature and grows more and more unto the stature of the fulness of Christ.

The Holy Ghost is also called the Spirit of Power. His influence is the great moral dynamic. The Lord said to His disciples, on His departure, "Wait at Jerusalem until you are endowed with power." They waited ten days, with one accord in prayer, until it came. It came from Heaven with a sound as of a rushing mighty wind; and there appeared unto them cloven tongues, like as of fire; and they were all filled with the Holy Ghost (Acts 2:1-4). This was their qualification for the work of the kingdom.

It was a great promise that Christ gave to His disciples, "He that believes on Me, the works that I do shall he do also; and greater works than these shall he do, because I go unto My Father" (John 14:12). Greater works than those of Jesus! Yes; because His was the work of preparation. A fortnight had not passed after His ascension, when one of His disciples preached the gospel with such power that his hearers, pricked to the heart, cried out, "Men and brethren, What shall we do?" And three thousand were gathered into the kingdom that day. Greater works? Why not? "For it is not you who speak, but the Spirit speaks in you" (Matthew 10:19-20). Ah, when we are willing to receive the fulness of His promise of power we shall work such wonders as we have never dreamed of.

August 9: His Nature
by George Matheson
Excerpted from "The Gospel of the Spirit in Nature", *Voices of the Spirit*, published by A. C. Armstrong & Son, New York, New York in 1892

By His Spirit He has decorated the heavens.
Job 26:13

The heavens are garnished by the Spirit of the Son of Man—the Spirit of the Cross. The beauty of the heavens is the beauty of sacrifice. Nothing shines by its own light. The radiance of everything is a borrowed radiance; all things live by the life of others. One star differs from another star in glory, yet the one cannot say to the other, "I have no need of you." The universe depends on each one as much as each one depends on the universe. If one of the least of these should perish there would be a crash of all worlds. What is that law which I call gravity but the sign of the Son of Man in Heaven. It is the gospel of self-surrender in nature. It is the inability of any world to be its own center, the necessity of every world to center in something else. The eyes of all wait upon the Father, and He gives them their food in due season, but He takes care that it is not the interest of any to receive its bread alone. The Power that has garnished the heavens is the Spirit of Him whose many members constitute one body.

O You who tells the number of the stars, help me to realize that You call them all by name—the name that is above every name. Help me to see in the unity of the starry heavens a picture of that higher unity—our membership in You. I speak of the heavens declaring Your glory; what do I mean by that? What is Your glory? Is it the splendor of lights and the blending of colors? Is it the flashing of comets and the radiance of suns? Is it the vastness of spaces and the immeasurableness of distances? All this is but a mechanic's glory. You are Spirit, and Your glory must be the glory of the Spirit. The glory of the Spirit is sacrifice, and it is by telling of sacrifice that the heavens declare Your glory. When I look up at the stars, it sometimes seems as if Your gospel is a contradiction to nature; I say "What is man that You are mindful of him?" Teach me that these stars are themselves the promise of Your mindfulness. Teach me that the heavens themselves declare the wonders of the Cross. Inspire me with the thought that the beauty which I see in nature is the same beauty which I behold in Calvary. Reveal to me that, alike in the firmament as on the earth, the many are made one by giving the one for the many; so shall I know that it is Your Spirit who has garnished the heavens.

August 10: His Necessity
by George Matheson
Excerpted from "The Worldly Necessity of the Spirit", *Voices of the Spirit*, published by A. C. Armstrong & Son, New York, New York in 1892

If He gathers unto Himself His Spirit and His breath, all flesh shall perish together, and man shall turn again unto dust.
Job 34:14-15

Is it so! I never knew that man was so dependent on the Spirit of God. I always knew indeed that the Spirit was necessary to man's salvation, but it never occurred to me that he was required even to keep up the flesh. I understood well enough that His removal would shut out a man from the other world, but I never thought that His removal would make it impossible to live in this. Yet this is what the Bible says. It tells me that the Divine Spirit is necessary even to the life of the human. It tells me that if the Spirit of God were gathered back to Himself, there would be a simultaneous collapse of the world called secular, that the products of materialism would disappear with the death of spiritualism, that the institutions of earth would fade in the vanishing of the breath of Heaven, that in the extinction of grace supreme "all flesh would perish together."

O Divine Spirit, life would be unbearable without You. The very fact that I am not consumed by the world is a proof that You are in the world. I have never seen anything at its worst. Bad men would be infinitely more bad but for You. The ship of life is tossing but it is anchored. I often complain of the storm, and say "Verily You are a God who hides Himself." If You did hide Yourself even for a moment I would know what it is to have a storm. My very complaining shows that the storm is not natural to me, that there is more good than evil in Your universe. You are Yourself the good that outweighs the evil. You are the balance of all discords; You are the compensation of all losses; You are the restraint of all violence; You are the limit of all vices. You are the oil of every troubled water; You are the still small voice of every rolling thunder; You are the rainbow of promise in every threatening cloud. Without You we can do nothing even in our own department; only in Your life does our life become endurable. Abide with us, for our natural strength fades into evening; if You take away Your breath, all flesh shall perish together.

August 11: His Newness - 1
by Andrew Murray
Excerpted from "The Newness of the Spirit", *The Spirit of Christ*, published by A. D. F. Randolph & Co., New York, New York in 1888

But now we have been released from the law, having died to that which held us captive; so that we serve in newness of the Spirit, and not in oldness of the letter.
Romans 7:6

If you are led by the Spirit, you are not under the law.
Galatians 5:18

The work of the indwelling Spirit is to glorify Christ and reveal Him within us. Corresponding to Christ's threefold office of Prophet, Priest, and King, we find that the work of the Indwelling Spirit in the believer is set before us in three aspects, as Enlightening, Sanctifying, and Strengthening. Of the Enlightening it is that Christ especially speaks in His farewell discourse, when He promises Him as the Spirit of Truth, who will bear witness of Him, will guide into all Truth, will take of Christ's and declare it unto us. In the Epistles to the Romans and Galatians His work as Sanctifying is especially prominent: This was what was needed in churches just brought out of the depths of heathenism. In the Epistles to the Corinthians, where wisdom was so sought and prized, the two aspects are combined; they are taught that the Spirit can only enlighten as He sanctifies (1 Corinthians 2; 3:1-3,

16; 2 Corinthians 3). In the Acts of the Apostles, as we might expect, His Strengthening for work is in the foreground; as the promised Spirit of Power He equips for a bold and blessed testimony in the midst of persecution and difficulty.

In the Epistle to the Church at Rome, the capital of the world, Paul was called by God to give a full and systematic exposition of His gospel and the scheme of redemption. In this the work of the Holy Spirit must needs have an important place. In giving his text or theme (Romans 1:17), "The righteous shall live by faith," he paves the way for what he was to expound, that through Faith both Righteousness and Life would come. In the first part of his argument, to verse 11, he teaches what the Righteousness of faith is. He then proceeds in verses 12-21 to prove how this Righteousness is rooted in our living connection with the second Adam, and in a justification of Life. In the individual (6:1-13) this Life comes through the believing acceptance of Christ's death to sin and His life to God as ours, and the willing surrender (6:14-23) to be servants of God and of righteousness. Proceeding to show that in Christ we are not only dead to sin, but to the law too as the strength of sin. He comes naturally to the new law which His gospel brings to take the place of the old, the law of the Spirit of life in Christ Jesus.

August 12: His Newness - 2
by Andrew Murray

In the description Paul gives of the life of a believer, who is still held in bondage of the law, and seeks to fulfil it, there are three expressions in which the characteristic marks of that state are summed up. The first is, the word flesh: "I am carnal (fleshly), sold under sin. In me, that is, in my flesh, dwells no good thing" (Romans 7:14, 18). If we want to understand the word carnal, we must refer to Paul's exposition of it in 1 Corinthians 3:1-3. He uses it there of Christians, who, though regenerate, have not yielded themselves to the Spirit entirely, so as to become spiritual. They have the Spirit, but allow the flesh to prevail. And so there is a difference between Christians, as they bear their name, carnal or spiritual, from the element that is strongest in them. As long as they have the Spirit, but, owing to whatever cause, do not accept fully His mighty deliverance, and so strive in their own strength, they do not and cannot become spiritual. Paul here describes the regenerate man, as he is in himself. He lives by the Spirit, but, according to Galatians 5:25, does not walk by the Spirit. He has the new spirit within him, according to Ezekiel 36:26, but he has not intelligently and practically accepted God's own Spirit to dwell and rule within that spirit, as the life of His life. He is still carnal.

The second expression we find in verse 18: "To will is present with me, but how to do that which is good is not." In every possible variety of expression Paul (Romans 7:15-21) attempts to make clear the painful state of utter impotence in which the law, the effort to fulfil it, leaves a man in this way: "The good which I would, I do not; but the evil which I would not, that I do." Willing, but not doing, such is the service of God in the oldness of the letter, in the life before Pentecost (see Matthew 26:41). The renewed spirit of the man has accepted and consented to the will of God; but the secret of power to do, the Spirit of God, as indwelling, is not yet known. In those, on the contrary, who know what the life in the Spirit is, God works both to will and to do; the Christian testifies, "I can do all things in Him that strengthens me." But this is only possible through faith and the Holy Spirit. As long as the believer has not consciously been made free from the law with its, "He that does these things shall live through them," continual failure will attend his efforts to do the will of God. He may even delight in the law of God after the inward man, but the power is lacking. It is only when he submits to the law of faith, "He that lives shall do these things," because he knows that he has been made free from the law, that he may be joined to Another, to the living Jesus, working in him through His Holy Spirit, that he will indeed bring forth fruit unto God (see Romans 7:4).

August 13: His Oil - 1
by A. B. Simpson
Excerpted from "A Pot of Oil", *When the Comforter Came*, published by The Alliance Press Company, New York, New York in 1911

"What do you have in the house?" Nothing except a pot of oil."
2 Kings 4:2

The passage before us is a striking object lesson of the Holy Ghost in His all-sufficiency for the supplying of every source of need.

First, we have, in the case of this poor widow, an example of great need. Her situation was one of debt, danger, distress, and of complete helplessness.

Nearly all the great examples of faith and victorious grace which we find in the Scriptures came out of situations of extremity and distress. God loves hard places, and faith is usually born of danger and extremity.

Was there, then, nothing left for her? Was she entirely without resources? "Tell me, what do you have in the house?" And she answered, "Your servant has nothing, except a pot of oil." To her that seemed nothing, and yet it contained the supply of all her need.

But that little pot of oil was not a little thing. It represented the power of the Holy Ghost, the infinite attribute of God Himself.

We need not stop to prove that oil is the Scriptural symbol of the Holy Spirit. And so this little vessel of oil represented the presence and power of the Spirit, which every believer may have, and in some measure does have, and which, if we only know how to use Him, is equal to every possible situation and need of our Christian life. But in how many cases is this an unrealized power and an unemployed force?

There is a grim story told of a poor Scotch woman who went to her pastor in her extremity, and told him of her poverty. He kindly asked her if she had no friend or member of her family who could support or help her, and she said she had a son, a bonny lad, but he was in India, in the service of the government. "But does he not write to you?" "Oh, he often writes me, and sends the kindest letters, and such pretty pictures in them. But I am too proud to tell him how poor I am, and, of course, I have not expected him to send me money." "Would you mind showing me some of the pictures?" said the minister. And so Janet went to her Bible, and brought out from between the leaves a great number of Bank of England notes, laid away with the greatest care. "These," she said, "are the pictures." The minister smiled, and said, "Janet, you are richer than I am. These are bank notes; and every one of them might have been turned into money, and you have had all your needs supplied. You have had a fortune in your Bible without knowing it."

August 14: His Oil - 2
by A. B. Simpson

Alas, beloved, many of us have fortunes in our Bibles without knowing it, or using our infinite resources! The Holy Spirit is given to us to be used for every sort of need, and yet, with all the power of Heaven at our call, many of us are going about in starvation, simply because we do not know our treasure, and do not use our redemption rights.

But the widow must make room. She must get vessels, and empty vessels, to hold the supply which is about to be revealed. And so our greatest need is to make room for God.

Again, there must be faith to count upon God and go forward expecting Him to meet our need. And so she did not wait till the oil was running over from her little pot. But she provided the vessels in advance and acted as though she had an unbounded supply.

She showed her faith by beginning to pour out the contents of the little pot into the larger vessel.

And as she poured, it continued to flow and overflow until every vessel was filled, and still that little pot was running, and it might have been running still if there had been room enough to hold its multiplying stream.

So faith must go forward and act out its confidence and risk itself by doing something and putting itself in the place where God must meet it with actual help. It was when the water at Cana was poured out that it became wine. It was when the man stretched out his hand that it was healed. It was as the lepers went on their way that they were made whole. It was as the father went back to his home that the messenger was sent to tell him that his son was alive.

There is yet another lesson, the most important of all: "Go, sell the oil, and live, you and your children on the rest." The oil was but the representative of value, and was convertible into everything that she could need. And so the Holy Ghost is convertible into everything that we can require.

There is a parallel passage in the Gospels of Matthew and Luke which teaches a great lesson. In the one passage it reads, "If you, being evil, know how to give good gifts unto your children, how much more shall your Father who is in Heaven give the Holy Spirit to them that ask Him." In the parallel passage in the other Gospel, instead of the Holy Spirit, it reads, "Give good things to them that ask Him." That is to say, the Holy Ghost gives all good things and He is equivalent to anything and everything that we need.

The oil did not stop until the woman stopped; God was stilling working when her faith reached its limit. And the same God is working still.

August 15: His Outpouring
by Andrew Murray

Excerpted from "The Outpouring of the Spirit", *The Spirit of Christ*, published by A. D. F. Randolph & Co., New York, New York in 1888

And when the day of Pentecost was fully come, they were all filled with the Holy Ghost, and began to speak, as the Spirit gave them utterance.
Acts 2:1-4

In the outpouring of the Holy Spirit, the work of Christ culminates. The adorable mystery of the Incarnation in Bethlehem, the great Redemption accomplished on Calvary, the revelation of Christ as the Son of God in the power of the Eternal Life by the Resurrection, His entrance into glory in the Ascension—these are all preliminary stages; their goal and their crown was the coming down of the Holy Spirit. As Pentecost is the last, it is the greatest of the Christian feasts; in it the others find their realization and their fulfilment. It is because the Church has hardly acknowledged this, and has not seen that the glory of Pentecost is the highest glory of the Father and the Son, that the Holy Spirit has not yet been able to reveal and glorify the Son in her as He would like. Let us see if we can realize what Pentecost means.

God made man in His own image, and for His likeness, with the distinct objective that he should become like Himself. Man was to be a temple for God to dwell in; he was to become the home in which God could rest. The closest and most intimate union, the indwelling of love: This was what the Holy One longed for, and looked forward to. What was very feebly set forth in type in the temple in Israel became a Divine reality in Jesus of Nazareth: God had found a Man in whom He could rest, whose whole being was opened to the rule of His will and the fellowship of His love. In Him there was a human nature, possessed by the Divine Spirit; and such God would have had all men to be. And such all would be, who accepted of this Jesus and His Spirit as their life. His death was to remove the curse and power of sin, and make it possible for them to receive His Spirit. His resurrection was the entrance of human nature, free from all the weakness of the flesh, into the life of Deity, the Divine Spirit-life. His ascension was admittance as Man into the very glory of God; the participation by human nature of perfect fellowship with God in glory in the unity of the Spirit. And yet, with all this, the work was not yet complete. Something, the chief thing, was still lacking. How could the Father dwell in men even as He had dwelt in Christ? This was the great question to which Pentecost gives the answer.

Out of the depths of Godhead, the Holy Spirit is sent forth in a new character and a new power, such as He never had before. In creation and nature He came forth from God as the Spirit of Life. In the creation of man especially He acted as the power in which his god-likeness was grounded, and after his fall still testified for God. In Israel He appeared as the Spirit of the theocracy, distinctly inspiring and equipping certain men for their work.

August 16: His Patience - 1
by Thomas Guthrie
Excerpted from "The Christian's Patience", *The Way to Life Sermons*, published by E. B. Treat & Company, New York, New York in 1891

I waited patiently for the Lord.
Psalm 40:1

Patience is not to be confused with apathy, sluggishness or laziness. There are circumstances which justify urgency. For example, we do not walk, but rush out of a house on fire. If anyone has been poisoned, or having burst a blood-vessel is bleeding to death, we do not stroll, we run for a physician; and, hardly taking time to tell our story, hurry them off to the scene of danger. Such impatience, if it can be called that, is even more necessary in the interests of the soul than of the body. Its case is far more urgent; its danger is very much greater. Hours here may involve the loss of eternity—no, one moment too late may be forever too late.

Those who wait most patiently on the Lord may be placed in circumstances where the more they believe the busier they will be; and the more they hope, the more they will hurry. Awakened at the dead of night by a loud knocking at the door and by Lot, with terror in his face, and quick speech on his tongue, crying, "Up; get out of this place for the Lord will destroy this city," his sons-in-law lay still and laughed at the old man; thinking him mad—wrong in the head. At any rate, they would wait a little; there would be time enough to seek safety when they saw danger; and thus, like many, they perished through unbelief. So did Lot, almost—like many others, better at giving advice than taking it and administering wise counsel than practicing it. And he would have died, but the angels hurried the lingerer out of the city, crying, as God does to all sinners in the way of destruction, and to all saints in the way of temptation, Escape for your life and do not look back!

What a contrast between Lot with his defective faith and lingering steps, and David on that day when he went to meet Goliath. Never were two antagonists more unequally matched—the one a giant, the other a mere youth; the one accustomed to war and crowned with its bloody honors, the other familiar only with the quiet scenes of pastoral life; the one clothed from head to heel in polished armor, the other clothed in shepherd's attire; the one waving a spear shafted like a weaver's beam (possibly 10'-15' in length) to send it whistling through the air and pin its victim to the ground, the other with no weapon more formidable than a few smooth stones and a slingshot. Yet, and just because he had faith in God, David was in a sense impatient. Eager for battle, burning to redeem God's honor and wipe out this disgrace from the army of Israel, when the giant, enraged at what he took to be the child's disrespect, stalked out. And David, we are told, ran to meet him. Patient waiting for the Lord is quite consistent with boldness in design, and energy and promptness in action; and only inconsistent with those unbelieving, impulsive, ungovernable, headlong, headstrong passions which breed impatience, and lead people to run before Providence instead of waiting on it.

August 17: His Patience - 2
by Thomas Guthrie

Let's observe the conduct of Abraham. On his leaving Ur of the Chaldeans to wander as a pilgrim in the land of Canaan, God had promised that he should become the father of a great nation. "Lift up your eyes," He said to him one day, "and look northward, and southward, and eastward, and westward." And when Abraham had scanned the wide horizon from the hills of Moab beyond Jordan to the sea that lies gleaming in the bay of Carmel, and from the snows of Lebanon to the sands of the burning desert, "All the land you see," said the Lord, "I will give it to you, and to your descendants after you; and I will make your descendants as numerous as the dust of the earth, so that if a person can number the dust of the earth, then your descendants shall also be numbered: Arise and walk through the land, I will give it to you" [Genesis 13:14-17].

Well, years pass after that. Time rolls on and erodes Sarah's beauty, writing wrinkles on both their brows. Old age has come upon them, and their bed is childless. Now where is the hope for the descendants that are like the dust of the earth? It is the privilege of faith to hope against hope. Abraham should have believed that He who formed a child in the Virgin's womb, and who, as Jesus said, could raise up children for Abraham from the stones of the street, would cause fruit to grow on the withered tree and sooner change the ordinary course of nature than fail in His word. But Abraham, at Sarah's suggestion, formed an unholy alliance with an Egyptian, thereby sowing discord in his house, and setting an example for his descendants which the best of them were too prone to follow. Though he is the father of the faithful, in this he ran before Providence, not waiting patiently on the Lord.

Look at David's own example of waiting for the Lord. It was impatience, springing from unbelief, which cost Saul his kingdom. Merchants in times of bad trade, or other trying circumstances, instead of trusting in God to bring them through their difficulties, or sustain them under them, have instead chosen fraud; or a poor man, instead of trusting Providence with the supply of his needs and committing his children to the care of Him who hears the young ravens cry, hard pinched and pressed, decides to steal. And so, hard pressed by the Philistines, and wearied waiting for Samuel's return so that the sacrifices might be offered and counsel sought with God, Saul did a forbidden thing—he took upon himself the priestly office which, as he was king, he had no right or authority to do—in his impatience was sinning against the Lord. The smoke of the profane sacrifice offered by this rash, impetuous man is still floating in a grey cloud up to the sky when Samuel appears—and says as he points to the ashes and the altar, "You have done foolishly: now your kingdom shall not continue" [1 Samuel 13:13]. Unhappy and unfortunate man! Like many others who do not wait patiently on the Lord, Saul, in trying to save his fortune, lost it.

August 18: His Patience - 3
by Thomas Guthrie

Saul was tempted to yield to impatience. And how much more and more often was his illustrious successor tempted? On that day David was sent for and called from the flock to meet Samuel in his father's house, wondering what they wanted with a lad like him, he came in with a shepherd's staff in his hand — most unlike a future king — to receive on bended knee the royal and sacred oil from the prophet's hand. He then knew that he was to be king. And though, when a running as a fugitive for his life from Saul, a beggar for bread, an exile from his country, hunted like a wild beast from swamp to mountain, from their crags to their caves, his hope of ever reaching the throne seemed as faint as that of a ship ever reaching land when it lies un-masted and waterlogged, a floating hulk with a starving crew on the waves of a shoreless sea. Yet David hoped in the Lord and waited patiently for God's way to put him in possession of the kingdom.

At least twice Saul was within his reach. Twice, when one blow of his hand would have settled the controversy and hastened the event and would have put him in immediate possession of the crown, he restrained himself by wrapping his soul in patience. In that dark cave, where Saul had no idea about who stood beside him and could touch him and could have killed him at a stroke. And also in that field where the king slept unaware of who stood over him—one who had only to give the sign and the spear of Abishai, already raised, would have pinned Saul to the ground—David could say in truth, "I waited patiently for the Lord." Amply rewarded for years of enduring faith and hope, when the long, looked-for day came that the nation called him to the throne, in him patience had her perfect work.

Consider thoroughly how we are to wait patiently on God. We are to wait patiently on Providence in the common affairs of life.

Many failures in business may be attributed to the neglect of this. People are impatient to get on in life; to acquire a skill; to be rich. The slow but sure methods by which all great things are accomplished in the ordinary course of Providence are too slow for them; so they engage in rash and reckless schemes—building up a business with "unready mortar," and without a solid foundation of funds. The result is that when some shock, like an earthquake, shakes the commercial world, their fortunes topple over to bury the business owner in their ruins.

We are to take and do our part in life's common affairs. But the gospel which calls us to that, though it does not allow us to cast our work on God, encourages us to cast its cares on Him. Cast your burden on the Lord, for He will carry it; and in ordinary circumstances it is not the work that is the burden. On the contrary, work is a blessing.

August 19: His Patience - 4
by Thomas Guthrie

*Commit your ways unto the Lord; trust also in Him,
and He shall bring it to pass.*
Psalm 37:5

By waiting on Him we will therefore be armed with patience, and will find faith in His Providence to be a sevenfold shield against the cares that are the misery of other other's lives, and against temptations that lead many into sin. For between a heathen torn with anxieties and tossed with fears, and a child of God who waits on Providence, believing that God reigns over all, there is such a difference as there is between a brawling, foaming, roaring flood that, rushing along its rugged channel, leaps with mad haste from crag to crag, and the placid river that, with heaven in its bosom and beauty flowering on its banks, pursues a noiseless, peaceful, useful course onward to its parent sea. Blessed is the person who trusts in the Lord. It is better to trust in the Lord than to put confidence in people; it is better to trust in the Lord than to put confidence in princes; for they that trust in the Lord shall be as Mount Zion which cannot be moved. "Wait on the Lord, and be of good courage, and He shall strengthen your heart. Wait, I say, on the Lord" [Psalm 27:14].

We are to wait patiently on God under the trials of life. "Is this not David, the king of the land? Did they not sing one to another of him in dances, saying, Saul has slain his thousands, and David his tens of thousands" [1 Samuel 18:7]. Fame breeds envy, and sometimes also brings danger with it. So David found out when these words of the men of Gath fell on his startled ear. There, under Achish its king, he had sought protection from Saul, and was much like the man in prophecy who, in fleeing from a bear, was met by a lion; when leaning on a wall, was stung by a serpent. He had gone down into the den of the very lioness that he had robbed of her cub; for Goliath, who had fallen before his slingshot, had been the pride of Gath — her greatest and most famous son. Was this an act of rashness or of faith? Where now is the man whose faith, rising with the trial, once said, "He that delivered me from the paw of the lion and the paw of the bear will deliver me from the hand of this Philistine!" [1 Samuel 17:37]? Where is the man who said, "Though a host should encamp against me, yet I will not fear!" [Psalm 27:3]? Now, instead, there he is, letting his spit fall on his beard, scratching on the doors of the gate, playing the madman; passing himself off as a fool! Was this a way for a man of God to seek safety in danger? He took his own way of getting out of the trial rather than waiting patiently for God to deliver him. And what a contrast to his former self, or to the calm and lofty bearing of Daniel when he went down like a hero into the den of lions. Daniel trusted in the Lord — in the time of trial he waited on his God; and was alive the next day to send up this grand answer to the anxious king, "My God has sent His angel, and shut the lions' mouths so that they have not hurt me" [Daniel 6:22].

August 20: His Patience - 5
by Thomas Guthrie

And those who wait on God sincerely, prayerfully, patiently in their trials, shall have the same tale to tell; the same experience — He will shut the lions' mouths that they shall not hurt them. In the trials He sends or permits, God does not willingly afflict; and has no more pleasure in seeing His people suffer than a father in the tears of the boy he corrects; than a kind surgeon, with bloody knife in his hand but tenderness in his heart, in his patient's groans. Believe that! And though to be brought to poverty, to suffer days of despair and wakeful nights; to sit weeping amid the ruins of your fondest domestic hopes; or to shed tears of less bitter sorrow on the graves of your dead, is not joyous but grievous — very grievous — believe that!

Oh, see God's hand in everything and believe that all things shall work together for your good, and you will learn to thank Him for the bitter as well as for the sweet; for your crosses as well are for your comforts; for medicine as for meat; for the withering, biting, winter-frosts that kill the weeds as for the dewy nights and sunny days that ripen the fields of corn. The young lions may lack and suffer hunger, but they that wait on the Lord shall need no good thing. Who is among you that fears the Lord, and obeys the voice of His servant, walks in darkness and has no light? Let them trust in the name of the Lord and stay upon their God.

We are to wait patiently on God to complete our sanctification. We cannot be too dedicated or too diligent in wanting to be sanctified; also, we cannot be too persistent, but we may be too impatient. Yielding to impatience we may be depressed and ready to abandon that hope which, inspiring courage in the soldier, contributes so much to win the fight; which sustains the workers in their labor, the sailors on their watch, the mother by the sick bed, the most wretched in their misery, and in spiritual matters is both a prelude and a means of success.

Consider that all great works progress slowly. All of God's works, with exceptional cases, both in nature and grace, certainly are so. So when we lapse into sin, fall back, make little perceptible progress, we should be grieved and sorry, but not depressed — as if God had abandoned either us or His work of grace in our hearts. To the devil standing with his foot on us, we are not to give up ourselves as captives, but say, Do not rejoice over me, my enemy, for when I fall I shall rise again. And to our souls, we are to say with David, "Why are you depressed, my soul, why is my spirit disquieted within me? Hope in God, for I shall yet praise Him, who is the health of my appearance, and my God" [Psalm 42:11].

August 21: His Patience - 6
by Thomas Guthrie

Why should the work of the Holy Spirit differ from God's other works? Minutes elapse between the dawn and the day; days elapse between the opening bud and the full blown flower; months elapse between spring's green blade and autumn's golden corn; years elapse between feeble infancy and steadfast maturity; centuries elapsed between the hope generated in the heart of Eve and the child born of Mary's womb; and long ages elapsed between the period when God laid the foundations of this world and that when, passing up through many stages, it was completed. God looked on all the works of His hands, and proclaimed them to be very good.

Progress in sanctification may, in fact, be going on when you do not see it; even perhaps when it seems to be going backwards. Take comfort! "The kingdom of God does not come with observation" [Luke 17:20]. The river may appear to be flowing away from the sea, when, turning around the base of some opposing hill, it is continues to pursue an onward course. God works in strange, mysterious, silent, unnoticed ways. Unseen and unnoticed the rains wash away the ground below the stone that shall one day, on a sudden leap from its seat, roll to the bottom of the hill. Quietly and slowly the root grows in the crack that shall one day all of a sudden split the rock and reveal its long-continued, silent, secret, but mighty power. The work of sanctification may be going on in a deep, growing sense of the evil of sin, produced perhaps by our very sin; in deeper humility, in a low view of ourselves, in greater self-abasement; in a more entire dependence on Christ for righteousness, and on the Holy Spirit for the work of grace; in feelings that fill us with pain and regret and godly sorrow, making us "eat our Passover with bitter herbs." Like a patient who, through the power of returning life, begins to feel and complain about all their pains, when we think we are growing worse we may actually be growing better and making substantial progress when we seem to be making none. Do not be depressed! Progression is the ordinary law of God's government.

It is minute by minute that morning's grey dawn brightens up into a perfect day; it is ring by ring that the oak grows into the monarch of the forest; it is inch by inch and foot by foot that the tide, which bears navies on its waves comes creeping in on the shore. And, not like the act of justification, our sanctification is a work of God's free grace and is under the same law of progress. More or less rapid, it is a thing of steps and stages. Therefore, while praying earnestly and working diligently, live hopefully and wait patiently.

August 22: His Peace - 1
by George Matheson
Excerpted from "The Peace of the Spirit", *Voices of the Spirit*, published by A. C. Armstrong & Son, New York, New York in 1892

And the Spirit of the Lord shall rest upon Him.
Isaiah 11:2

Alone among the sons of men the Spirit came to Christ in the form of rest. To us it always comes in the form of unrest. The beginnings of new life ever make us restless. We are disquieted by the novelty of our own vision, we are pained by its unlikeness to our present selves. Why is youth the time of unrest? It is because youth carries in its bosom a life higher than its own — the germ of that coming adult for whose coming it is not yet ready. God's Spirit also comes as a seed in the bosom of a life not His own. He comes into the heart while the heart is yet in winter; He sings as a swallow in the cold. He is too big for His environment, He has seen too much for His surroundings; so He beats against the bars and struggles to be free.

But far otherwise was it with Christ. When the Spirit came to Him, He came to no foreign soil; His heart was ready for Him. There was no struggle between the year that was coming and the year that was going; the Dove from Heaven rested in the pure waters of an already prepared soul. There was no strife between the breath of the Divine Spirit and the atmosphere of the earthly wilderness; He was the Spirit that led Him into the wilderness. He was the underlying rest that conquered for Him the outward tempest. He gave calmness on the dizzy height. He smoothed a passage through the sea; He multiplied sustenance in a desert land. He bore the solitary burden of the garden; He endured the universal burden of the cross. It was a peace eternal, a peace continuous, a peace independent of war; the Spirit rested on Him.

Son of Man, let me enter into Your rest. Fulfill to me Your latest promise, send me Your peace. I often get Your Spirit in flashes—in moments of transfiguration, in heights of Pisgah. But I want more than His flashes; I want His abiding rest. I want Him to come to me as a permanent power, to be with me always even unto the end of the world. I want Him to be something which the world can neither give nor take away, which the hosannahs of Jerusalem cannot create nor the tears of Gethsemane destroy. That is what You have promised me, that is what I wait for. Nothing less will make life tolerable to me; nothing more remains to make it perfect. Your peace passes all understanding because it is unchanged amid the changing; give me also this fadeless bloom. Grant me too the power to pass from the opened Heaven into the clouded wilderness and to hear undimmed the voice, "This is My beloved Son." The Dove that lighted on me at the Jordan must abide with me in the desert; the desert will be a Paradise when Your Spirit has rested upon me.

August 23: His Peace - 2
by George Matheson
Excerpted from "The Road to the Spirit's Peace", *Voices of the Spirit*, published by A. C. Armstrong & Son, New York, New York in 1892

And when He had said this, He breathed on them, and said unto them, "Receive the Holy Ghost."
John 20:22

"When He had said this." Said what? You will find it in the previous verse. "Peace be unto you: as My Father has sent Me, even so send I you." It was not till He had said this that Christ breathed upon them. Before He gave them the gift of the Spirit's peace He had to tell them the kind of peace they must expect; otherwise they would have been disappointed. He had to tell them that His peace meant what the world calls dispeace — submission to a sacrifice, "as My Father has sent Me, even so send I you." How had the Father sent Him? From the height to the depths, from Heaven to earth, from joy to tribulation, from life to death. The peace which His Father gave Him was a peace that could descend the valley, a peace that could meet the darkness, a peace that could bear the cross. Before I can receive that peace I must be prepared for it. I must learn that His mission is to be my mission too — not the life of luxurious self-indulgence, but the beatitude of the poor in spirit.

Son of Man, I shall only get Your peace by moving in Your sphere. Your peace came to You by going where Your Father sent You. You did not get it first and then go into Gethsemane; it was in Gethsemane You found it. It came to You by doing the Father's will, came through persistent struggle, came by determination not to yield. So must it be with me. You will not send me Your peace until You have sent me on the path of sacrifice; Your Olivet will only come to me on the steps of Your Calvary. Your will must precede Your reward, I must serve You before I can rejoice in You. Obedience first, then liberty; the cross first, then the crown; the wilderness first, then Nebo; the mission of sacrifice first, then the breath of the free Spirit. You shall breathe Your peace into my soul when You have sent me where Your Father sent You.

August 24: His Penalizing
by George Matheson
Excerpted from "The Penalties of the Spirit", *Voices of the Spirit*,
published by A. C. Armstrong & Son, New York, New York in 1892

He that despised Moses' law died without mercy, under two or three witnesses; of how much worse punishment shall he be thought worthy, who has outraged the Spirit of grace?
Hebrews 10:28-29

The thought is that there is no penalty so great as the punishment inflicted by the Spirit. If I am only convicted by outward witnesses, if I do not feel the pain from within, it is only my body that suffers. But if I am convicted by the witness of my own heart, if I am confronted by the stings of a violated conscience, my punishment is sore indeed. There is no pain like spiritual pain; there is no spiritual pain like the sense of having done wrong. If I have outraged the law of love in my own soul, it is no solace to me that there are not outward witnesses of my deed. It is no consolation to me that eye has not seen it, that ear has not heard it, that visible tribunal shall not avenge it. It is the reverse; if I could only get outward punishment it would be a relief. Why have men in all ages sought penance? Why have they wounded themselves, lacerated themselves, starved themselves? It is that thereby they may avert the greater penalty—the stroke of a wounded conscience. Not by accident is it written that the first punishment was not physical. Why is no man allowed to kill Cain? It is to teach the world at the beginning that the penalties of the Spirit are in God's sight heavier than the penalties of the Law.

My soul, is there any escape for you? The stroke of the outer law was sharp but it was short-lived; one brief pain and all was over. But the remorse for deeds misdone: Can there be any end to that? Yes, there can. There is One who has been coming up behind you, lifting the crosses you have left by the wayside. There is One who has been gathering your misdeeds into His kingdom and making them work for good. There is One who has been not only forgiving your past, not only cancelling your past, but atoning for your past. The crosses left by you on the wayside have not merely been lifted, but have been beaten into the steps of a golden ladder on which the world instead of stumbling shall rise; the dungeon you made for Joseph has become the road to his throne. Would you have your past unspoken? Would you have your deeds undone? Would you have the sense of being a child again—with the page still to write, the race still to run, the road still to traverse? Come then to Him who crucifies your misspent years. Come to Him who beats your sword into a plow, your spear into a pruning hook. Come to Him who makes the wrath of the wicked to praise Him. Come to Him who turns the water of the past into wine and tells you that you are born anew. The penalties of the outraged Spirit shall be crucified on the bosom of the Son of Man.

August 25: His Pentecost - 1
by W. M. Clow
Excerpted from "The Pentecost of the Soul", *The Evangel of the Strait Gate*, published by Hodder and Stoughton, London, England in 1916

"And when He is come, He will convince the world of sin, and of righteousness, and of judgment."
John 16:8

In these mystic words Jesus revealed the coming of a new era in the religious life of humanity through the advent of the Holy Ghost. By that advent the heedless world would be given a deeper consciousness of sin, a nobler concept of righteousness, and a final assurance of the condemnation of God upon all who do evil. There had been rare spirits in earlier ages who had passed through an illuminating spiritual experience. A poignant sorrow after sin, a vision of an austere holiness, and a confident conviction that there is a God who judges in the earth, breathes through the words of the Hebrew prophets. The Spirit of God has ever been moving upon the face of the waters of the soul. But all past experiences of the religious nature would be surpassed in that day when the Spirit of God would descend upon the spirit of man in a more personal, more intimate, and more potent filling than any enraptured psalmist had known. That prophecy was fulfilled on the day of Pentecost. As Christ's little company waited in the hush of desire, and lifted up their hearts in prayer, the Divine Personality came upon them. Their eyes were opened to see the invisible, and their energies were raised to power. Their hearts burned within them, and their tongues were gifted with a strange eloquence. But the greater marvel was this, that as they preached Jesus, who had lived and died and risen again, callous consciences were quickened, long chilled hearts were renewed, and men who had lived in darkness and loved its deeds were given a new conviction of sin, and righteousness, and judgment. That was the first of the days of the new era in religious life. Down all the course of time this keener conviction has been visiting a careless and godless world, and the cry of the penitent has been heard from long silent lips.

This Pentecost in history is really the Pentecost of the soul. There is a day when the man who has been attempting the narrow way finds himself at the strait gate. The Word of God has come to him. The Divine condemnation has been passed upon his sin. The message of the grace of God in Christ has been heard, and its echoes abide in his soul. He has assented and hesitated, relented and hardened, again and again. He has been in the Slough of Despond [term used in *Pilgrim's Progress* by John Bunyan], and has come out on the other side. Then, in a strange silence, the inner world of his soul is aware of the advent of the Spirit, and he finds himself on the threshold of a new life. Some have spoken of this hour as a mood of reflection; others, as an inexpressible tenderness of feeling; others, as an impulse into which the whole force of holy desire was poured; others, with a finer conception, have named it the Heavenly vision. But this was the common certainty, that God had become the supreme reality, and that His longing in the call of Christ rang through the soul.

August 26: His Pentecost - 2
by W. M. Clow

No one can flee from God's Spirit. Though we make our bed in Hell, He is there. Sometimes He brings the soul to repentance by His judgments. Again He rouses the conscience by His law. And again He woos the soul by the attraction of moral loveliness. Yet how often do these fail! How often do men stride on in their wrongdoing, absorbed in the gluttony of coarse desires. But now, in this new era, the heinousness of sin is brought in upon the conscience by the Spirit of God, using that new and more potent truth of Christ, in whom men have not believed.

What is the meaning of this conviction of sin when it is disbelief in Christ? All conviction of sin depends not merely on its inherent wrong, but on its aggravation. The pitiless cruelties of an ignorant heathen man, or the dishonesties and blasphemies of a gutter outcast, are not offenses so black as the self-indulgent gratifications of a man encompassed by sanctities, gifted with an inherited spiritual sensibility, and nurtured in the fear of God. Sin is the more heinous as it is committed against knowledge, and light, and love. When a man perceives that his evil doing has been a defiance to holiness, and that his life has been a course of willful disloyalty to love, he is convicted of his sin, often with an anguish of remorse. God's Spirit uses the holiness and the long-suffering love of Christ to bring in that conviction of the soul.

We know the spiritual darkness of the leaders of Israel in those days when Christ walked in the Holy Land clothed upon with the apparel of His perfect moral beauty. Their condemnation was found upon the lips of Him whose compassion for the lost and castaway never failed. But their covetousness, and pride, and hypocrisy, and merciless craft, blacken the pages of the Gospels as they evoked Christ's moral anger. Yet these rulers and leaders who knew the words of the law, and chanted its sentences every day, were not convicted of sin. They consummated their iniquity when they crucified Christ and went down from the sight of the cross with mockery. But when Peter, in the power of the Holy Ghost, recalled that Life whose holiness they had denied, whose grace and mercy they had slandered, and when he pointed to its crowning infamy, "Him, you have taken, and by wicked hands have crucified and slain," their sin stood out before them. They were all abashed. And some were pricked in their hearts, and cried, "Men and brethren, what shall we do?" They were convicted of sin because they had not believed in Christ. That is, to all time, the crowning iniquity. To live and move under the very shadow of holiness and yet remain unconcerned, to see infinite patience and infinite pity pouring out its treasures of grace and yet to turn away unmoved to greed and hate and lust, to be in the presence of a love which agonizes over our sins and yields up its life to redeem us from them, and yet to look on with callous indifference, there is no iniquity so awful as that. The man who does not believe in Christ stands with those who set up His cross and ordered men to drive in the nails.

August 27: His Pentecost - 3
by W. M. Clow

"He will convince the world of righteousness." It is too possible to be convinced of sin but not of righteousness. The world is full of men who are assured of the power and prevalence of evil. "All men are liars," wrote the Psalmist, and a man of the world has affirmed that every man has his price. A modern poet has told us the story of the man whose conviction of sin destroyed his conviction of righteousness. He discovered, after her death, that his mother, whose faith had been his bulwark against the sea of doubt, had lived a life of secret fraud. In the shock of the discovery of so black a sin in a heart he deemed so pure, all belief in righteousness was lost.

Men have grown cynical and become misanthropic and bitter in speech as they have lost faith in righteous ness. Some, indeed, have passed into a mortal horror, as is suggested by Nathaniel Hawthorne [American writer, 1804-1864] in his weird fancy of *The Minister's Veil*, where a morbidly sensitive soul covered his face with a veil he wore all through life, even on his dying bed, because of an unbearable sense of secret sin which quenched his belief in righteousness.

He will convince the world of righteousness, "because I go unto My Father, and you shall see Me no more." That word can be understood from our experience. When we have loved those whom we have lost, our memory and our judgment are busy with the estimate of their moral worth. Every man, though he is almost inarticulate and cannot find the words to express his conviction, hears the melodies of an *In Memoriam* when his trusted friend has gone to the Father and he sees him no more. From Telemachus [martyr], trampled to his death in the Colosseum, down to the last brave young missionary, who left home and love and alluring distinction behind, and now lies buried beside an African lake, how many martyr spirits pass before our minds, and we see them now clothed on with sanctity? The man who follows his father and mother to the grave, or he who stands beside his wife's casket to look on the face, once so often shadowed by love's anxieties, and now calm and free from care, not only realizes with keen rebuke his ingratitude, but he is convinced of the truth, the purity, the honor, the self-denial against which he so often sinned.

After the same fashion the Holy Spirit takes of the things of Christ and shows them to men. It is a fact of history that, since Jesus has gone to the Father and the world has seen Him no more, righteousness has been discerned as it never was before. The Spirit has "glorified" Jesus.

So the soul discerns the righteousness of Christ, and becomes persuaded that righteousness is the true grace of the soul. The Spirit has been glorifying Christ down all the centuries. We know Him and see Him as they did not who touched Him with their hands.

August 28: His Place - 1
by Andrew Murray
Excerpted from "The Place of the Indwelling", *The Spirit of Christ*, published by A. D. F. Randolph & Co., New York, New York in 1888

In studying the teaching of Scripture on the indwelling of the Holy Spirit, it is of great consequence to see clearly what it tells us of the place where the Spirit dwells, and the mode in which He works. And to this end we need to be especially careful to seek correct views as to the difference between the soul and the spirit of man, and their mutual relation.

In the history of man's creation we read, "The Lord God formed man of the dust of the ground" — thus was his body made — "and breathed into his nostrils the breath" or spirit "of life" thus his spirit came from God; "and man became a living soul." The Spirit quickening the body made man a living soul, a living person with the consciousness of himself. The soul was the meeting place, the point of union between body and spirit. Through the holy man, the living soul, stood related to the external world of sense; could influence it, or be influenced by it. Through the spirit he stood related to the spiritual world and the Spirit of God, whence he had his origin; could be the recipient and the minister of its life and power. Standing thus midway between two worlds, belonging to both, the soul had the power of determining itself, of choosing or refusing the objects by which it was surrounded, and to which it stood related.

In the constitution of these three parts of man's nature, the spirit, as linking him with the Divine, was the highest; the body, connecting him with the sensible and animal, the lowest; intermediate stood the soul, partaker of the nature of the others, the bond that united them, and through which they could act on each other. Its work, as the central power, was to maintain them in their due relation; to keep the body, as the lowest, in subjection to the spirit; itself to receive through the spirit, as the higher, from the Divine Spirit what was waiting it for its perfection; and so to pass down, even to the body, that by which it might be partaker of the Spirit's perfection, and become a spiritual body.

The wondrous gifts with which the soul was endowed, especially those of consciousness and self-determination, or mind and will, were just the mold or vessel into which the life of the Spirit, the real substance and truth of the Divine life, was to be received and assimilated. They were a God-given capacity for making the knowledge and the will of God its own. In doing this, the personal life of the soul would have become filled and possessed with the life of the Spirit, the whole man would have become spiritual.

August 29: His Place - 2
by Andrew Murray

Instead of the whole person becoming spiritual, we know how the opposite of this took place. The soul yielded to the solicitations of sense, and became its slave, so that the Spirit no longer ruled, but vainly strove to vindicate for God His place, until God said, "My Spirit shall not strive with man forever, for that he also is flesh," wholly under the power of the flesh. The spirit in man became dormant—a capacity for knowing and serving God which would have to wait its time for deliverance and quickening. The soul ruled instead of the spirit, and the great mark of all religion, even in its most earnest struggles after God, is that it is the soul, man's own energy without the Divine Spirit, putting forth its effort to find and to please God.

In regeneration it is this spirit of man which is quickened again and renewed. The word regeneration, or being born again, Scripture uses as that change whereby the soul passes from death to life, effected like the natural birth, at once and once for all. The word renewed is used of that continuous and progressive work by which the life of the Spirit of God enters more fully into our life, and asserts its supremacy through our entire nature.

In the regenerate man the original relation between the soul and the spirit has been restored. The spirit of man has been quickened to become a habitation of God's Spirit, who is now to teach and to lead, by communicating as a Divine life, as something substantial and real, the Truth, the actual good things which Christ has for us. This Divine leading into the Truth by the Spirit of God takes place not in our soul or mind, in the first place, but in our spirit, in the inner recesses of a life deeper than mind or will. And it takes place only as the soul, in the confession of how blinded it has become, of how slowly its faculties really become spiritual and Divinely enlightened, in the willingness to be foolish and ignorant, and in teachableness to wait on God's Spirit to give His Truth in the life, yields itself to that complete supremacy of the Spirit which was its original destiny.

And now comes the most important lesson, not easy to learn, for the sake of which we have at some length spoken of the relation between the soul and spirit. The greatest danger the religion of the Church or the individual has to dread is the inordinate activity of the soul, with its power of mind and will. It has been so long accustomed to rule, that even when in conversion it has surrendered to Jesus, it too easily imagines that it is now its work to carry out that surrender, and serve the King it has accepted. Many a believer has no conception of the reality of the Spirit's indwelling, and of the extent to which He must get the mastery of the soul, that is, of our whole self in all our feeling and thinking and willing, so as to purge out all confidence in the flesh, and work that teachableness and submissiveness which is indispensable to the Spirit's doing His work.

August 30: His Power - 1
by Louis Albert Banks
Excerpted from "The Gift of Power", *The Fisherman and His Friends*, published by Funk & Wagnalls Company, New York, New York in 1896

"But you shall receive power, when the Holy Ghost is come upon you."
Acts 1:8

Power is what we want—power to halt the tide of sin and iniquity; power to make men pause and consider the certain disaster of the downward power to arouse men who are asleep in trespasses and in sins; power to clutch the candle of the Lord that is lighted with the devil's fire and snatch it as "a brand from the burning;" power to turn a wrong world upside down; power to make Jesus live again in our lives; power to make Him so real and so charming that men shall be drawn away from their sins and find freedom and purity in Him. Jesus said to the disciples, "You shall receive power, after the Holy Ghost is come upon you."

As we look into the New Testament we see that this was true everywhere during the ministry of Jesus and in the establishing of the Christian Church. It was when Jesus was full of the Holy Ghost that He returned from the Jordan River and went up into the wilderness and won His great victory over the devil. On the day of Pentecost it was, when they were all "filled with the Holy Ghost," that Peter and his one hundred and twenty fellow workers had such wondrous power in the presentation of the truth that the wicked, prejudiced Jews yielded to their preaching of the cross of Christ on every side, and three thousand of them were added to the Church in a single day.

It was when Peter and John were "full of the Holy Ghost" that they healed the lame man, and were so full of holy boldness that the people, perceiving that they were unlearned and ignorant men, marveled and "took knowledge of them that they had been with Jesus." It was when the early Christians were gathered together in prayer, and the place was shaken where they assembled together, and "they were all filled with the Holy Ghost," that it is said about them, "They spoke the word of…God with boldness. And the multitude of them that believed were of one heart and of one soul, and with great power gave the apostles witness of the resurrection of the Lord Jesus: and great grace was upon them all."

We are told in the description given of Stephen that he was "a man full of faith and of the Holy Ghost." We are not astonished after that to hear that he was full of power and "did great wonders and miracles among the people," and that the multitude "were not able to resist the wisdom and the spirit by which he spoke."

When Saul was stricken down with conviction of sin, on the way to Damascus, and Ananias came to him to lead him into the light, it is said that he was "filled with the Holy Ghost." After that it is only natural to read that he "increased the more in strength, and confounded the Jews…proving that this is very Christ."

August 31: His Power - 2
by Louis Albert Banks

It is said of Barnabas that "He was a good man, and full of the Holy Ghost and of faith;" and it follows then, as a matter of course, in the record, "much people was added unto the Lord." At Iconium "the disciples were filled with joy and with the Holy Ghost," and the result of the work carried forward in such a spirit was that "a great multitude both of the Jews and also of the Greeks believed."

The same power has been with the Church in its days of triumph in every age. The men who have accomplished wondrous things for the salvation of souls have been those who have received power because the Holy Ghost was upon them. Freeman Clarke [American minister, 1810-1888] well says that there is always a tendency in religion to relapse into mechanism—to multiply ceremonies and lose the spirit. Ever, as the winter of unbelief chills the soul and the river of religious life sinks in its channel, the ice of forms accumulates along its shores. Then the Lord sends a new prophet, to whom religion is not a form, but one who sees with his own eyes God as a Heavenly presence in nature and life; who has the vision, the faculty Divine. What a long and glorious procession there are of them—a line of torch-bearers who have kept the Divine life aglow in the Church! Such men as Paul, Augustine, Bernard, Savonarola, Huss, Wycliffe, Luther; and, in the later days, such men as Fox the Quaker, Whitefield and the Wesleys, Finney and Edwards, and Moody. Such men are Divinely ordained to call people away from dusty books and dry forms to the open vision of a new heaven and new earth. Their power is not their own. It is not the power of genius, or learning, or logic, or eloquence. It is the power of the Holy Spirit. They see God face to face. They see Him in Christ, as Whittier [American Quaker poet, 1807-1892] saw Him when he sang: "Our friend, our brother, and our Lord! What shall thy service be? Nor name, nor form, nor ritual word, But simply following thee!"

This power we want! A power that will make us irresistible as the messengers of the Son of God. A power that will melt down all our icicles of indifference and change our natures into impetuous torrents of loving enthusiasm. The disciples on the day of Pentecost were such marvels of fervor and earnestness that some of the people thought they were intoxicated with strong drink; but Peter replied that it was not the effect of wine but the power of the Holy Spirit working within them. They were carried away by that Divine Spirit; they were, to use a foreign phrase, "God-intoxicated men." When the people were astonished at the enthusiasm of Paul, he exclaimed, "The love of Christ compels us." Few men won more souls to Christ in his day than Richard Baxter [English theologian, 1615-1691]. The secret of all his success was the power of the Holy Ghost which was upon him. That it was which gave him his unbounded enthusiasm. His biographer says Baxter would have set the world on fire while another was lighting a match. "He preached as though he ne'er should preach again, and as a dying man to dying men."

September 1: His Power - 3
by Louis Albert Banks

Dr. O. P. Gifford tells the story of a mighty revival which was in progress in a Wesleyan chapel. The rector of the Established Church dropped in one evening, as he was bound to do, the chapel being within the limits of his parish. Scandalized by the excitement, he rebuked the zealous Wesleyans, saying, "This is all wrong, all wrong. When Solomon built his temple there was heard neither the sound of hammer, nor saw, nor chisel. You make too much noise here." The chapel preacher replied, "Oh, but that's all right; we are not building here, we are just blasting, getting out lively stones for the temple. Christ is the Master-builder." The preacher was right; he was using dynamite, destroying the kingdom of darkness. Something of this Paul must have done when his enemies declared, "These that have turned the world upside down have come here also." A touch of the dynamic energy of the Holy Spirit shook the prison wherein Paul and Silas sung psalms and prayed to God.

Friends, this is what the Christianity of today lacks, what you and I lack—dynamic energy. Books as dark as those of Ephesus need to be piled in the public squares, leaders as corrupt as Felix and Festus ought to be faced, hypocrisy as vile as that of Simon Magus ought to be unmasked, sins as flagrant as those at Rome and Corinth demand attention. Oh, for the promised dynamite of the Holy Spirit! This power which we lack, and which we may have because it is promised, has its source outside the Church and human life altogether. "You shall receive power" — not generated from within, not attained to by straining present powers, or enlarging present capacities. We cannot whip ourselves into a state of power, as though we were eggs; strike the fire from ourselves by any flint and steel arrangement; lift ourselves into it by force of will; educate ourselves into it by culture of heart or head. The dynamic power is without; we are to receive it. Though itself such a mighty cause, it is also an effect; the power lies in the Holy Spirit. "You shall receive power when the Holy Spirit comes upon you."

Do you ask how we can receive this power? The answer is by obedience and prayer. When Jesus came to be baptized by John in the Jordan He said to John, "It is proper for us to do this to fulfill all righteousness." And it is recorded that "Jesus also being baptized, and praying, Heaven was opened, and the Holy Ghost descended in bodily shape like a dove upon Him." Thus it was through obedience and prayer that Jesus passed from being Jesus the carpenter of Nazareth, to be Jesus the Christ, the Savior of the world. Then He began to do mighty works. We shall get power by following the example of our Lord.

Let us not forget that the Holy Spirit, in answer to prayer, is able and willing to convict of sin even those who have long withstood His grace. If so, I beg of you not to delay, not to grieve the Holy Spirit, but to yield to His gracious influence and accept Jesus Christ as your Savior.

September 2: His Power - 4
by John Henry Jowett
Excepted from "The Power of the Holy Spirit", *Things That Matter Most*, published by Fleming H. Revell Company, New York, New York in 1913

When the apostles received the power of the Holy Spirit what difference did it make to them? What kind of dynamic does the Holy Spirit bring to people? What change takes place in the lives of men and women today when they become companions of the Holy Spirit? What infirmities do they leave behind? What new equipment do they gain? I turn to the records of apostolic life and I put my inquiries there. What happened to these men? What kind of power did they receive when they had received the Holy Spirit?

First of all, then, I find an extraordinary power of spiritual understanding. I know not how to express what I see. The apostles have a certain powerful feeling for God. They have a keen spiritual sense which discerns the realities of the unseen. It is as though their souls have developed latent feelers for the Divine. If we compare their dullness in the earlier days before the Holy Spirit was received, with their alertness afterwards, we shall see that the difference is most marked. The Master Himself describes them as "slow of heart." Their perceptions are blunt. They are dull to catch the spiritual side of things. But now when we turn to the record in the Acts of the Apostles we find this powerful sense of the Divine presence. It is as though a man has been sitting in a room with another man, but was only dimly aware of his presence; and then there came to him a refinement of his senses, and he gained a perfect assurance and a vivid knowledge of the other's company. The spiritual senses of these men were awakened, and they became aware of the "all-aboutness" of God. They have an intimate power of correspondence with Him which makes the unseen Lord a most real and intimate Friend. And along with this sense of the Divine presence there is a refined perception of the Divine will. Everywhere in the apostolic life there is a tender and refined correspondence with the mind of God. Everywhere communications are being made between the Divine and human, and the human is strongly grasping the Divine. Sentences like these abound everywhere: "The angel of the Lord said unto me"; "The Spirit said to Philip, Go near"; "And the Lord said to Ananias"; "The Spirit said unto Peter." There is everywhere this suggestion of an intimate walk and an intimate knowledge of God's will. Is not this a power to be coveted, and a power to be desired? And it is a power given by the baptism of the Holy Spirit.

I look again at the lives of these apostles, and I find them distinguished by magnificent force of character. In the early days they were timid, pliable, unfaithful. In supreme crises they deserted their Master and fled. They were as reeds shaken by the wind. The wind that blew upon them from the haunts of desolation, the keen, perilous winds of persecution, made these disciples bend before their opposition.

September 3: His Power - 5
by John Henry Jowett

The second element in a forceful character is heat, the fire of a quenchless enthusiasm. And they certainly had this fire in glorious strength and abundance. The Acts of the Apostles is a burning book. There is no cold or lukewarm patch from end to end. The disciples had been baptized with fire, with the holy, glowing enthusiasm caught from the altar of God. They had this central fire, from which every other purpose and faculty in life gets its strength. This fire in the apostles' soul was like a furnace-fire in a great ocean liner, which drives her through the tempests and through the engulfing deep. Nothing could stop these men! Nothing could hinder their going. "We can only speak about the things that we have seen and heard." "We must obey God rather than man." This strong imperative rings throughout all their doings and all their speech. They have heat, and they have light, because they were baptized by the power of the Holy Ghost.

And I look again into the lives of these men who had been redeemed by the power of the Holy Ghost, and I find the energies of a glorious optimism. There is no more buoyant and exhilarating book in the literature than the book of The Acts. If we sit down and read it at a sitting we shall feel something of the swift and hopeful pace of its movement. I do not know that in their earlier days we should have described the disciples as "children of light." They easily lost heart, and the cloudy days filled them with dismay. But now, after they have received the Holy Spirit, we find them facing a hostile world. They are face to face with obstructions, with persecutions, with threats of imprisonment and death. But nowhere do we find a despairing or a hopeless note. Ever and everywhere they are optimists in spirit. And what is an optimist? A person who can scent the coming harvest when the snow is on the ground; who can "feel the days before him." They can live in the distant June in the dingy days of December. That is an optimist, a person who can believe in the best in the arrogant and aggressive presence of the worst. He can be imprisoned in the desolations of Patmos and yet can see "the Holy City, the New Jerusalem coming down out of Heaven from God." He can look at a poor, wayward, sinful Samaritan woman whose life is scorched like a blasted field, and He can say, "The fields are ripe already unto harvest." And this power of optimism is always operative in the apostolic life. I find it in the springiness of their soul. You cannot break their spirit. You cannot hold them down in dull despair. "They laid their hands on apostles and put them in the common prison." And what happened after that? The morning after their release I read, "They entered into the temple early in the morning and taught." And here is another part of the record: "When they had called the apostles, and had beaten them, they commanded that they should not speak in the name of Jesus, and let them go. And they departed from the presence of the council, rejoicing that they were counted worthy to suffer for His sake." These men could not be held down. The spirit of optimism was ever dominant.

September 4: His Power - 6
by John Timothy Stone

"But you shall receive power when the Holy Spirit is come upon you."
Acts 1:8

Our Lord and Master states these words regarding the Holy Spirit with gracious wisdom and profound insight. He knew that He was soon to leave those who were dependent upon Him, and whose faith had been largely centered in His personality and leadership. He had for this great world, and for the ever-increasing Church which He loved, a legacy far greater than He Himself could ever give had He remained on the earth, the Man of Nazareth and the leader of the twelve. A limited circle would come into personal and vital association with Him, but the Invisible and Eternal, Omnipresent Spirit was to make His dwelling place in human hearts, and every Christian body was to become His indwelling temple.

We believe in God the Father, God the Son, and God the Holy Spirit. And may I ask this now: Why we do not appreciate and appropriate the presence and power of the Holy Spirit, according to the promises of our Lord and Master?

The preface of our text is very human. The wonderful experiences of the resurrection had not taken from Christ's followers the curiosity and craving for the outward manifestation of His glory. They were impatient. Time, place and events filled their minds. When would this Victor over death and the grave "restore again the kingdom to Israel"? We can picture our risen Lord with calm and deliberate voice, replying to them, "It is not for you to know times or seasons, which the Father has set within His own authority. But you shall receive power when the Holy Spirit is come unto you; and you shall be My witnesses."

The one great truth which Christ would impart to those early followers, so soon to be left without His personality and presence in leadership, was the truth of the reality of the Holy Spirit, and the power which was to be theirs through Him.

Throughout the centuries and ages of the Christian Church this theme has been without a rival, and still we seem to evade and postpone it, perhaps because so many have erred in narrowing and limiting and misconstruing it; perhaps because we have feared to tread such holy ground. The Church of Christ has needed this truth, and needs it more than ever in this age in which we live, so filled with its complexity of thought; so eager to know the truth and apply it practically to life; so willing to search into the deep things of human philosophy and material science and discover new relationships, adjustments and appliances of truth.

September 5: His Power - 7
by John Timothy Stone

Because Joseph, Moses, Joshua, Daniel, David, Elijah, John the Baptist, Stephen and Paul were men singled out in their day as embodiments of God's Holy Spirit, men in whom the Spirit of God dwelt, they were men of matchless power. Others were brilliant, individualistic, scholarly, efficient, attractive, magnanimous. But these great leaders whom God selected were men who had more than eminent, or pre-eminent, gifts or culture. They were men of holy life; men whose secret strength came from personal contact with the Almighty; men of whom kings and peasantry cried out: "Can we find such a man as this, a man in whom the Spirit of God is?"

Moses was forced to flee to the pinnacled heights of the Sinai wilderness; Joseph was sold to the Ishmaelites by his angered brothers; David fled from cave to cave, pursued by an envying Saul; Stephen sank beneath the stones hurled by an infuriated religious mob. But the world knew and knows that these men were God's choice, who in life and death led in the reconstruction and reorganization of society—men who turned from human philosophy to Divine truth. They were men of power.

The last great promise that Christ made us, when men heard His words as they came from lips which the eye could see, was the promise of the power of His Holy Spirit Who would come and remain with us, instruct, comfort, strengthen, and accomplish for and through us. This power of the Holy Spirit was to be given first in the common-place duties of life. Those early disciples were zealous for the restoration of Israel's great kingdom. Christ calls them back to simplicity in service. What He needed was witnessing. The world did not know Him. Only a little circle understood the mission of Jesus of Nazareth, and the power of the Holy Spirit was to be theirs so that they should witness, beginning where they were, in Jerusalem; then in Judaea; then to the despised and neglected Samaritans; then even to the uttermost parts of the world.

From the study of our subject we find that men have felt that the outpouring of God's Spirit upon a community has too frequently implied a great and extraordinary movement—one which is out of the ordinary; unnatural, extensive, exceptional, commanding—when the presence of God's Spirit should be the natural expression of His indwelling power, that we may accomplish the ordinary tasks of life with faithful regularity and simplicity. God does not require exceptional gifts to do His work well. Not many wise or mighty men have been chosen. Many a person who has been unconscious of gifts has been used of God in the hastening of His kingdom. Ten thousand men had brighter prospects, and more brilliant training than John Bunyan [English pastor/writer, 1628-1688] in the Bedford jail. Charles Spurgeon and D. L. Moody were not youths of such remarkable promise. It is not so much what a person is without the Spirit of God that counts, but what a person becomes when the Spirit of God abides within them, and God, with His power, uses them as His vessel.

September 6: His Practicality
by George Matheson
Excerpted from "The Practicalness of the Spirit", *Voices of the Spirit*, published by A. C. Armstrong & Son, New York, New York in 1892

And Pharaoh said unto his servants, "Can we find such a one as this is, a man in whom the Spirit of God is?"
Genesis 11:38

One would have thought the fact would have been a disqualification in the eyes of Pharaoh. Pharaoh was a worldling; how could he respect that which was unworldly? All his motives were guided by the interests of the hour, how could he welcome a man who belonged to the immensities and eternities? It is because eternity includes the present hour, and He who has the Spirit of eternity has also the Spirit of the time. Do you think that an atheist master would consent to have an atheist servant? No, he would know that the temporal work would not be done well. He who would do well the temporal work must be beyond the time. No man can steer his way through the ocean of life whose eye is not on the stars. Would you be fit for your service? Then you must be higher than your service. Life would be too much for you if you did not see ahead of it. You are saved by hope. You cannot be a man of the world without a balanced mind, and a balanced mind is a mind at peace. God's peace is not something to die with; it is something to live by. Without it you are only half a man—unfit for Egypt, unfit for

Pharaoh, unfit for the coming famine. With it, you are more a man of the time than those who call themselves abreast of the age; he who would be abreast of the age must already have outrun it, for the world that now is, is lighted by the world to come.

Spirit of Christ, equip me for the earth on which I dwell. I used to ask that You would prepare me for death; Your main purpose is to prepare me for life. I used to pray that You would make me ready for the things that are unseen and eternal; Your summer is the ripeness for the things that are seen and temporal. I am growing more impressed with the solemnity of living than of dying. I am growing more impressed with the need of You in things common than in things transcendental. I am in need of You not to help me *out* of the world but to help me *in* the world. I need You both for the seven years of plenty and for the seven years of famine. Without You I cannot bear either the one or the other. Be my pillar of cloud by day; be my pillar of fire by night. Teach me my nothingness in the hour of my prosperity; tell me in my adversity that I am something to You. Redeem from dust alike my evenings and my mornings that I may claim as Your gifts not only angels and principalities but the world and life as well. The day of common work shall be the Lord's day, when I can say like the man of Patmos, "I was in the Spirit."

September 7: His Praying - 1
by Charles G. Finney
Excerpted from "Spirit of Prayer", *Lectures on Revivals of Religion*, published by Fleming H. Revell Company, New York, New York in 1868

In like manner the Spirit also helps our infirmity: for we know not how to pray as we ought; but the Spirit Himself makes intercession for us with groanings that cannot be uttered; and He that searches the hearts knows what is the mind of the Spirit, because He makes intercession for the saints according to God.
Romans 8:26-27

Some have supposed that the Spirit spoken of in the text means our own spirit — our own mind. But a little attention to the text will show plainly that this is not the meaning. "The Spirit helps our infirmities" would then read, "Our own spirit helps the infirmities of our own spirit," and "Our own spirit likewise makes intercession for our own spirit." You see you can make no sense of it on that supposition. It is evident from the manner in which the text is introduced, that the Spirit referred to is the Holy Ghost: "For if you live after the flesh, you shall die; but if you through the Spirit do mortify the deeds of the body, you shall live. For as many as are led by the Spirit of God, they are the sons of God. For you have not received the spirit of bondage again to fear; but you have received the spirit of adoption, whereby we cry, Abba, Father. The Spirit Himself bears witness with our spirit, that we are the children of God." And the text is plainly speaking of the same Spirit.

What the Spirit does. Answer—He intercedes for the saints. "He makes intercession for us," and "helps our infirmities," when "we do not know what to pray for as we ought." He helps Christians to pray according to the will of God, or for the things that God desires them to pray for.

Why is the Holy Spirit thus employed? Because of our ignorance. Because we know not what we should pray for as we ought. We are so ignorant both of the will of God, revealed in the Bible, and of His unrevealed will, as we ought to learn it from His providence. People are vastly ignorant both of the promises and prophecies of the Bible, and blind to the providence of God. And they are still more in the dark about those points of which God has said nothing but by the leadings of His Spirit. You recollect that I named these four sources of evidence on which to ground faith in prayer—promises, prophecies, providences, and the Holy Spirit. When all other means fail of leading us to the knowledge of what we ought to pray for, the Spirit does it.

How does He make intercession for the saints? In what mode does He operate, so as to help our infirmities? Not by superseding the use of our faculties. It is not by praying for us, while we do nothing. He prays for us, by exciting our own faculties. Not that He immediately suggests to us words, or guides our language. But He enlightens our minds, and makes the truth take hold of our souls.

September 8: His Praying - 2
by Charles G. Finney

The Spirit makes the Christian feel the value of souls, and the guilt and danger of sinners in their present condition. It is amazing how dark and stupid Christians often are about this. Even Christian parents let their children go right down to Hell before their eyes, and scarcely seem to exercise a single feeling, or put forth an effort to save them. And why? Because they are so blind to what Hell is, so unbelieving about the Bible, so ignorant of the precious promise which God has made to faithful parents. They grieve the Spirit of God away, and it is in vain to try to make them pray for their children, while the Spirit of God is away from them.

He leads Christians to understand and apply the promises of Scripture. It is wonderful that in no age have Christians been able fully to apply the promises of Scripture to the events of life, as they go along. This is not because the promises themselves are obscure. The promises themselves are plain enough. But there has always been a wonderful disposition to overlook the Scriptures, as a source of light respecting the passing events of life. How astonished the apostles were at Christ's application of so many prophecies to Himself! They seemed to be continually ready to exclaim, "Astonishing! Can it be so? We never understood it before." Those who have witnessed the manner in which the apostles, influenced and inspired by the Holy Ghost, applied the Old Testament to gospel times, have not been amazed at the richness of meaning which they found in the Scriptures? So it has been with many a Christian; while deeply engaged in prayer, he has seen that passages of Scripture are appropriate which he never thought of before, as having any such application.

The Spirit leads Christians to desire and pray for things of which nothing is specifically said in the Word of God. God is willing to say yes is a general truth. So it is a general truth that He is willing to answer prayer. But how shall I know the will of God respecting that individual, whether I can pray in faith according to the will of God for the conversion and salvation of that individual, or not? Here the agency of the Spirit comes in, to lead the minds of God's people to pray for those individuals, and at those times, when God is prepared to bless them. When we know not what to pray for, the Holy Spirit leads the mind to dwell on some object, to consider its situation, to realize its value, and to feel for it, and pray, and travail in birth, till the object is attained. This sort of experience I know is less common in cities than it is in some parts of the country, because of the infinite number of things to divert the attention and grieve the Spirit in cities. I have had much opportunity to know how it has been in some sections.

In this manner the Spirit of God leads individual Christians to pray for things which they would not pray for, unless they were led by the Spirit. And thus they pray for things according to the will of God.

September 9: His Praying - 3
by Andrew Murray
Excerpted from "The Spirit of Prayer", *The Spirit of Christ*, published by A. D. F. Randolph & Co., New York, New York in 1888

In like manner the Spirit also helps our infirmity: for we know not how to pray as we ought; but the Spirit Himself makes intercession for us with groanings that cannot be uttered; and He that searches the hearts knows what is the mind of the Spirit, because He makes intercession for the saints according to God.
Romans 8:26-27

Of the offices of the Holy Spirit, one that leads us most deeply into the understanding of His place in the Divine economy of grace, and into the mystery of the Holy Trinity, is the work He does as the Spirit of prayer. We have the Father to whom we pray, and who hears prayer. We have the Son through whom we pray, and through whom, in union with whom, we receive and really appropriate the answer. And we have the Holy Spirit in whom we pray, who prays in us according to the will of God, with such deeply hidden, unutterable sighing, that God has to search the hearts to know what is the mind of the Spirit. Just as wonderful and real as is the Divine work of God on the Throne, graciously hearing, and, by His mighty power, effectively answering prayer; just as Divine as is the work of the Son interceding and securing and transmitting the answer from above, is the work of the

Holy Spirit in us in the prayer which waits and obtains the answer. The intercession within is as Divine as the intercession above. Let us try and understand why this should be so, and what it teaches.

In the creation of the world we see how it was the work of the Spirit to put Himself into contact with the dark and lifeless matter of chaos, and by His quickening energy to impart to it the power of life and fruitfulness. It was only after it had been thus vitalized by Him, that the Word of God gave it form, and called forth all the different types of life and beauty we now see. So, too, again in the creation of man it was the Spirit that was breathed into the body that had been formed from the ground, and that thus united itself with what would otherwise be dead matter. Even so, in the person of Jesus it is the Spirit through whose work a body was prepared for Him, through whom His body again was quickened from the grave, as it is through Him that our bodies are the temples of God, and the very members of our body the members of Christ. We think of the Spirit in connection with the spiritual nature of the Divine Being, far removed from the grossness and feebleness of matter; we forget that it is the very work of the Spirit especially to unite Himself with what is material, to lift it up into His own Spirit nature, and so to develop what will be the highest type of perfection, a spiritual body.

September 10: His Praying - 4
by Andrew Murray

This view of the Spirit's work is essential to the understanding of the place He takes in the Divine work of redemption. In each part of that work there is a special place assigned to each of the Three Persons of the Holy Trinity. In the Father we have the unseen God, the Author of all. In the Son God revealed, made manifest, and brought near; He is the Form of God. In the Spirit of God we have the Indwelling God — the Power of God dwelling in the human body and working in it what the Father and the Son have for us. Not only in the individual, but in the Church as a whole, what the Father has purposed, and the Son has procured, can be appropriated and take effect in the body of Christ only through the continual intervention and active operation of the Holy Spirit.

This is especially true of intercessory prayer. The coming of the kingdom of God, the increase of grace and knowledge and holiness in believers, their growing devotion to God's work and power for that work, the effective working of God's power on the unconverted through the means of grace — all this waits to come to us from God through Christ. But it cannot come except as it is looked for and desired, asked and expected, believed and hoped for. And this is now the wonderful position the Holy Ghost occupies, that to Him has been assigned the task of preparing the body of Christ to reach out and receive and hold fast what has been provided in the fulness of Christ the Head. For the communication of the Father's love and blessing the Son and the Spirit must both work. The Son receives from the Father, reveals and brings near, as it were, descends from above; the Spirit from within awakens the soul to come out and meet its Lord. As indispensable as the unceasing intercession of Christ asking and receiving from the Father above, is the unceasing intercession of the Spirit within, asking and accepting from the Son what the Father gives.

Very wonderful is the light that is cast upon this holy mystery by the words of our text. In the life of faith and prayer there are operations of the Spirit in which the Word of God is made clear to our understanding, and our faith knows to express what it needs and asks. But there are also operations of the Spirit, deeper down than thoughts or feelings, where He works desires and yearnings in our spirit, in the secret springs of life and being, which God only can discover and understand. Of this nature is the real thirst for God Himself, the Living God, the longing to know the love "that passes knowledge," and to be "filled with all the fulness of God," the hope in "Him who is able to do exceeding abundantly above all we can ask or think," even "what has not entered the heart of man to conceive." When these aspirations indeed take possession of us, we begin to pray for what cannot be expressed, and our only comfort is that the Spirit prays with His unutterable yearnings in a region and a language which the Heart Searcher alone knows and understands.

September 11: His Preceding
by George Matheson
Excerpted from "The Precedence of the Spirit", *Voices of the Spirit*, published by A. C. Armstrong & Son, New York, New York in 1892

The Spirit of God moved upon the face of the waters.
Genesis 1:2

Before God said "Let there be light," He said "Let there be Spirit." It was the keynote of all His voices to the human soul. It is no use to bring the light until you have brought the Spirit. Light will not make the waters of life glad unless the spirit of joy has already moved them. Light is only outward and the joy of the soul has its seat within. It is in vain you promise me the herb of the field and the bird of the air and the fish of the sea. It is in vain even that you bring me into contact with my fellow-men made in the image of God. If the Spirit has not moved on the face of the waters there can be no gladness in my face. That which makes me glad is not what I get but what I am, and what I am depends on the Spirit. Therefore it was well that the Spirit should come before all His gifts—before the light, before the firmament, before the herb of the field. It was well that the joy in the heart should precede the joy in the universe. It was well that before the light could rise, the Spirit should move on the face of the waters.

O Divine Spirit whose breath preceded all things, I am seeking to invert the order of Your work. I am asking for other things before You. I am crying for light, for sun and moon and star, for the green herb, for the bird of Heaven. I am forgetting that without You the light would not charm, the grass would not grow, the bird would not sing. Come Yourself first of all and move upon the face of the waters. Come and give to the light its charm, to the herb its greenness, to the bird its song. Come and let me see the image of God in my brother man, that I may learn to love him as my other self and in the joy of love may find universal joy. Without You the days of my creation are evenings without mornings; the night-less Sabbath shall have dawned when You shall move upon the waters.

September 12: His Preparing
by I. L. Kephart
Excerpted from "What He Does—His Characteristics", *The Holy Spirit in the Devout Life*, published by United Brethren Publishing House, Dayton, Ohio in 1904

The devout life, Spirit-filled, recognizes this earth-life as a time of preparation for the life which is to come. Too many professed Christians live as if life in this world were the only thing to live for. Pleasure, the latest styles, social amusements, the theaters, with them must have the right of way. Not so with the devout Christian. With him, as the Apostle Peter exhorted, life here is the time to "give diligence, to make your calling and election sure," to aid his Divine Master in establishing the kingdom of righteousness in this world. For him this life is the time for character-building, by rendering faithful service in the holy cause of saving souls from death; and the time of rest is to be in the glory world beyond, where Christ has gone to prepare a place for all those to whom He can say, "Come you blessed by My Father," etc. (Matthew 25:34-40).

To the devout Christian all the teachings of our Divine Lord and the apostles concerning service—working out our salvation, being faithful unto death, cutting down the barren fig-tree, taking the talent away from him who failed to improve it, the going away in to everlasting punishment, and turning the wicked into Hell—are solemn realities, and they, endowed by the Holy Spirit, endeavor to behave accordingly. Glad of the opportunity to cooperate with Jesus, they work. Believing that the judgments of the Lord are true and certain, and "knowing the terror of the Lord," they lovingly do all they can to persuade men to flee from the wrath to come (2 Corinthians 5:11).

With the devout Christian it is not enough to have received the Holy Spirit; he cannot rest without using Him. In fact, it is through using Him in promoting and effecting the salvation of men that he retains Him and becomes more and more efficient in using the power He imparts.

Plato well said, "A man who would be happy must not only have the good things, but he must also use them; there is no advantage in merely having them." This truth, aptly expressed by that eminent pagan philosopher, is a sterling reality to the devout Christian in regard to his being the fortunate possessor of the Holy Spirit. The joy accompanying a knowledge of his Possession would soon vanish did he not use, to the glory of God, the power with which that Possession equips him. And right here we have the secret of the deplorable fact that many new converts soon lapse from their first love into a state of joylessness, doubt, uncertainty, and spiritual death.

Paul's was truly a devout life, a life wonderfully endowed with capital with which to do business for the Lord, and the largeness of his endowment and the superiority of his work both in quantity and quality, was due to the fact that he believed God (Acts 27:25), and diligently and with great zeal and boldness, used the capital with which the Holy Spirit endowed him.

September 13: His Presence
by Andrew Murray
Excerpted from "On the Presence of the Spirit in the Church, Note I, The Paraclete", *The Spirit of Christ*, published by A. D. F. Randolph & Co., New York, New York in 1888

The present enjoyment of the Spirit is but an earnest, a gift beforehand, a pledge of the coming fulness. The Apostle Paul speaks (Romans 8:23) of those "which have the first-fruits of the Spirit," and in his other epistles he uses equivalent expressions (Ephesians 1:13; 4:30; 2 Corinthians 1:22; 5:5). What can be meant by such words but that the spiritual life is a continual progression, receiving, with its widening capacities, richer gifts of the wisdom and holiness of God? The Church is in its infancy as to valuation of spiritual blessing. It is, too, so much engaged in controversy that it can hardly be preparing itself for the completion of the holy promise. By mistaking the part for the whole, it is in danger of settling itself into premature satisfaction, as if it had exhausted the possibilities of prayer!

Will it be uncharitable to suggest that the Church is too much engaged in that worst and most scourging of all worldliness, the elevation of one sect above another, and the angry defense of forms, which are just transient conveniences? What is delaying the outpouring of the fulness of the Spirit? There is indeed a still sterner inquiry, which cannot be put without emotion, yet it may not be honestly suppressed. Is not the presence of the Holy Ghost in the Church less distinct today than in the apostolic age? Certainly, there is not much appearance of Pentecostal inspiration in contemporary Christianity. Why has not a Church eighteen hundred years old a fuller realization of the witness of the Holy Ghost than had the Church of the first century? Has the Church accomplished all the purpose of God, and passed the zenith of her light and beauty?

September 14: His Prohibitions
by George Matheson
Excerpted from "The Prohibitions of the Spirit", *Voices of the Spirit*, published by A. C. Armstrong & Son, New York, New York in 1892

After they were come to Mysia, they attempted to go into Bithynia: but the Spirit did not allow them.
Acts 16:7

What a strange prohibition! These men were going into Bithynia just to do Christ's work and the door is shut to them by Christ's own Spirit. I too have experienced this in certain moments. I have sometimes found myself interrupted in what seemed to me a career of usefulness. Opposition came and forced me to go back, or sickness came and compelled me to retire into a desert place apart. It was hard at such times to leave my work undone when I believed that work to be the service of the Spirit. But I came to remember that the Spirit has not only a service of work but a service of waiting. I came to see that in the Kingdom of Christ there are not only times for action but times in which to restrain from acting. I came to learn that the desert place apart is often the most useful spot in the varied life of man—more rich in harvest than the seasons in which the corn and wine abounded. I have been taught by the songs of the night to thank the blessed Spirit that many a darling Bithynia had to be left unvisited by me.

And so, Divine Spirit, I would still be led by You. Still there come to me disappointed prospects of usefulness. Today the door seems to open into life and work for You; tomorrow it closes before me just as I am about to enter. Teach me to see another door in the very inaction of the hour. Help me to find in the very prohibition thus to serve You a new opening into Your service. Inspire me with the knowledge that a man may at times be called to do his duty by doing nothing, to work by keeping still, to serve by waiting. Awaken me to the conviction that there are moments of solitary rest which are more rich in their result to humanity than centuries of busy strife. When I remember the power of the still small voice I shall not murmur that sometimes the Spirit allows me not to go.

September 15: His Promise - 1
by Charles H. Spurgeon

Excerpted from "The Covenant Promise of the Spirit", *Twelve Sermons on the Holy Spirit*, published by Fleming H. Revell Company, New York, New York in 1855

"And I will put My Spirit within you."
Ezekiel 36:27

No preface is needed; and the largeness of our subject forbids our wasting time in beating about the bush. I shall try to do two things: First, I would commend the text; and, secondly, I would in some measure expound the text.

First, as for the commendation of the text, the tongues of men and of angels might fail. To call it a golden sentence would be much too commonplace. To liken it to a pearl of great price would be too poor a comparison. We cannot feel, much less speak, too much in praise of that great God who has put this clause into the covenant of His grace. In that covenant every sentence is more precious than Heaven and earth; and this line is not the least among His choice words of promise: "I will put My Spirit within you."

I would begin by saying that this is a gracious word. It was spoken to a graceless people, to a people who had followed "their own way," and refused the way of God; a people who had already provoked something more than ordinary anger in the Judge of all the earth; for He Himself said (verse 18), "I poured My fury upon them." These people, even under chastisement, caused the holy name of God to be profaned among the heathen, wherever they went. They had been highly favored, but they abused their privileges, and behaved worse than those who never knew the Lord. They sinned wantonly, willfully, wickedly, proudly and presumptuously; and by this they greatly provoked the Lord. Yet to them He made such a promise as this: "I will put My Spirit within you." Surely, where sin abounded grace did much more abound.

Clearly this is a word of grace, for the law says nothing of this kind. Turn to the law of Moses and see if there is any word spoken therein concerning the putting of the Spirit within men to cause them to walk in God's statutes. The law proclaims the statutes; but the gospel alone promises the Spirit by which the statutes will be obeyed. The law commands and makes us know what God requires of us; but the gospel goes further, and inclines us to obey the will of the Lord, and enables us practically to walk in His ways. Under the dominion of grace the Lord works in us to will and to do of His own good pleasure.

So great a boon as this could never come to any man by merit. A man might so act as to deserve a reward of a certain kind, in measure suited to his commendable action; but the Holy Spirit can never be the wage of human service: The idea verges upon blasphemy. Can any man deserve that Christ should die for him? Who would dream of such a thing? Can any man deserve that the Holy Ghost should dwell in him, and work holiness in him? The greatness of the blessing lifts it high above the range of merit.

September 16: His Promise - 2
by Charles H. Spurgeon

We see that if the Holy Ghost is bestowed, it must be by an act of Divine grace — grace infinite in bounty, exceeding all that we could have imagined. "Grace o'er sin abounding" is here seen in clearest light. "I will put My Spirit within you" is a promise which drops with graces as the honeycomb with honey. Listen to the Divine music which pours from this word of love. I hear the soft melody of grace, grace, grace, and nothing else but grace. Glory be to God, who gives to sinners the indwelling of His Spirit.

Note, next, that it is a Divine word: "I will put My Spirit within you." Who but the Lord could speak after this fashion? Can one man put the Spirit of God within another? Could all the Church combined breathe the Spirit of God into a single sinner's heart? To put any good thing into the deceitful heart of man is a great achievement; but to put the Spirit of God into the heart, truly this is the finger of God. No, here I may say, the Lord has made bare His arm, and displayed the fulness of His mighty power. To put the Spirit of God into our nature is a work unique to the Godhead, and to do this within the nature of a free agent, such as man, is marvelous. Who but Jehovah, the God of Israel, can speak after this royal style, and, beyond all dispute, declare, "I will put My Spirit within you"? Men must always surround their resolves with conditions and uncertainties; but since omnipotence is at the back of every promise of God, He speaks like a king; yes, in a style which is only fit for the eternal God. He purposes and promises, and He as surely performs. Sure, then, is this sacred saying, "I will put My Spirit within you." O sinner, if we poor creatures had the saving of you, we should break down in the attempt; but, behold, the Lord Himself comes on the scene, and the work is done! All the difficulties are removed by this one sentence, "I will put My Spirit within you."

We have worked with our spirit, we have wept over you, and we have entreated you; but we have failed. Lo, there comes One into the matter who will not fail, with whom nothing is impossible; and He begins His work by saying, "I will put My Spirit within you." The word is of grace and of God; regard it, then, as a pledge from the God of grace.

To me there is much charm in the further thought that this is an individual and personal word. The Lord means, "I will put My Spirit within you," that is to say, within you, as individuals, "put My spirit within you" one by one. This must be so since the connection requires it. We read in verse 26, "A new heart will I also give you." Now, a new heart can only be given to one person. Each man needs a heart of his own, and each man must have a new heart for himself. "And a new spirit will I put within you." Within each one this must be done. "And I will take away the stony heart out of your flesh, and I will give you a heart of flesh"—these are all personal, individual operations of grace.

September 17: His Prosperity
by George Matheson
Excerpted from "The Prosperity of the Spirit", *Voices of the Spirit*, published by A. C. Armstrong & Son, New York, New York in 1892

And the Spirit of God came upon Azariah the son of Oded: and he went out to meet Asa, and said unto him, "Hear me, Asa, and all Judah and Benjamin; The Lord is with you, while you are with Him."
2 Chronicles 15:1-2

I thought inspiration was the revelation of something new. I thought it should tell us something nobody knew before. Why then send the Spirit to a man to utter such a truism as this, "The Lord is with you, while you are with Him"? It is because these words are only a truism to him who has received the Spirit. He who has not received the Spirit would deem them the wildest paradox. He would look at the men of God, and say, "Where is to them the promise of His coming?" He would say to the Son of Man, "Come down from the cross and we will believe in You." He would ask if the favor of God was consistent with being mocked, and scourged, and crucified, with being despised and rejected of men, with having nowhere to lay the weary head. We know that it is consistent, but why? Because we have the fruit of the Spirit. We have learned by Christian experience that the valley may be exalted, that the crooked may be made straight, and the rough places plain. We have learned by Christian experience that there is a peace which passes understanding, which the world cannot give and never can take away. But that knowledge is itself a gift of the Spirit. Is it not written, "The secret of the Lord is with them that fear Him"? To all outside it is a secret. A song in the night, a stream in the desert, a light in the valley, a rainbow in the flood — these are not the truisms of the natural mind. Inspiration alone can reveal the prosperity of the soul; the Spirit alone can tell us that God is with us while we are with Him.

Spirit of Christ, only in Your inspiration can I know that the righteous prosper. Seen in the light of the world, those that are with You appear to have the worst of it. But the light of the world cannot reveal the glories of Gethsemane. It can disclose the sweat drops and the tears and the darkness. It can reveal the Suppliant pouring out His petition with the voice of strong crying. It can show that the prayer is seemingly unanswered, and the passing of the cup denied. But it cannot disclose the peace that comes with the cup. It cannot detect the angel of strength that follows the surrendered will. It cannot photograph the rod and the staff that even in the valley of the shadow of death enable a man to say, "You are with me." Create Yourself that sublime vision, O Spirit of the Cross. Usher me into the joy of my Lord — the joy that could speak of its fulness at the very foot of Calvary. Inspire me with the peace which is independent of circumstances, which in the hour of death can say, "Let not your heart be troubled." Then and not till then shall the paradox become a truism, then and not till then shall I understand the promise, "The Lord is with you, while you are with Him."

September 18: His Qualifying
by George Matheson
Excerpted from "The Qualification for the Spirit", *Voices of the Spirit*, published by A. C. Armstrong & Son, New York, New York in 1892

"For I will pour water upon him that is thirsty, and floods upon the dry ground: I will pour My Spirit upon your seed."
Isaiah 44:3

That which makes me capable of receiving God's Spirit is not my feeling of boundlessness, but my struggle with limitations. That which makes me greater than the beasts of the field is not my superior strength, but my superior insight into my own weakness. My greatness is my sense of needs unsatisfied. Everything about me which makes me human is a form of thirst. My speculation is the thirst of my understanding. My love is the thirst of my heart. My aspiration is the thirst of my fancy. My prayer is the thirst of my spirit. I am a bundle of longings, and my longings are all prophecies. I could not long for anything if I had reached finality. Why do I seek so many things that are not here? Why do I not sing through the world as the bird sings through the sky? It is because the sky is the bird's environment; the world is not my environment. If it were, I too would sing. But there is that within me which is not met by anything around me. My eye is not satisfied with its seeing, nor my ear with its hearing. My intellect is not filled with its knowledge, nor my heart with its love. I seek a perfect beauty, a perfect music, a perfect wisdom, a perfect soul. My thirst is the prophecy of an environment yet to be.

I long for Your Spirit, O Lord, and thereby I know that You too long for me. Nothing but Yourself can enclose the aspirations of my heart, because nothing but myself can meet the desires of Yours. I am incomplete without You, because without me Your fulness has not come. Come to my heart and we shall dwell together, I in You and You in me. Come to my heart and its hungering shall be filled, and Your love shall be satisfied, and we shall be one. Come to my heart and there shall be a union of earth and Heaven; day and night shall meet together, omnipotence and frailty shall embrace each other. I hope for Your Spirit because I thirst for You.

September 19: His Quenching - 1
by Theodore L. Cuyler
Excerpted from "Quench not the Spirit", *The Cedar Christian and Other Practical Papers and Personal Sketches*, published by Robert Carter and Brothers, New York, New York in 1864

If a party of Arctic explorers, after a long, perilous march through driving snowstorms, were to find themselves under the overhang of a rock or an ice-mound for the night, how carefully would they draw forth the single match or bit of tinder that was to keep them from perishing. All depends on that one match. How they hover around it to protect the first faint flicker from the wind. "Be careful, be c-a-r-e-f-u-l," says the anxious leader, with suspended breath, as he watches the spark light into a little blaze, and the blaze slowly creep up until it takes hold of twigs and begins to ignite the heap of driftwood. To put out that flame is suicide. To fan it is the first instinct of self-preservation. And when the seed of fire has grown into a crackling flame, illuminating rock, and ice, and fur-clad men with a reddish glow, they all thank God that no careless hand was permitted to quench the fire on which their lives depended.

Why are inquiring souls to take heed not to "quench the Spirit"? One: Because the Holy Spirit is the soul's Enlightener. Do not put out the light is Paul's tender caution. A sinner's heart is by nature enveloped in darkness. As absence of light makes darkness, so absence of spiritual knowledge makes ignorance, and absence of godliness makes depravity. This midnight of the heart can only be illuminated by the incoming of the Spirit. It is one of the blessed offices of Him whom "the Father sends to teach you all things," and to "guide you into all truth." It is His work to reveal the iniquity of the heart, It is His to show the sinner his besetting sin, and to make known its exceeding wickedness. It is His, too, to reveal the way of salvation. As the Alpine traveler at night needs the lantern at his waist to find his way to the lodge, so does the inquirer for salvation need the Divine Enlightener to guide his trembling footsteps to Calvary. Do not put out the light.

Two: The Spirit resembles fire because He melts the flinty heart. A "heart of stone" is the Bible's description of the stubborn sinner. There is no contrition, no tenderness, no godly love in it. It needs melting. A stubborn heart is first so softened as to feel the truth; then to weep over sin; then to be pliable and moldable; then so flexible as to be "formed anew" into a shape that pleases the Lord Jesus Christ. This melting process is accomplished by the Holy Ghost. Just what the fire accomplishes in the foundry the infinite Spirit of love accomplishes in a convicted soul. As the Holy Spirit alone can melt you into repentance, alone can subdue your stubbornness, and mold you into obedience to God, as He alone can transform your hard, ungrateful deformity into the "beauty of holiness," we plead with you, awakened friend, quench not the fire.

September 20: His Quenching - 2
by Theodore L. Cuyler

Three: The third office of the Spirit is that of a Purifier. Have you ever witnessed the smelting process by which the dross is burned away and the pure metal is made to flow into the clay receptacle? Then you have witnessed a vivid illustration of the Spirit's work in sanctification. How the corruption runs away under the blessed action of Divine love! How the dross goes off! How the graces burnish into brightness! How that which hides the pure gold is eliminated! Oh, you who yearn for a better life, for conquests over indwelling sin, for the incoming of holiness, as you love your souls, quench not the Spirit.

Four: One other agency of God's Spirit we glance at; it is the heating, soul-propelling power. Every heart is more or less frozen by selfishness—more or less sluggish to the claims of Heavenly blessing. Now, what is accomplished in the engine room of an ocean steamship when a flame is kindled under the dead mass of coal in the furnace, is accomplished in the cold, selfish heart of man, when the Divine Spirit brings in the new inspiration of love for Christ. The mass kindles; the soul moves; the powers begin their play; the whole man gets in motion; and as long as the fire of holy love burns on in the depths of the soul, so long do men see the steady, triumphant march of a life of radiant zeal and Christ-like character.

This was the fire from Heaven that descended at Pentecost. It was the young Church's inspiration that propelled it to the spiritual conquest of the globe. Here is the one greatest, sorest, saddest lack of our modern Churches. Pulpit and pew alike need the blessed propulsion which God's Spirit alone can kindle.

Do you not see by this time, my unconverted friend, how much your very life depends on the Spirit's influence? Already have you felt His power. In all your guilt for past wasted hours of selfishness and sin—in all your aspiring for a better life—you felt that power. He it was who thrilled you under that solemn discourse in God's house, until your conscience reeled as the reed is smitten under a mighty wind. He startled you on that bed of sickness, when eternity came near and looked you in the face. He melted your heart under the pleading appeal and the touching prayer of that faithful friend, who yearned for your salvation. He came with that affectionate pastor to your fireside, and warned you to flee from the wrath to come. He spoke to you out of that hollow tomb that opened for your departed, and told you to prepare to meet your God. A Monitor has He been to you. He waits to be a Teacher, a Comforter, a Purifier, a Sanctifier of your soul. Dare you grieve Him away? Oh, as you value your present peace and your hope of future salvation—as you desire life, and joy, and glory everlasting—as you would shun the agonies of Hell and secure the blessedness of Heaven—we beg you, quench not the Spirit!

September 21: His Quickening - 1
by A. B. Simpson
Excerpted from "The Quickening Spirit", *When the Comforter Came*, published by The Alliance Press Company, New York, New York in 1911

If the Spirit of Him who raised up Jesus from the dead dwells in you, He that raised up Christ from the dead shall also quicken your mortal bodies by His Spirit who dwells in you.
Romans 7:11

This text reveals the Comforter as the Quickener or Author of life. The verse depends for its force upon the place we give it in the plan of redemption and the true exegesis of the passage. It has been usual to refer it to the future resurrection and to the work of the Holy Spirit in calling to immortal life the dead bodies of the saints of God. But there are the strongest reasons in the passage itself and the analogy of Scripture against this view.

In the first place the Holy Spirit is not represented in the Scriptures as the Agent in the final resurrection. It is the Lord Jesus who shall raise the dead by His own direct voice. "The dead shall hear the voice of the Son of God and they that hear shall live."

In the next place the Spirit is represented as now dwelling in the body that He quickens. This could not be true of the dead. The Holy Spirit is never represented as dwelling in a dead body. "God is not the God of the dead, but of the living." It must therefore be the bodies of living persons that the Holy Spirit is here said to quicken.

Further, the bodies here quickened are described as "mortal bodies." Now a mortal body is not a dead body, but a body liable to death.

Once more, the word "quicken" does not necessarily mean the resurrection of the dead body. In this very book of Romans it is applied to the quickening of Abraham's body (4:17), when he was old and his strength was renewed for the birth of Isaac. It means the invigorating, vitalizing, stimulating of a body weak and failing, and precisely applies to the healing of disease by the touch of the Holy Spirit.

And this appears to be the obvious meaning of the passage. The Apostle has just been speaking of the work of the Holy Ghost in sanctifying the soul and directing and controlling the believer's walk and life. Naturally, therefore, he next refers to the Holy Spirit's work for the Christian's body and tells us that He who is a new and Divine law of life for the soul is just as much the Quickener of the weak and mortal body. If He dwells in the house He will repair it and take good care of it.

September 22: His Quickening - 2
by A. B. Simpson

We are introduced to God's great secret of true physical life. It is not nerve force, muscular force, the effect of food and air and constitution, although all these have their place and none of them must be neglected or despised; but it is a direct infusion into our mortal frame and our vital centers of a supernatural and Divine vitality through the Holy Ghost. It is something not communicated by drugs or electrical applications, or even air and food, but it is life from the primal source of life, the Creator Himself. It is another kind of life, a higher kind of life, an added life; that very life of which the same writer says in 2 Corinthians 4:2: "The life also of Jesus is manifested in our mortal flesh."

Now have we any precedents for this in the Scriptures? Certainly. We go back to the story of Samson, and we find that his strength was not produced by muscle and bone or weight and size, but by the Holy Spirit. When the Spirit began "to move upon him," he suddenly developed into gigantic strength and slew his enemies and carried away the gates of their cities and laughed at their strength and numbers. And when by disobedience he lost the Holy Spirit and sank into self-indulgence and sin his body became as weak as a child's and his enemies blinded him and made sport of him.

I once found myself in an abandoned office where I had some work to do at night, but where I had neither light nor heat. I lit a match and tried to light the gas, but the pipes had been taken out. I then searched for lamps and candles but there were none. Finally I went to a closet where I had been accustomed to keep old newspapers, and I felt sure if I could throw these in the grate I would have at least temporary light. But the newspapers had already been thrown into the grate and there was nothing left but a heap of black and lifeless ashes. Then I discovered a small bottle of kerosene. I poured it in on the ashes in the grate and lo, they blazed up and lit the room and dispelled the chill, and I was able to finish my work with comfort. As often as the grate fire began to go down all I had to do was to pour a little fresh oil upon it. That is the parable of the Spirit's quickening life in our mortal bodies. Our natural bodies may be like that heap of dead ashes. But if the Spirit is dwelling in us we shall live by His life till our work is done.

September 23: His Rapture
by George Matheson
Excerpted from "The Rapture of the Spirit", *Voices of the Spirit*, published by A. C. Armstrong & Son, New York, New York in 1892

And he carried me away in the Spirit to a great and high mountain, and showed me that great city, the holy Jerusalem, descending out of Heaven from God.
Revelation 21:10

There are times of inward rapture in which I am quite carried away—caught up to meet the Lord in the air. Like Moses I stand upon a great and high mountain, and the desert is forgotten and the promised land is near. I could not live but for these glints of sunshine. When the night is very dark and the desert is very dreary, I say to myself, "Remember what you saw on the mountain; you will come out of the desert; there is a city somewhere." And truly I am right, my mountain moments are the test of what I shall be. It matters not how seldom they come; if they came only once, they would still predict the capacity of my wings. Sometimes in the early year you can hear only the note of a single bird, and all the rest is silence. Yet the bird and not the silence is the coming reality; a little while and nature will take up the song and be sung altogether. Even so is it with my mountain moments. My songs may be few, but they are few because the year is early; they and not the silences are the realities of the ripening hour. A whole lifetime in the desert is outweighed by one sight of the city of God.

Spirit Divine, in whose presence is fulness of joy and at whose right hand there are pleasures forevermore, send into my spring premonitions of the summer gold. Send me in advance "days of Heaven upon earth" — days of warmth above their season, days of sunshine brighter than their time. I have known You in Your hours of conflict moving on the face of the chaotic waters. I have known You in Your hours of calmness descending dove-like on the banks of Jordan. Am I not to know You in yet one stage more — Your stage of overflowing joy? The struggle with chaos is noble; the peace of Jordan's dove is beautiful; but do You not have moments in which You transcend even these? Do You not have moments in which my soul is "carried away," transported, surprised out of itself? Do You not have moments in which the prophet precedes the Messianic age and tells me beforehand of the glory that shall be revealed, when the desert dwindles into a span and eternity alone is real? Such moments I ask of You. By these and not by its shadows shall I measure life. Mount Ararat was dry when all beside was flooded, but Mount Ararat was the reality and all beside was vanishing away. When Your sunlight touches the summits of the mountain I know that before long there shall be light in the city too.

September 24: His Realization
by Edward Irving
Excerpted from "Christ's Life the Realization of the Spirit's Work",
Miscellanies, published by Alexander Strahan, London, England in 1866

The work of the Holy Ghost in the human nature of Christ, from His conception unto His baptism, was to fulfill all the righteousness of the law; and I think that word which He spoke at His baptism, "It is proper for us to do this to fulfill all righteousness," is the amen with which He concluded that great accomplishment. The baptism of John was the isthmus which connected the fulfillment of the law upon the one hand, with the opening of the spiritual and evangelical holiness upon the other: to which our Lord alludes, in these words: "The kingdom of Heaven suffers violence from the baptism of John until now, and the violent take it by force;" giving them to understand that the baptism of John had initiated into the kingdom, as the baptism of Moses in the cloud, and in the sea, initiated into the law. From the anointing with the descending of the Holy Spirit in the form of a dove, I believe that our Lord entered upon a higher and holier walk than mere law-fulfilling, giving to us the example of that spiritual holiness which knows no law but the law of liberty; that is, the will inclined unto the will of God.

Therefore it was that our Lord broke the Sabbath without offense; and touched lepers, and otherwise offended the law; and therefore, also, He went up to the feasts, or went not up, according to His mind. And many things besides He did, which are all expressed in these two similarities, of which, when challenged for this neglect, He made use of: "No man puts new wine into old bottles; no man puts a piece of new cloth onto an old garment;" signifying that the spirit of His discipleship, of which He was then performing the initiation, would not piece on to, much less be contained within, the old worn-out commandments of Moses. Besides, the works which He did by the Spirit were the self-same works which the Spirit in the apostles did. And it is continually written, He set us an example that we should follow His steps.

He had the Spirit lifting Him into a high communion with His Father, to the end of showing Him the regenerate Church, and what should be the measure of their enjoyment; and this being accomplished, I say again, He was let plumb down into the former measure of the Spirit, to swim in the tempestuous ocean, which all the elements of moral disorder could raise around Him. Fearful chaos! awful valley of the shadow of death! season of the hour and power of darkness! Thus have we two measures of the Spirit: The first for law-keeping, to be in lieu of the obedience of those elect ones before, who had believed on Him under the law, or, as it is written, "for the transgressions that were under the first covenant;" the second measure of the Spirit being for an example unto us of that baptism of the Holy Spirit with which we should be baptized.

September 25: His Receiving
by A. B. Simpson
Excerpted from "How to Receive the Comforter", *When the Comforter Came*, published by The Alliance Press Company, New York, New York in 1911

> *"Receive the Holy Ghost."*
> John 20:22

One: The first condition of receiving the Spirit is a deep and intense desire.

Two: The empty are always filled. "He has filled the hungry with good things, but the rich He has sent away empty." "Blessed are the poor in spirit, for theirs is the kingdom of Heaven." Every great blessing begins with a great sacrifice, a great severance, a great dispossessing. "He brought them out that He might bring them in."

Three: The open heart shall be filled. "Open your mouth wide and I will fill it." We know what it is for the flower-cup to close its petals and also to open to the sunlight, the dew and the refreshing shower. The heart has its susceptibilities and receptive sensibilities, but often it is so tightened up with unbelief, doubt, fear, and self-consciousness that it cannot take in the love which God is waiting to pour out. Like the mother who found her long-lost child after years of separation, but the child could not recognize the mother, and as she tried to awaken its response and to pour out the full tides of her bursting heart and found no recognition, but only the dull stare of strangeness and suspicion, her heart broke in grief and agony. So the heart of God has more to give us than we can receive.

Four: Again, we are called by waiting upon the Lord in prayer, and especially in continued prayer. It was after they had waited upon the Lord that they were all filled with the Holy Ghost. Prayer is not only an asking, but also a receiving. Many of us do not wait long enough before the Lord to get filled. You can take your breakfast in half an hour, but you cannot be filled with the Holy Spirit as quickly.

Five: Service for God and for others is perhaps the most effective condition of receiving continually the fullness of the Spirit. As we pour out the blessing God will pour it in. And our blessing should always be twice blessed.

Above all the best way to be filled with the Spirit is to be true to the great trust for which He was given—the evangelization of the world. "You shall receive the power of the Holy Ghost coming upon you and you shall be witness unto Me…unto the uttermost part of the world." Perhaps this is the secret of our poverty—that we have tried to hoard our blessing, and let the world perish through our selfishness. Freely you have received, freely give.

September 26: His Recognizing
by George Matheson
Excerpted from "The Spirit's Recognition of Christ", *Voices of the Spirit*, published by A. C. Armstrong & Son, New York, New York in 1892

No man can say that Jesus is the Lord, but by the Holy Ghost.
1 Corinthians 12:3

The thought is a beautiful one. Paul says that all worship is participation in that which we adore. And truly he is right. Worship is the homage of the heart, and the heart can only pay homage to that which is already in it. If I admire the beauties of Shakespeare I must be myself a Shakespeare. However much I acknowledge his lordship over me I can only do so by reason of a kindred spirit; the light which shows him to be above me is his own light in me. I may be a mute inglorious poet; I may never be able to write a line in my life; never fit to give forth one note of song. But if my heart has thrilled to the accents of Shakespeare, if my soul has bowed down before the majesty of that which it instantaneously feels but could never have expressed, I have already the clear and certain evidence that the seed of the same genius sleeps in me.

My soul, are you seeking a test of whether you have the Spirit of Christ? Are you desiring to know whether the life that dwelt in Him dwells in you? You need not wait long for an answer. There is a test for you which is infallible, unimpeachable. Is Christ to you an object of admiration?

Does there rise within you a thrill of rapture at the sound of His footsteps passing by? Does there wake within you a flutter of the heart as His voice reaches your ear? Does there vibrate within you a chord of music as His accents fall upon your way? Does there swell within you an infinite longing to be like Him, to be near Him, to be one with Him? Do you feel yourself to be poorer than before, lower in your own eyes than before He had crossed your path? Then you are already like Him, you already have His Spirit. You are like Him because you see Him as He is—beautiful. If you were not like Him it would be impossible for you to see His beauty; you would be able to look only on His disfigured face. But you have seen beneath that. You have bowed before a glory not made with hands. You have recognized a kingdom amid the emblems of the dust. You have revered a lordship hidden in a servant's form. You have detected a loveliness that concealed itself in the miry clay. Therefore you are like Him; you have the impression of His image in yourself, for that which you love is already half your own. No man can say that Christ is Lord but by participation of His own Spirit.

September 27: His Redeeming
by George Matheson
Excerpted from "The Spirit Seeking the Body", *Voices of the Spirit*, published by A. C. Armstrong & Son, New York, New York in 1892

And not only they, but ourselves also, which have the first-fruits of the Spirit, even we ourselves groan within ourselves, waiting for the adoption, the redemption of our body.
Romans 8:23

The idea is a very striking one. Even we—those who have the first-fruits of the Spirit—are not satisfied without the redemption of the body too. Even we, who are supposed to have our souls anchored in another world, are not content to let the present world go. It is not enough for us to believe, as we do believe, that there are regions beyond the seen and temporal; we want the region that is seen and temporal to be itself redeemed and glorified. It is not enough for us to know that there is a sacred as well as a secular life; we want the secular life to be made itself sacred. It is not enough for us to recognize that there is a city not built with hands; we want to feel that every village of the world was meant to be a street of that city. We want to see the deep things of God thrown up upon the surface of society, to behold the life of the Spirit permeating the life of the flesh, to find the impression of eternity stamped upon the forms of time. We wait for the creation itself to be delivered from bondage into freedom. We wait for the time when we shall have pleasure without hurt, knowledge without detriment, research without shaking, criticism without irreverence, culture without coldness, contact with impurity without sin. We, the people of the Spirit, desire most of all the redemption of the body.

Spirit Divine, make the body Divine too. Redeem this outer man from the sense of bondage. Give me an enlarged liberty of action, an extended sphere of locomotion, a wider boundary of possession. Give me the power to visit more places without injury, to do more things without harm, to taste more pleasures without corruption. Give me the grace to walk through the cornfields on Sunday and yet to keep Sunday even in my walking. Give me the strength to go to the marriage feast of Cana, and yet to make a sacrament even of the nuptial joy. Give me the purity to sit down in the social circle of Bethany and yet to preserve the heart unencumbered by social cares. Give me, above all, the spotlessness of soul that can touch the world and remain unspotted still—exposed, yet undefiled, attacked, yet free from tarnish, tempted, yet without sin. The Spirit indeed is willing; but I groan within myself for the redemption of the body.

September 28: His Regenerating - 1
by George Matheson
Excerpted from "The Spirit's Mode of Regeneration", *Voices of the Spirit*, published by A. C. Armstrong & Son, New York, New York in 1892

The grass withers, the flower fades: because the Spirit of the Lord blows upon it: surely the people are grass.
Isaiah 40:7

What! the Spirit a destroyer! I thought He was the source of life. I would have expected it to have been written, "The grass withers because the Spirit of the Lord does not blow upon it." Here for the first time the breath of the Spirit is said to give not life but death. Yes, but is not death the prelude to life? "That which you sow is not enlivened except it dies." I used to think it strange that among the gods of the Hindus there was one worshipped as "the Destroyer;" is not the Spirit here worshipped as the Destroyer—the One who withers the grass. And is it not well that the grass should wither? Is not grass the very emblem of temporariness, the very principle of death? Is not to say that the grass shall wither, equivalent to saying that death shall die? The flowering of the flesh is killing the Word of the Lord within me; if that Word is to endure forever, the flowering of the flesh must fade. What power shall make it fade, what but the Spirit Divine? Shall the Breath that gave life to the waters do otherwise than destroy the adversary of His own gift? Shall He not blow upon the flesh that impedes the immortal life, shall He not breathe upon the grass that buries the Word of the Lord?

O You Divine Destroyer, You crucifier of sin, You abolisher of death, we worship You. Spirit of Calvary, Spirit of the redeeming Christ, blow upon our deadness that it may die. Wither all in my heart that would wither Your Word. Wither its pride, its self-seeking, its vanity. Wither its malice, its hatred, its envy, its uncharitableness. Wither its preference for the seen and temporal, its estimation of the dross above the gold. Wither its hopes of being happy through the love of self, its prospects of avoiding misery through forgetfulness of others. Wither the gourd that shuts out the larger view, that prevents me from seeing the woes of Nineveh. When You blow upon the grass, mortality shall be swallowed up in life; when the flower of the flesh shall fade, Your Word shall endure forever.

September 29: His Regenerating - 2
by W. B. Godbey
Excerpted from "The Holy Spirit, Our Regenerator", *Work of the Holy Spirit*, published by Pickett Publishing Co., Louisville, Kentucky in 1902

You has He quickened who were dead in trespasses and sins.
Ephesians 2:1

The word "quicken" here is *edzoo opoieese*, from *zooll* (life) and *poioo* (to make). Therefore it means to create spiritual life in the dead soul, precisely as Jesus created physical life in the dead body of Lazarus. Ignorant people tell us the days of miracles are past. Every soul born of the Spirit is miraculously and supernaturally raised from the dead. The grand, fundamental, salient truth of the Bible is its conspicuous supernaturalism in the resurrection of the soul out of spiritual death into the life of God in regeneration, and the extermination of the death element out of us in entire sanctification.

As the Executive of the new creation, the Holy Spirit, with superabounding love and sympathy, is anxious to regenerate every human spirit in all the world, but before the sinner's repentance He is inhibited by the Divine law which says, "The soul that sins it shall die." That law has been fully and abundantly satisfied by the work of Christ; yet the Spirit, in harmony with the Divine economy, must withhold this creative intervention, till the sinner in utter and eternal abandonment by solid evangelical repentance, exercises the faith accomplished by the Spirit in the heart in the appropriation of the vicarious atonement to his own soul. This done, He comes at lightning speed into the heart and rears up the stupendous work of the new creation, dispensing to that soul the resurrection power. This supernatural intervention of the Holy Ghost in regeneration is fundamental in the grand superstructure of Christian experience. If you do not have it—solid, clear, radical and unmistakable—collapse and dilapidation will strew your pilgrimage with debris, over which others will stumble, and vast bewilderment will follow, fraught with immense detriment to souls. So, be sure your foundation is all right, and then proceed to erect the gorgeous superstructure of experiential and practical holiness.

September 30: His Rejection - 1
by Arthur T. Pierson
Excerpted from "The Reception and Rejection of the Spirit", *The Acts of the Holy Spirit*, published by Fleming H. Revell Company, New York, New York in 1895

No blessing, though it is the richest God can give and the most needy man can have, is forced upon our acceptance. It is a fact fraught with solemn significance that the Book which thus opens with the Holy Spirit, and is pervaded throughout with His presence and power, also closes with Him, only the promise of the first chapter turns into a warning in the last. Notwithstanding the marvels, accomplished in this first generation of Church history, there were some who called themselves God's people and prided themselves on their "election," who were blind and deaf and hard-hearted and lost their golden opportunity. Even when such a man as Paul the aged expounded and testified the kingdom of God, persuading concerning Jesus, both out of the law of Moses and out of the prophets, from morning till evening, it is sadly recorded that, while "some believed the things which were spoken" (Acts 28:1), "some believed not." And, as they departed, not to give simple faith its blessed exercise in believing and trusting, but to indulge their wayward minds and have great reasonings among themselves, Paul gave utterance once more to that awful Isaiah rebuke of the prophet Isaiah, which is more forcible, and probably more intelligible, if translated so as to bring out the voluntary element in this willful rejection of testimony [Isaiah 6:9-10]:

> "Go unto this people, and say,
> Hearing you will hear, and will not understand;
> And seeing you will see, and will not perceive:
> For the heart of this people is calloused,
> And their ears are dull of hearing,
> And their eyes have they closed;
> Lest they should see with their eyes,
> And hear with their ears,
> And understand with their heart,
> And should turn about,
> And I should heal them."

Is it possible that, even in our own day, with the burning chapters of the Acts of the Holy Ghost open before our eyes, compelling us to read their perpetual lesson, we may yet come under the same condemnation? Is it possible that the heart of believers is callous, and their ears are dull of hearing, and their eyes they have closed; so that while they cannot but see this marvelous testimony, they have no real spiritual perception, understanding, or disposition to accept the teaching of this Book? Can it be that the Church of Christ has practically denied to the Spirit of God His rightful seat of authority and administration, and put in His place a usurper—the spirit of this world, which works in the children of disobedience? It is a solemn question, which—without daring, or even desiring, to bring against any of God's professed people a railing accusation—we can only ask every believer, minister of Christ, and church, to consider; for it is to this inquiry that all our studies of this Book of Acts must finally lead.

October 1: His Rejection - 2
by Arthur T. Pierson

Certain it is that the power of the Holy Spirit no longer pervades our witness and work as of old. We have risen from these studies of the Acts of the Holy Spirit with an unquenchable desire to see this power once more manifested. We are not zealous or jealous for the particular form and mode in which the Spirit's presence shall be exhibited, nor that the exact signs and wonders of the apostolic age should be revived. God has infinite variety of manifestation, and the particular modes of that manifestation may vary as the times and needs change. But the Holy Spirit given that He may abide with the Church forever; and we cannot believe that so glorious and Divine a person as the Spirit of God dwells in the Church and yet gives no unmistakable sign or signal of His presence. There has been promised one "everlasting sign that shall not be cut off" (Isaiah 55:13). The thorn shall still be displaced by the fir tree, and the brier by the myrtle tree; plants of godliness shall spring up in unpromising soils and bear celestial fruit, that He may be glorified (Isaiah 60:21; 61:2).

If the Spirit dwells in the body of Christ, and is left free to work His own will, He will quicken the whole body. Members will have a new care one for another, suffering and rejoicing together. There will be a holy jealousy for the welfare and happiness of all who belong to the mystical body, and an earnest and loving cooperation in all holy work. All schism, whether manifest in inward estrangement or in outward separation, becomes impossible where the Spirit of Love prevails; all heresy becomes impossible so far as the Spirit of Truth indwells; and all apathy and inactivity in the face of a dying world will give way to sympathetic activity when and so far as the Spirit of Life thrills the body; even as all ignorance of God and superstitious worship of forms flee like owls of the night when the Spirit of Light shines. In a word, all needs of the Church are met so surely and speedily as the Holy Ghost, who still abides in the Church as God's only earthly temple, resumes by the consent and cooperation of disciples his normal control, actively guiding into all truth and duty.

God's name is "I AM"—a mystic name indeed; yet whatever else it means, it can mean no less than this: One everlasting, unchanging NOW. He is "the same yesterday, and today, and forever." What He was, He is; what He has done, He can do, will do, does, whether or not His being and doing are seen or known by us. Like the sun, His shining is perpetual. We may get into the dark, but the light is essentially undimmed. We may shut out the light, but it is struggling to reach us behind the shutters. The Church of God may pass into eclipse behind the world's shadow, but the sun is still as radiant and glorious. "There is in God no variableness, neither shadow of turning." His past deeds, however wonderful, are the promise, prophecy, and proof of what He wills to do and waits to do when our conditions make it possible.

October 2: His Renewing
by J. R. Macduff
Excerpted from "Second Morning", *The Morning Watches and Night Watches*, published by James Nisbet & Co., London, England in 1883

Create in me a clean heart, O God, and renew
a right spirit within me.
Psalm 51:10

Almighty God, who has preserved me during the unconscious hours of slumber, I desire to dedicate my waking moments and thoughts to You. Do preoccupy my mind with holy and Heavenly things. May I be enabled throughout this day, by the help of Your Holy Spirit, to exclude all that is vain and frivolous and sinful, and to have my affections centered on You, as my best portion and chiefest joy. As Your Spirit of old did brood over the face of the waters, may that same blessed Spirit descend in all the plenty of His Heavenly graces, that the gloom of a deeper moral chaos may be dispersed, and that mine may be the beauty and happiness and gladness of a soul that has been transformed from darkness to light, and from the power of sin and Satan unto God.

Forbid, blessed Lord, that I should be resting in anything short of this new creation. May my old nature be crucified and, as one alive from the dead may I walk with Jesus in newness of life. May the new life infused by Your Spirit, urge me to higher achievements and more Heavenly aspirations. May I be enabled to see the world in its true light—its pleasures fading, its hopes delusive, its friendships perishable. May I be more solemnly and habitually impressed by the surpassing magnitude of "the things not seen." May I give evidence of the reality of a renewal of heart by a more entire and consistent dedication of the life. May my soul become a temple of the Holy Ghost; may "Holiness to the Lord" be its superscription. May I be led to feel that there can be no true joy but what emanates from Yourself, the fountain and fulness of all joy—the God in whom "all my wellsprings" are.

Whatever may be the discipline You are employing for this inward heart transformation, let me be willing to submit to it. Let me lie passive in the arms of Your mercy, saying, "Undertake You for me." May it be mine to bear all, and endure all, and rejoice in all—adoring a Father's hand, and trusting a Father's faithfulness—feeling secure in a Father's tried love.

Do shine upon my ways. May I this day get nearer Heaven. May I feel at its close that I have done something for God—something to promote the great end for which existence was given me—the glory of Your Holy Name. Bless all my beloved friends. Unite us together in bonds of holy fellowship and at last, in Your presence, may we be permitted to drink together of the streams of everlasting love. And all I ask is for Jesus' sake. Amen.

October 3: His Requiring – 1
by John Macneil
Excerpted from "Surrender", *The Spirit-Filled Life*, published by Marshall Brothers Ltd., London, England in 1894

Consecration involves surrender—total absolute, unconditional, irreversible. This is Paul's teaching in Romans: "I beseech you therefore, brethren, by the mercies of God, that you present your bodies a living sacrifice, holy, acceptable unto God, which is your reasonable service" (Romans 12:1). These people had already given their souls to God, and now the apostle insists on their giving their "bodies" too. "Yield yourselves unto God as those that are alive from the dead" (Romans 6:13). Life first, then sacrifice. Have we life in Christ? Then it is imperative that we "yield," "present" ourselves unto God. It is not a matter of individual choice or taste or convenience; but everyone who has been quickened from the death in trespasses and sins is commanded, yes, commanded, to "present himself to God." Have you obeyed this command? If not, why not? God excuses no one. Had it not better be attended to now? Yes, before you read another line!

It follows as a corollary that if we yield ourselves, we yield everything else to God; nothing is withheld. What loss we suffer because we will hold back some little thing! A little child was one day playing with a very valuable vase, when he put his hand into it and could not withdraw it. His father, too, tried his best to get it out, but all in vain. They were talking of breaking the vase, when the father said, "Now, my son, make one more try; open your hand and hold your fingers out straight, as you see me doing, and then pull." To their astonishment the little fellow said, "Oh no, pa; I couldn't put out my fingers like that, for if I did, I would drop my penny." He had been holding on to a penny all the time! No wonder he could not withdraw his hand. How many of us are like him!

Now let us note that the verb translated "yield" (Romans 6:13) and "present" (Romans 12:1) is not in the present tense in the original, as if Paul said "be yielding," "keep presenting," but it is in the *aorist* tense, the general force of which is a definite act, something done and finished with. So that when the command, "Present yourself to God," is complied with as far as one's light goes, the person is entitled to regard the transaction as a completed act and to say, "Yes, I have presented myself to God." Then Faith presses on the heels of that statement and says, "God has accepted what I have thus presented." It is absolutely necessary that Faith be in lively exercise on this point, for what will be the practical outcome of all my presenting if I do not believe that God takes what I give? "Him who comes unto Me I will in nowise cast out" is just as appropriate to the saint seeking full salvation as to the sinner seeking pardon. It is failure here, failure to comprehend by faith the fact that God receives what I present, that has blocked progress for so many of God's people who are truly desiring to live consecrated lives. From this it will be seen that consecration is a crisis in the life of the believer, just as cleansing is, and not a process; but it, too, "is a crisis in order to a process."

October 4: His Requiring – 2
by John Macneil

Consecration implies and involves transference of ownership. Many a Christian is living today as if he were his own; but the consecrated heart endorses the statement of the Divine Word: "You are not your own, for you are bought with a price: therefore glorify God in your body and in your spirit, which are God's" (1 Corinthians 6:19-20). The consecrated man looks upon himself as the absolute property of the Lord who bought him, and his whole life is lived in the light of this fact.

Consecration involves the "glorifying" of Christ, the "enthroning" Him, the crowning of Jesus "Lord of all" in our own heart and life. "Crown Him, crown Him, Lord of all"'; "and," says Dr. Hudson Taylor, "if you do not crown Him Lord *of all*, you do not crown Him Lord *at all*." This view of consecration, with its accompanying results, is beautifully illustrated for us in John 7:38-39, "He who believes on Me, as the scripture has said, out of his belly shall flow rivers of living water. But this He spoke of the Spirit, which they who believe on Him were to receive: for the Spirit was not yet given; because Jesus was not yet glorified." The flowing forth of the rivers—just the outflow, the overflow of the infilling Spirit—was dependent on Jesus being "glorified." Jesus had not yet reached the throne, and so the Spirit had not yet been given. The reason why they had not come to Pentecost was that as yet there was no Ascension. Ascension preceded Pentecost. Let us learn it by root of heart, that every Pentecost since the first has, in like manner, been preceded by an Ascension. Do we know Pentecost experientially for ourselves? If not the reason is close at hand. Jesus has not been "glorified" by us, not enthroned in our hearts. He may be in the heart, He may even be in the throne room, but He has not been placed upon the throne! There has never been a coronation day in our lives, when "in full and glad surrender" we placed the crown on the many crowned Head, crying, "Crown Him, crown Him Lord of all!" "And he showed me a river of water of life, bright as crystal, proceeding out of the throne of God and of the Lamb" (Revelation 22:1).

When Christ reached the throne at the Father's right hand, from underneath His throne the river began to flow, the Holy Ghost was given, His Church received her Pentecost. "Being by the right hand of God...He has poured forth this" Acts 2:33). So when Christ is "exalted," "enthroned," "glorified" in the heart, from underneath His throne will the rivers begin to flow according to promise; but, no Ascension, no Pentecost; and let us remember, as has been already stated, that though life begins at the Cross, service does not begin till Pentecost. No Pentecost, no service worthy of the name!

October 5: His Requiring – 3
by John Macneil

We need not be concerned as to how the rivers are flowing from us, or troubled as to what channels they are flowing in. They flowed from Peter in one way, and from Paul in quite another, and from Barnabas in yet another; "diversities" of ways. We need not trouble at all about the rivers, and the direction of their flow; our concern is to "glorify Jesus," to see that He is on the throne; and it becomes His business then to see that the rivers are flowing; and there is not the slightest danger that the blessed business with which He charges Himself will be neglected!

Our life and service will be enriched beyond telling by enthroning Christ. This, of course, involves the breaking of all our idols, for He will not share His throne with any. When Mahmoud, conqueror of India, had taken the city of Gujarat he proceeded, as was his custom, to destroy the idols. There was one, fifteen feet high, which its priests and devotees begged him to spare. He was deaf to their entreaties, and seizing a hammer he struck it one blow when, to his amazement from the shattered image there rained down at his feet a shower of gems, pearls and diamonds—treasure of fabulous value, which had been hidden within it! Had he spared the idol he would have lost all this wealth. Let us not spare our idols. It is in our interest to demolish them. If we shatter them there will rain about our hearts the very treasures of Heaven, the gifts and graces of the Holy Spirit; but if we spare our idol we will miss riches unsearchable.

The consecrated life is a Christ-centered life, the only truly-centered life; every other life is eccentric: yet how often do we hear worldly people or worldly-minded Christians (what a contradiction in terms!) criticizing some devoted Spirit-filled man or woman as "so eccentric," simply because of their loyalty to Christ their King! When all the while it is the critics that are "eccentric"—off the true center. Indeed, so eccentric did the first Spirit-filled band appear, that "others mocking said, they are filled with new wine"; so they were "full of new wine," the "new wine" of the kingdom! And in God's sight these drunken, eccentric men were the only truly-centered, spiritually-adjusted men in the throng!

October 6: His Rest - 1
by George Matheson
Excerpted from "The Spirit in Patmos", *Voices of the Spirit*,
published by A. C. Armstrong & Son, New York, New York in 1892

I was in the Spirit on the Lord's Day.
Revelation 1:10

Wonderful triumph of love! — to keep even in Patmos the spirit of Sabbath rest. He was not only "in the Spirit," but he was "in the Spirit on the Lord's Day" — the Spirit in its deepest rest. But what a strange rest that was! It was rest amid the storm. The Spirit that overshadowed him was brooding over the face of the waters. It was an hour of darkness, an hour of chaos, an hour of desolation — yet he found rest, Sabbath rest. How can we explain this? Is there any key to the mystery of the Apostle John's peace in storm? Yes; we find it on the very threshold: "Behold, He comes with clouds." All the clouds of this world are to him Christ's coming; that is the secret of his calm. However dark life is, however stormy it is, however desolate it is, he feels that the darkness and the storm and the desolateness are steps of Christ's coming, and that in this light one day "every eye shall see Him." It is that which keeps the seer of Patmos calm — the knowledge that Christ is here now, and that tomorrow He shall be proved to have been here. Above the sound of the trumpets, above the outpouring of the vials, above the voices and thundering and lightning of human calamity, there floats ever in his ear the resistless music "the Lord God omnipotent reigns."

O Spirit, let me also hear that music, that even in Patmos I may have the Sabbath rest. Clouds and darkness are around me; trumpets are sounding, seals are opening, vials are outpouring their flows of bitterness. But all these are Your chariots, O my God; You make the clouds Your chariots; You come with clouds. May I not rest in Your chariot of clouds as Elijah rested in Your chariot of fire? May I not ascend to Heaven by the same means wherewith You descended to the earth? Why should I not even in Patmos keep my Sabbath? My love will not be perfected until it can keep its Sabbath there. I want to be able to hear You moving on the face of my waters; I want to be able to know You behind my cloud and care. Mine is a poor Sabbath if it does not come after the chaos; mine is an unfinished love if it has never lived in Patmos. I am not satisfied till I can say of my love "it is finished." I am not content till I can hear Your footsteps in the storm. I have not reached the summer of my soul until I can meet You in the clouds of Heaven and say of these clouds, "It is the Lord's day."

October 7: His Rest - 2
by George Matheson
Excerpted from "The Nature of the Spirit's Rest", *Voices of the Spirit*, published by A. C. Armstrong & Son, New York, New York in 1892

"Blessed are the dead who die in the Lord from now on."
"Blessed indeed, says the Spirit, "that they may rest from their labors, for their deeds follow them."
Revelation 14:13

What a strange contradiction: I would have expected the words to be "they rested from their labors and their works do not follow them." Ah! but I forget that this is the Spirit's rest: "Yes, says the Spirit." When the Spirit says "yes," I enter into work just because I lose the sense of labor. The Spirit's "yes" is love; it is the consent of the will. It is where my love is weak that my labor is most burdensome and my work most incomplete. But when I enter into the Spirit's "yes," I enter into a rest that makes me strong; I forget the sense of toil, I fly over the ground, I bound across the fields of duty. The rest of the Spirit is always followed by action. When I lie down on the bosom of God I wake up to my own energies. Why does the Son of Man say, "I must work the works of Him that sent Me"? Why, indeed, but because He "is in the bosom of the Father." Do you think that He could have borne so much outward toil if it had not been for His fulness of inward rest? No; it was the rested soul that made the active body; it was the stable will that made the moving power; it was the waveless heart that bore upon its ocean breast the burdens of the world. His spirit had ceased from its labors; therefore His works followed Him.

My brothers and sisters, are you in times of sorrow longing for the rest of the grave? God desires no such rest for you. The rest of the grave is for a body; a soul must have the rest of the Spirit. Do you think that death is to be a cessation of work? No; only of labor. That which makes your life a toil is not your work but your weariness. If you could only cease to be tired, your works would follow you everywhere. God offers you in death not less work but work more abundantly — work that achieves more because it feels no strain. "There shall be no night there" — no sense of reaction from the burden and heat of the day. Yours shall be the blessedness, not of sleep, but of waking, not of dreams, but of doing, not of apathy, but of feeling. Yours shall be the blessedness of love — the action of the heart. Yours shall be the blessedness of ministration — the labor of love. Yours shall be the blessedness of having one will with the Divine — the state in which service is identical with liberty, and where obedience becomes the free person's vital air. You shall resume your abandoned works when you have attained the Spirit's rest.

October 8: His Restraining - 1
by Arthur T. Pierson
Excerpted from "The Restraint and Constraint of the Spirit", *The Acts of the Holy Spirit*, published by Fleming H. Revell Company, New York, New York in 1895

This is a new character or function of the Spirit. Paul and Timothy were "forbidden by the Holy Ghost to preach the Word in Asia," and when they tried to go into Bithynia, "the Spirit did not allow them." The language is explicit. Why thus hindered or diverted does not clearly appear, unless this territory was reserved for other laborers, other methods, other times. For some reason, which it is easy to conjecture were we now dealing with conjectures, God's set and full time had not come. And so, notwithstanding their purpose and endeavor, they were "forbidden," "not allowed." We are twice told that the restraint was of the Holy Spirit.

Side by side with this act of restraint we must, however, place what immediately follows. Paul is guided by a vision to go into Macedonia. The vision must have been very vivid and unmistakable, for he adds, "Immediately we undertook to go into Macedonia, assuredly gathering that the Lord had called us to preach the gospel unto them." And so confident was he of the call that although, instead of the open doors he had looked for, he and Silas found the strange welcome of the cruel whip, the inner prison, and the torturing stocks, they made the prison cell echo and ring with midnight songs of praise, until the Philippian jail became Heaven's gate!

Here again we are taught a new and vital lesson. The Holy Spirit is shown to us in another of His acts of administration: The double guidance of Paul and his companion; on the one hand prohibition and restraint, on the other permission and constraint. They are forbidden in one direction, invited in another; one way the Spirit says, "Do not go;" the other He calls, "Come." He had a mission for them to accomplish in introducing the gospel into Europe. Many a time in history has supernatural restraint and constraint changed the course of God's servants. David Livingstone [Scottish missionary, 1813-1873] planned to go into China, but God did not allow him, and sent him to Africa to be its missionary general, statesman, explorer. Before him, William Carey [English missionary, 1761-1834] planned to go to the Great Polynesia in the South Seas, but God guided him to India to lay foundations for giving a vernacular Bible to one sixth of the people of the world. Adoniram Judson [American missionary, 1788-1850] did go to India, but was driven to Burma, where he built up an apostolic church for all the age. Barnabas Shaw [English missionary, 1788-1857] was thrust out from Boerland [South Africa], and trusted to God's guidance, not knowing where he was headed until the twenty-eighth day brought to him the chief of Namaqualand [Namibia], his "man of Macedonia," who literally said, "Come over and help us." How many secrets of leading are yet to be brought to light, thousands of God's servants having been forbidden by Him to follow out their plans, because He has had some unexpected open door of service to set before them!

October 9: His Restraining - 2
by Arthur T. Pierson

We need to trust Him for guidance and rejoice equally in His restraints and constraints; because if we had infinite wisdom and love to guide us, we should not by one hair's-breadth change His perfect plan for our lives!

In the case of Lydia, "whose heart the Lord opened, that she attended unto the things which were spoken of by Paul" (Acts 16:14), though no direct mention is made of the Spirit, it was one of His acts to open her ears and heart to the gospel. Here again may be read between the lines the Spirit's working, as also in the strongly contrasted case of the jailer at Philippi, and later on in the active search of the Bereans into the Holy Scriptures, so that many of them believed. In Paul's "stirred" spirit at Athens, a mightier Spirit was at work; and in the conversion of Dionysius and Damaris, who, even in the idolatrous, philosophical, and self-sufficient Grecian capital, believed and followed Paul, we may see the brooding influence of that same Creator Spirit who over the primal chaos hovered to bring life out of the abyss of death.

We meet in the eighteenth chapter, verse five, a phrase: "Paul was pressed in the spirit"; and we are told that Apollos was "fervent in the spirit," as also that Paul "purposed in the spirit." These and some other kindred expressions have been thought by some wise Bible students to refer to the Holy Spirit's acting on the mind and heart, creating a holy pressure which must find vent in testimony, a spiritual passion and fervor which must be relieved by preaching and teaching, or a purpose which was not of the will of man nor of the will of the flesh, but of the will of God. However this is, it is beyond all doubt that in all our inward moving of conviction and affection, of yearning and praying, of determination and decision, we may, in proportion as we maintain close fellowship with Him and are surrendered to Him for service, recognize with joyfulness His acting and motivating.

In this latter purpose of Paul to go to Jerusalem and Rome may be found a possible explanation of his steadfastness of resolve. When at Miletus he was held fast by the Ephesian elders, and in Caesarea Agabus prophesied that at the sacred city he should be bound and delivered over to the will of the Gentiles, so that he was tenderly begged not to go up to Jerusalem at all, he "would not be persuaded," and his entreating friends, compelled to desist, could only say, "The will of the Lord be done." Such persistence of purpose seems due not to mere obstinacy, for we are told that Paul went, "bound in the spirit." The same Holy Ghost, who witnessed in every city that bonds and afflictions awaited him, molded his purpose and kept him in the bonds of holy resolve and steadfastness of heart in doing and suffering the will of God, though, like his Master, he could say, "How am I straitened till it is accomplished!"

October 10: His Retrospection
by George Matheson
Excerpted from "The Retrospect of the Spirit", *Voices of the Spirit*, published by A. C. Armstrong & Son, New York, New York in 1892

Then the Spirit took me up, and I heard behind me a voice of a great rushing, saying, "Blessed be the glory of the Lord from His place."
Ezekiel 3:12

When the Spirit lifts me up I hear the voice of blessings behind me. From the place off my spiritual elevation I see the glory of the things I have passed by. My past life looks resplendent in the light of the new present. When I saw it in advance it seemed dark, but the moment it becomes a retrospective, the moment it lies behind me in the light of a higher experience, I see it to have been the best thing possible, I say of it, "Blessed be the glory of the Lord."

Spirit Divine, reveal to me the glory of the things behind me, teach me the providence of the events that have gone by. I trusted You while they were going by; I was content to walk by faith; I murmured not. But faith is not Your goal for me; it is sight. It is not enough that I should feel You to be my King; I must see the King in His beauty. It is not enough that I should experience Your strength in the wilderness; the wilderness must be made to blossom as the rose. It is not enough that an angel should support me in Gethsemane; Gethsemane itself must be glorified in the light of Olivet. I have not asked to trace You while Your chariot wheels were passing; but now that they are past, O Spirit, let me see Your face. Let me see You as Jacob saw You at Peniel—as a vindication of his struggle, as an explanation of his grief. Let me see You as Saul saw You at Tarsus—sending the future sunshine in the disguise of present darkness. Let me see You as John saw You at Patmos—revealing that the clouds of life were themselves just modes of Your coming. I shall not weep for the depression of the passing hour, if only when the time of Your uplifting comes, I shall see behind me the glory of the Lord.

October 11: His Revealing - 1
by Handley C. G. Moule

Excerpted from "Christ Revealed by the Holy Spirit", *Cathedral and University and Other Sermons*, published by Hodder and Stoughton, London, England in 1920

But as it is written, Eye has not seen, nor ear heard, neither have entered into the heart of man, the things which God has prepared for them that love Him. But God has revealed them unto us by His Spirit.
1 Corinthians 2:9-10

Paul's quotation of Isaiah plainly refers to the whole gift of salvation, not only to the bright eternal future of the saved. The words cannot exclude the thought of the glories of Heaven, which assuredly senses have not seen, nor imagination either, but which God has prepared for them that love Him. But neither can they exclude the wonders of grace on earth; which equally are things of eternal plan and preparation, and which here stand nearest in connection to the previous verse. For, according to that verse, it was not ignorance of the nature of Heaven, but ignorance of the nature of the Lord from Heaven, which allowed the Crucifixion. It was above all things ignorance of Him. Not ignorance of His existence, nor of a supernatural something that lay around Him, for these were things of admitted fact; but ignorance of Him. It was a failure of the soul, somehow or other, to grasp the "hidden wisdom" of His nature and His work. In short,

Paul's citation of the passage, or passages, of the prophet appears to bear upon the glorious total of redeeming mercy; not only, or mainly, upon glory, but also, and mainly, upon grace; as indeed it is the way of Scripture to bind the two everywhere into one strong series, and always to throw more emphasis and more illumination upon grace than upon glory; for grace is always less attractive to the imagination, and always more necessary for the will.

The discovery of the ways of grace, then, had been beyond the reach of senses and of mind. "The salvation which is in Christ Jesus" had not entered into the human heart, any more than it had shone visibly upon human eyes, or poured music into human ears. The understanding of it needed to be borne in upon the soul by the eternal Spirit. And by Him, to Paul and to his brethren, it had been so borne in. "God revealed them unto us by His Spirit."

One further remark, and one only, on the details of the text. What is the personal reference of the word "us" — "God has revealed them unto us"? The reference must be not to the Paul or the apostles exclusively, but to the saints at large. The context leads naturally this way. For the "hidden wisdom," once hidden but now revealed, of which the Christian teacher spoke among his mature, or "perfect," hearers, has just been described as "foreordained before the world unto our glory;" the glory certainly not of the teachers only but of the believing community. And again, those who have received the revelation of it are contrasted, not with a lower grade of believers, but just with the unenlightened enemies and murderers of the Lord of Glory.

October 12: His Revealing - 2
by Handley C. G. Moule

Listen to the words of the Son of God Himself, and let in their whole appeal upon your soul: "No man knows the Father except the Son, and he to whomsoever the Son will reveal Him;" "It is written in the prophets, And they shall all be taught of God; every man therefore that has heard, and has learned of the Father, comes unto Me;" "The world cannot receive the Spirit of truth, because it does not see Him, neither knows Him; but you know Him;" "He who has My commandments, and keeps them, he it is that loves Me; and he that loves Me shall be loved of My Father, and I will love him"—and ponder well the closing promise—"and will manifest Myself to him."

How perfectly in harmony this is with the narrative of the Acts, and with the Epistles, and the Apocalypse! From the Acts take one example. You read of Paul's first work in Europe. He sits teaching on a certain sabbath by the side of the river at Philippi, amid the circle of female worshippers; and we are informed of one conversion: Lydia believed and was baptized. What had happened in her soul? No mere reception of information, however authentic, nor of inferences, however compelling, but an inner light from God: "Her heart the Lord opened, to respond to the things spoken." Here again is a case fully in point to our enquiry of today. It is a case for all time. The element of miracle, in the ordinary sense, which might have seemed to restrict the significance to an exceptional period, is wholly absent. Lydia witnessed no miracle before, or at, her conversion, that we read of. Nothing could have been more perfectly natural in externals than that occasion. But from the point of view of Scripture it was supernatural as well. To be sure, Lydia listened with her own ears, and reflected with her own mind, and accepted with her own will; let us be very sure of that; but her inner being was drawn towards the gospel, and made conscious of its glory, by a power not her own; it was God, revealing, through the Spirit. And the very simplicity of the narration, and the incidental comment of this remarkable feature in it, commend this case to the enquirer into the ways of salvation as a wide-reaching example. The heart that effectively attends to the things which God has prepared for them that love Him, does not for one moment cease to be itself; it never thinks and feels with faculties, so to speak, imported and injected, if such things could be; no, but its perceptions and feelings take the Divinely healthy line they do, thanks to a Divine power, strong and special, which has been at work upon the inner world; "that heart, the Lord has opened."

Just so it is in the words close to the text, "We have received the Spirit which is from God, that we may know the things which are freely given to us of God." Just so it is again, in the words of 2 Corinthians 4:6: "God shined in our hearts, to the lighting up of the knowledge of the glory of God in the face of Jesus Christ."

October 13: His Revealing - 3
by Isaak A. Dorner

Excerpted from "The Difference Between the Revelation of God in Christ, and In the Holy Spirit, Note B", from the book by Andrew Murray entitled *The Spirit of Christ*, published by A. D. F. Randolph & Co., New York, New York in 1888

The character of Christ's substitution is not negative, nor repressive of personality, but productive. He is not content with the existence in Himself of the fulness of the spiritual life, into which His people are absorbed by faith. Believers are themselves to live and love as free personalities; Christ's redeeming purpose is directed to the creation, by the Holy Spirit whom He sends, of new personalities in whom Christ gains a settled, established being. But by this very means God exists in them after a new manner; new, not only because the power of redemption inherent only in God's being in Christ, but new also because, although Christ remains the Principle of this life, this life shapes itself in freedom and distinctness from Christ. Only by means of such freedom can the bond between Christ and man, instead of remaining a one-sided one, become two-sided, and therefore all the firmer — the reciprocal relationship of love.

But, at the same time, the fulness of the Spirit of light and life, grace and truth, which dwells objectively in Christ, no longer remains merely objective to the world, but lives and unfolds itself in the world, as a living treasure of salvation.

Through the Holy Spirit it comes to pass that Christ's impulse is not simply continued and extended to men, but becomes an indigenous impulse in them, a new focus being formed for naturalized Divine powers. As a new Divine principle, the Holy Spirit creates, though not substantially new faculties, a new will, knowledge, feeling a new self-consciousness. In brief, He creates a new person, dissolving the old union-point of the faculties, and creating a new pure union of the same. The new personality is formed in inner resemblance to the second Adam, on the same family type, so to speak. Everything by which the new personality, in its independence, makes itself known, is ascribed by Holy Scripture to this third Divine principle.

Through the Holy Spirit the believer has the consciousness of himself as a new man, and the power and living impulse of a new holy life, that is free in God. He is the spirit of joy and freedom, in opposition to the letter; subjection to the Divine impulse is now, in the blending of necessity and freedom, without spontaneous impulse; mere passivity and receptiveness are transformed into spontaneity, no, productiveness and independence. Through the Holy Spirit the individual personality is thus raised to complete charismatic personality. By all these means the Holy Spirit plants and cherishes the one relatively independent factor — the presupposition of the origin of the Church, namely, the new believing personality.

October 14: His Revival - 1
by A. B. Simpson
Excerpted from "The Spirit of Revival", *When the Comforter Came*, published by The Alliance Press Company, New York, New York in 1911

I will pour water on him who is thirsty and floods upon the dry ground.
Isaiah 44:3

Two forms of the Spirit's operations are here set forth, the ordinary and the extraordinary. Even the ordinary work of the Spirit is expressed by the strongest figure, "I will pour water," but His extraordinary ministry is described by a more emphatic figure, "I will pour floods upon the dry ground." These floods represent the occasional outpouring of the Spirit of God in seasons of great revival which the Church is witnessing now in many places and which earnest Christian hearts are longing to see everywhere.

Such seasons of mighty blessing are powerful witnesses for God, awakening the attention of a careless world and compelling even the most skeptical and indifferent to recognize the reality and power of the gospel of Jesus Christ. Such seasons, for a time at least, lift up a standard against the enemy and check the prevalence and power of evil as no mere human words or authorities ever can. God becomes His own witness and the scoffer and the sinner are awed and humbled before the majesty of the Lord. Let us pray for such a mighty outpouring of the Holy Ghost in our day. We are justified in expecting such manifestations of Divine power especially as the coming of our Lord draws near. These are to be the very signs that will herald His return, "I will pour out My Spirit upon all flesh," He says, "and I will show signs and wonders before the coming of that great and notable day of the Lord."

The prophet describes the individual blessing that will follow these gracious outpourings.

Conversion. "One shall say, I am the Lord's" (Isaiah 44:5). The Holy Spirit will lead souls, one by one, to Christ. How beautiful it is to read in the account of the Welsh revival of people springing up all over the meeting, spontaneously and confessing the Savior they had just found. It was not through preaching, but through personal dealing with the Holy Spirit who was present, pleading with souls all over the place, and they yielded and confessed Him one by one just as they settled the great transaction. Anyone can be saved the moment he is ready to confess Christ as his Savior: "If you shall confess with your mouth the Lord Jesus and believe in your heart that God has raised Him from the dead, you shall be saved." This is a personal confession directly to God and He accepts it and records the name of the confessor in the Lamb's book of life.

October 15: His Revival - 2
by A. B. Simpson

Two: Confession. "Another shall call himself by the name of Jacob" (Isaiah 44:5). This undoubtedly represents the identifying of the individual with the Lord's people. When the Holy Spirit truly leads souls to Christ, they always want to belong to His people. How quickly all severe criticism about churches and church members disappears and the true and humble spirit turns to the children of God for fellowship, sympathy and help. It is the duty of the young convert to attach himself to the fold of Christ, and although there may be many imperfections in the visible Church, yet it is far safer to be inside than outside, and all who truly love the Master will want to be identified with some branch of His cause.

Three: Consecration. "Another shall subscribe with his hand unto the Lord" (Isaiah 44:5). This represents that closer covenant into which it is the privilege of the individual soul to enter with the Lord Jesus. Dr. Phillip Dodridge [English minister, 1702-1751] recommends to young Christians to write down their covenant and formally sign it and ratify it, and then preserve it, and he suggests a very solemn form in which the soul may give itself to the Lord and claim His covenant blessing.

There is no doubt that such personal covenants have brought great blessing to those that have faith fully kept them and as we look back upon the records of our own lives we shall find that even where we have failed "He abides faithful."

Four: Higher spiritual blessing. The next clause, "and surname himself by the name of Israel" (Isaiah 44:5), seems to express the highest spiritual experiences. Israel stands for much more than Jacob. It marks the second stage of the patriarch's spiritual life when the Supplanter became the Prince of God. When the Holy Spirit comes, He leads the willing heart in the deeper and highest things of God. He shows the young convert that it is his privilege to be baptized with the Holy Ghost, to receive the Lord Jesus as an indwelling presence, to be delivered from the power of self and sin, and to enter into a life of abiding victory, rest and power.

Indeed, these are among the richest fruits of every true revival, and no wise Christian worker will be satisfied until the souls committed to his care have been led into all the fulness of Christ. This is presented here as a voluntary act and as the privilege of all who are willing to rise to it. God does not force His best things upon us, but offers them to our holy ambition.

Shall we, as we realize this mighty promise, rise to it for ourselves and claim, even as we read these lines, these showers of blessing, these floods of power and these glorious fruits for our own individual Christian life and the cause and kingdom of our Lord?

October 16: His Rock – 1
by A. B. Simpson
Excerpted from "The Rock and the River", *When the Comforter Came*, published by The Alliance Press Company, New York, New York in 1911

They drank of that rock that followed them and that Rock was Christ.
1 Corinthians 10:4

Among the beautiful types of spiritual truth in the Old Testament there is none more striking or significant than the rock in Horeb, of which we read in Exodus 17:2-7, and again in Numbers 20:8-12. The Rock in Horeb was a type of Jesus Christ, the Rock of Ages. The smiting of that rock set forth the death of Jesus on the cross under the stroke of Divine judgment. And the flowing of the waters from the rock when smitten foreshadowed the outpouring of the Holy Spirit in consequence of Christ's atoning death.

The Apostle John connects this with the piercing of Jesus' side by the Roman soldier when he says, "This He that came by water and blood, even Jesus Christ, not by water only, but by water and blood. And it is the Spirit that bears witness because the Spirit is truth." The Holy Spirit therefore was poured out at Pentecost in pursuance of Christ's finished work. The Comforter is closely associated with the precious blood in the Old Testament. The oil was always poured upon the blood and we cannot have the Holy Ghost apart from the cross of Jesus Christ. The water which flowed from the split rock suggests the cleansing, refreshing, satisfying influences of the blessed Comforter. He is for us the "Water of Life" so constantly referred to in the New Testament.

In the second passage referred to in Numbers we have an entirely different scene. A whole generation has passed since the rock was struck. Once more the people are famishing with thirst and once more Moses leads them at God's command to the rock. But this time the rock is not to be struck for it has been smitten once and is open still. Instead Moses is commanded to "speak to the rock," and the waters will flow forth abundantly. He is to use the language of faith and claim the blessing which is already waiting His acceptance. Instead of doing this Moses becomes excited and violently strikes the rock three times. God does not fail to respond by causing the water to flow in abundance, but He is grieved with Moses for his disobedience and haste and, in consequence of this, Moses is forbidden to enter the Land of Promise a few years later.

Now all this is full of deep spiritual teaching. This incident typifies our present relationship to the Holy Spirit. Pentecost has come. The Spirit is given. Heaven is opened. The water of life is flowing. We do not have to bring the Spirit now for He is here. We have only to "speak to the Rock."

October 17: His Rock – 2
by A. B. Simpson

We are to come in simple trust and claim the fulness of the Spirit who has been given, and as we open our hearts to drink, the water will flow at our bidding. There is no need for excitement or noisy demonstrations and incantations, but faith can calmly take what the Spirit is lovingly waiting to give.

> Speak to the Rock,
> id the waters flow,
> Doubt not the Spirit,
> Given long ago.
> Take what He waiteth
> Freely to bestow;
> Drink till thy being
> All His fulness know.

We pass on to the next chapter of Numbers and we find a still more striking and beautiful illustration of the Holy Spirit in chapter 21:16-18. Again they were suffering from thirst and no water appeared in sight. But this time they do not seek the rock, but gathered in a circle in the sand and with their rods dig a well, accompanying the digging with a song of faith and invocation, "Spring up, oh, well, sing you unto it." And as they dug and when they sang their song of faith, lo, the waters gushed up from subterranean fountains and they drank in abundance. The waters which had flowed from the stricken rock were evidently running as a subterranean river beneath their feet, and all they had to do was to tap the river and drink abundantly and be satisfied. This is what is meant by the "Rock that followed them." The Rock itself did not move, but the waters that flowed from it followed them all through the wilderness.

How full of simple and glorious meaning is this little picture! We may not always see the river of God's fulness flowing in our lives, nor be distinctly conscious of the Spirit's gracious presence. Often we shall be entirely without religious feeling or emotion, but the Holy Spirit is still there in the depths of our sub-conscious being and in the moment of need we can, like them, dig a well of faith and prayer, and best of all by song and praise, and lo, the fountains will gush forth, the living waters will flow, and our happy hearts will sing, "There is a river whose streams make glad the city of our God."

October 18: His Sacrifice
by George Matheson
Excerpted from "The Sacrifice of the Spirit", *Voices of the Spirit*, published by A. C. Armstrong & Son, New York, New York in 1892

Who through the eternal Spirit offered Himself.
Hebrews 9:14

"Offered Himself through the Spirit;" surely a strange mode of sacrifice. I would have expected it to have been said that Christ offered Himself through the pains of the flesh. No, but in God's sight this was not His offering. The deepest part of His sacrifice was invisible; it was the surrender of His will. The gift which He presented to the Father was not His pain but Himself—His willingness to suffer. What the Father loved was rather the painlessness than the pain. He delighted not so much in His sacrifice as in the joy of His sacrifice. It was offered "through the Spirit." It was not wrung out from a reluctant soul through obedience to an outward law; it came from the inner heart—from the impulse of undying love. It was a completed offering before Calvary began; it was seen by the Father before it was seen by the world. It was finished in the spirit before it began in the flesh—finished in that hour in which the Son of Man exclaimed, "Not as I will, but as You will." Man had to see the pain of His body; God was satisfied when "He poured out His soul."

Even so, my brother, is it with you. There are times in which you are impotent for all outward work, times in which you can offer no bodily sacrifice. Yours may be the path of obscurity; yours may be the season of poverty; yours may be the road apart from the world's highway. Yours may be the delicate frame that cannot run for God because it must rest for sustenance; there may be nothing for you to do but to look on and wish that you could serve. Yes, but can you do that? Is this wish indeed yours? Then your Father sees your sacrifice completed. It is not yet offered in the body, but it is offered "through the eternal Spirit." Like the sacrifice of Abraham it is accepted in its inwardness. You have brought up your gift to Mount Moriah and have laid it there before the Lord — laid it open in your heart, uncovered on the front of your bosom. Your Father sees it there and holds it already given. He accepts the offering of your will as an offering of your gift. He does not ask for the blood of Isaac when He has seen the blood of Abraham. He counts your faith unto you for righteousness, your devotion unto you for deed, for He knows that the sacrifice which lags behind in the flesh has been offered already in the eternal Spirit.

October 19: His Sanctifying - 1
by James Elder Cumming
Excerpted from "The Secret of Sanctification", *Through the Eternal Spirit*, published by Fleming H. Revell Company, Chicago, IL 1896

The law of the Spirit of Life in Christ Jesus made me free from the law of sin and of death.
Romans 8:2

Next to the work of glorifying Christ, the Sanctification of Believers must be regarded as having the chief place in the administration of the Church by the Spirit of God. The text at the head of this chapter speaks apparently only of freedom as given by the Holy Ghost. But it is freedom from the law of sin, under which, in Romans 7:23, Paul represents himself as having once been in "captivity." It stands here for the whole work of Sanctification, at least on its negative side, which consists in being set free from the dominion of sin, by the power of the Spirit, to serve God in newness of heart and life.

Many misunderstandings have gathered round the question, What is Sanctification? and how is it to be accomplished in the soul?

It is, then, a grievous mistake to suppose that the sanctification of the believer is a matter of course, as to which he need not trouble himself, but which will come of necessity, as the inevitable result of what has gone before.

It might be sufficient to reply to this notion, that it ignores the whole question of backsliding, which is not only a possible thing, but one of the most common and grievous facts of Christian experience. It may even be said that the course of some believers is little more than backsliding from the time of their conversion, so that their light becomes dim as the glowworm's spark, or even as "the smoking flax;" and the only comfort one has regarding them is in falling back on the thought that they "shall be saved," though "so as through fire."

So far from encouraging us to think that the new life of the soul in us will go on of itself, and of necessity, the New Testament continually warns Christians to "give all diligence" to "make their calling and election sure," to "watch and pray," to "give earnest heed" to the things that they have heard, to "hold fast that which they have, that no man take their crown;" and to "fear lest haply a promise being left of entering into His rest, any one should seem to have come short of it." Let every Christian beware of the folly of sitting down in unconcern, and leaving his renewed soul to take care of itself! The "lusting of the flesh" will in that case soon assert itself to his downfall.

October 20: His Sanctifying - 2
by James Elder Cumming

It is another and a more common mistake to suppose that the method of sanctification is to be simply that of gradual growth. This mistake tells against a Christian in two ways: it leads him to expect no positive holiness for a long period of years allowed for the growth in question; and it prevents him from taking any definite step towards holiness, so leading him back into the state of heedlessness and unconcern which has been already described. If the view which is at the root of this mistake were correct, no young Christian could be holy—contrary to the blessed fact that "grace abounding" is to be found in some of them which puts the oldest to shame. And what is to be said of the painful fact, far more common than is supposed, of no growth of holy character in men who have long been Christians? How many are forced to confess that they have been either standing still or positively going back! And how many must the Lord address as He did the Church at Ephesus: "I have this against you, that you left your First Love. Remember therefore from where have fallen, and repent, and do the first works" (Revelation 2:4-5).

As to gradual growth, moreover, there are two things to be said. The one is, that the growth of vegetable and animal life, if carefully looked at, is by no means the gradual and slow process which is often supposed. Take a tree, for instance. For a great part of the year its growth is stopped entirely; for another part its progress has become slow and insensible; while in a third part it shoots up with remarkable speed. In some years it grows only a little, in others a great deal. In other words, there are long periods in which nothing comparatively is gained; again, there are sudden outbursts of life, and it is a delusion to think only of a steady, slow process. So is it—though to an extent even more marked—in the Christian life. The growth is broken into stages, which are quite recognizable, as well as their causes.

The second remark to be made about growth is that it depends greatly on health. Sickness stops it. And such arrested growth is to be restored only by the cure of the disease which has brought it on the system. It is exactly so with the soul. When the soul is making no progress in holiness, or very little, delay is no remedy. The cause of halting must be removed, if the growth is to be resumed.

These are, no doubt, very elementary truths; yet, such has been the neglect of the subject, that they seem to be discoveries to many who are taught them.

October 21: His Sealing - 1
by A. B. Simpson
Excerpted from "The Sealing of the Holy Ghost", *When the Comforter Came*, published by The Alliance Press Company, New York, New York in 1911

After you believed you were sealed with that
Holy Spirit of promise.
Ephesians 1:13

The use of a seal in human business contracts and legal transactions is as old as human society.

The first thing suggested by a seal is Reality. The seal leaves a definite, visible and tangible mark that no one can mistake. So the Holy Spirit makes Christian experience actual, real and conscious. That which we have taken by simple faith now becomes a matter of living experience. This is what was meant when the Apostle John said, "The law was given by Moses, but grace and reality came by Jesus Christ." The law was only a "shadow of good things to come," a promise and a type of things that had not yet materialized. Jesus Christ brings to us, by the Holy Spirit, "the very substance" of those things. When the sinner believes in the Lord Jesus Christ his first step is to take by simple faith the promise of forgiveness and full salvation, and then to reckon upon God's Word, and "count the things that are not as though they were." But, after faith is tested and proved, the Holy Spirit brings to the heart the conscious witness of all that we have believed for, and sheds abroad the peace, love and joy of the Lord in our happy hearts, and we can say now, "I know Him whom I have believed." So, in all other experiences of faith, there is the twofold stage, first of believing and reckoning, and then of realizing and knowing.

The Scriptures themselves speak of two seals in this connection. First, there is our seal which faith places upon God's promise when it takes Him at His Word and counts Him true. "He who has believed on Him has set his seal that God is true." When we really believe God we commit ourselves to His Word as completely as when the notary puts his stamp upon a business contract.

But now having set our seal to the promise, God comes and adds His seal upon ours. "After you believed you were sealed with that Holy Spirit of promise." God makes real to our spiritual senses that which we accepted, without feeling, in naked faith, and now we know as well as believe. Hence the Apostle John declares, "He who believes on Him has the witness in himself." We have no right to look for the witness or for any inward sense of Divine acceptance until after we have first believed without it, and then God will surely give it.

October 22: His Sealing - 2
by A. B. Simpson

It is all right to tell people not to wait for feeling, but simply to take God at His Word. But there is a limit to this. After we have taken God at His Word there is a place for feeling, experience and all the fruits of the Spirit, which are love, joy, peace and a long catalogue of other spiritual experiences. Beloved friend, have you set your seal to God's Word, first for your salvation and then for every other blessing that you have a right to claim for spirit, soul and body? And have you also claimed and obtained the Holy Spirit's sealing and realizing touch, so that you can say with Peter, "We have believed and come to know that You are the Christ, the Son of God"? "We know that the Son of God is come, and has given us an understanding, that we may know Him that is true and we are in Him that is true, even in His Son Jesus Christ."

The second meaning of a seal is Security, Certainty and the guarantee of all contained in the sealed paper. The seal accredits the document and gives assurance that all the contracts will be fulfilled. And so the Holy Spirit as God's Seal gives to the heart full assurance of faith and the absolute certainty that we shall inherit all His covenant promises. There is undoubtedly a place into which the believer may come where doubt and fear have forever passed away and the spirit rests upon the "strong consolation" not only of God's promise, but of God's oath, as "an anchor of the soul, both sure and steadfast, and that enters into that within the veil." Henceforth its attitude is, "I know Him whom I have believed, and I am persuaded that He is able to keep that which I have committed unto Him against that day." This blessed experience is the result of full committal, entire consecration and, in consequence, the sealing of the Holy Ghost. Speaking of such an experience the Apostle Peter says, "Give diligence to make your calling and election sure, for if you do these things you shall never fall, for so an entrance shall be ministered unto you abundantly into the everlasting kingdom of our Lord and Savior Jesus Christ."

Once more, the seal implies Resemblance. It transmits its own image to the sensitive wax or the written page. It leaves a copy of its own face upon the object sealed. And so the Holy Spirit when He seals us not only makes the Lord Jesus real to our consciousness, but also the pattern and the very substance of our Christian character. He so unites us with Him that henceforth Jesus Himself lives in us, conforming us to His holy image and transforming and transfiguring us "into the same image from glory to glory even as by the glory of the Lord."

October 23: His Searching
by George Matheson
Excerpted from "The Spirit's Solutions of Mysteries", *Voices of the Spirit*, published by A. C. Armstrong & Son, New York, New York in 1892

For the Spirit searches all things, yes, the deep things of God.
1 Corinthians 2:10

There are mysteries which are quite unfathomable to everything but love. Why should the good Father send so many crosses to His children? We look in a hundred directions for the answer and from ninety and nine the answer does not come. Eye has not seen it; ear has not heard it; imagination has not conceived it. The crosses of life are the deep things of God, and thought cannot explore them. But love can; the Spirit of love can interpret the acts of love. You want to know why the Father gives you pain; the memory of parental love will search out that depth for you. Did you never get pain as a direct gift of parental love? Did you never receive a task when you wanted an hour of play, or sigh within school-house walls when you yearned for green fields? Yet your chains have become your wings; your tears have made your rainbow; your prison-house has led captivity captive. You would not part with that gift of pain for all the other gifts of your universe; it was a bondage that enlarged your soul.

Spirit of love, Spirit of the All-Father, You alone can interpret the dark places that surround You. Only when I learn that this world is Your school-house shall I find the vindication of its pain. I cannot penetrate the deep things of Joseph's dungeon except by the light of Your Fatherhood; it seems so hard to see the vanishing of youth through the iron entering into the soul. But the education of Your Fatherhood explains all. There is no gift of parental love like the iron of the soul—the strengthening of the inner man. It is love's brightest jewel given in its roughest chest. You cannot send it to me through the flowers of Eden; it can come only through the tears of Gethsemane. Your gift of iron to my soul interprets its Gethsemane. It justifies the long dark night with its deserted-ness and its agony. It vindicates the withered palm leaves, and the hushed hosannahs, and the fading of Jordan's morning glow. It explains the dropping of the curtain over that transfiguration glory which earth would fail to interpret as the promise of perpetual mountain heights. In the light of Your love the valleys are themselves exalted; the deep things, the dark things are illuminated by You.

October 24: His Seat
by George Matheson
Excerpted from "The Seat of the Spirit", *Voices of the Spirit*, published by A. C. Armstrong & Son, New York, New York in 1892

Strengthened with might by His Spirit in the inner man.
Ephesians 3:16

Paul's great concern is for the inner man; if he can only get that strengthened he feels that his work is done. And he is right. The inner man is the metropolis, the capital, the chief city; all the provinces take their tone from there. No man must begin with the provinces if he wants to make his fortune. In vain you adorn the body, in vain you amass the gold, in vain you seek the sights and sounds of beauty; the capital is the heart, and if the fashion of the heart is somber, the whole is sad. But if the fashion of the heart is bright, I have no fear for the provinces; these will soon follow. The body may be cheaply clad, the gold may be scarce and dim, the sights and sounds of beauty may be shut out by street and alley, but if in the heart there are voices of laughter, they will fill all the land. If there are songs in the metropolis, I shall not be able to keep down my singing. I shall sing through all the provinces; I shall sing in the cold and in the snow; I shall sing in the dark and in the rain; I shall sing amid my struggles for daily bread. The life of joy is everywhere when there is gladness in the inner man.

Therefore, You Divine Spirit, I come to You. I want to have my youth renewed within—at the heart. I know that the heart should be ever young, but mine is old; and because my heart is old the whole tree of life is withered. Often have I pondered these words of Yours: "If the salt has lost its savor, wherewith shall it be salted"—if the heart is old, if the principle of youth itself is withered, what can make us young? You, O Spirit, You can give me back my youth; You can restore my soul. The pastures are as green as ever, the waters are as quiet as the times of old, but the withering of my soul has robbed them of their morning's glow. Renew the sunshine of my heart; renew the childhood of my spirit. Give me back the freshness of the inward Spring—the buoyant expectation of tomorrow, the quenchless hope of the good time coming. Restore to me the elastic bounce that sorrow could not keep down, the lightness that burdens could not crush, the passion that coldness could not cool. Then shall the pastures grow green again; then shall the waters ripple peace once more, for the new creature shall make the new creation, and the restoration of the soul shall be the restitution of all things. My strength shall be renewed like the eagle's when You have strengthened my inner man.

October 25: His Secret - 1
by George Matheson
Excerpted from "The Secret of the Spirit's Revelation", *Voices of the Spirit*, published by A. C. Armstrong & Son, New York, New York in 1892

And it came to pass, that, when the Spirit rested upon them, they prophesied.
Numbers 11:25

When the Spirit rested upon them they prophesied; spiritual rest was mentally ceasing activity. It is ever so. My times of revelation are not my times of mental flutter. "Be still, and know that I am God," is the law of spiritual insight. Why did the Son of Man see Heaven opened and hear its voice of commendation? It was because the Spirit was "abiding upon Him." It was not a momentary flash, it was not a sudden outburst, it was not an excited rhapsody; it was the conviction of a dove-like calm. There are a hundred things lying at my feet which I cannot see for lack of calmness—lack of the dove-like rest. Why is Hagar in such distress in the desert? There is a well of water before her very eyes if she would only look at it. But she cannot look at it. It is not lack of sight that prevents her from seeing it; it is lack of spiritual rest. If she were only calm she would get a revelation, a revelation that has been waiting for her a long time, written on the desert sands. But she is not calm. Her heart is on fire, her nerves are in motion, her soul is ill at ease. She is a stranger to spiritual rest, and therefore she is a stranger to the actual outward comforts that are scattered at her door. When the Spirit has rested on her she will prophesy her own deliverance.

Spirit of rest, in Your light we shall see light. In the absence of Your light even our sunshine is darkness. Is it not written that in order to give a knowledge of the glorious light in the face of Jesus Christ, You had to shine "in our hearts?" If even the face of Christ could only have its glory seen through Your inward shining, what shall we say of the face of the universe? I am like Elijah under the shadows of Horeb; I underrate the number of my own sunbeams. It is stillness that I want most of all—power to stand and gaze on my actual surroundings. I am more disturbed by the earthquake than either by the thunder or by the fire. Speak peace to my soul, that I may awaken to the melodies that float around me. Speak peace to my soul, that in the hour of its rest I may see the ladder between earth and Heaven. I shall know that there are yet seven thousand who have not bowed the knee to Baal when You have inspired my spirit with Your still small voice.

October 26: His Secret - 2
by George D. Watson

Excerpted from "The Secret of Spiritual Power"", *The Secret of Spiritual Power*, published by The McDonald & Gill Co., Boston, Massachusetts in 1894

A great deal has been said and written upon the subject of spiritual power, and perhaps I can add nothing original upon the subject, but may help to stir up some pure minds by way of remembrance.

While attending a holiness convention in Star Hall, Manchester, England, one day, there opened up to my mind a series of thoughts as to the secret of God's power in man. In the first place, the secret of spiritual power consists in the union of the Holy Ghost with the purified faculties and natural energies of the human soul, and, on the human side, it consists in the utter abandonment of the soul to, and a heart cooperation with, the Holy Spirit. It is not eloquence, nor style, nor personal magnetism, nor psychology, nor the natural energy of the human soul, not even the energy of a purified soul. The soul may be purified, and yet as a mere creature, the creature faculties and creature powers do not have the power of God in soul-saving, in aggressive spiritual work, in bringing sinners to repentance, or believers into holiness. It is true that a human soul free from sin, as a mere creature, has a marvelous power above other unsaved souls, but as a creature, though it is holy, yet in itself does not possess that secret energy which can communicate conviction and lead to salvation. So that, however holy a man is, there must be joined on to him a Divine current, a supernatural energy which is emphatically Divine, and of which he is the vehicle and conductor. This Divine power is a secret unknown to the world, not accessible to the most learned sinners, misunderstood by carnal professors, utterly beyond the grasp of philosophers or scientists. Let us notice some Scripture proofs.

Jesus had a pure soul; from the very beginning of His being He was perfectly free from the fallen nature of Adam, and, as a mere man, He was superior in moral strength to all the men of the world. And yet it was not by His holy creature-strength that He did the works of His Father. The power that Jesus used in working miracles, in preaching sermons, in healing diseases, in casting out demons, in saving souls was not the power of His sinless soul, but it was the power flowing from the baptism of the Spirit upon His pure humanity. This is distinctly marked in the two periods of His life. From His infancy to His baptism in Jordan He was entirely holy, but performed no miracles, but when the Holy Ghost descended on Him, from that time on, He was the Anointed One, and worked under the perpetual unction that flowed through Him from the Holy Spirit. So that in addition to His holy creature-faculties, God poured into Him the fullness of the Spirit. We are told that when Jesus had gotten through with the temptation of the wilderness, He "returned to Galilee in the power of the Holy Ghost." This expression of returning in the "power of the Holy Ghost," implies that there was added unto Him a power which He did not possess as a mere pure man.

October 27: His Separating – 1
by Andrew Murray
Excerpted from "Separated Unto the Holy Ghost", *Absolute Surrender*, published by Fleming H. Revell Company, New York, New York in 1897

Now there were in the church that was at Antioch certain prophets and teachers; as Barnabas, and Simeon that was called Niger, and Lucius of Cyrene, and Manaen…and Saul. As they ministered to the Lord and fasted, the Holy Ghost said, "Separate unto Me Barnabas and Saul for the work whereunto I have called them." And when they had fasted and prayed, and laid their hands on them, they sent them away. So they, being sent forth by the Holy Ghost, departed unto Seleucia.
Acts 13:1-4

In the story of our text we shall find some precious thoughts to guide us as to what God would have of us, and what God would do for us. The great lesson of the verses quoted is this: The Holy Ghost is the Director of the work of God upon the earth. And what we should do if we are to work rightly for God, and if God is to bless our work, is to see that we stand in a right relation to the Holy Ghost, that we give Him every day the place of honor that belongs to Him, and that in all our work and (what is more) in all our private inner life, the Holy Ghost shall always have the first place. Let me point out to you some of the precious thoughts our passage suggests.

First of all, we see that God has His own plans with regard to His kingdom. His church at Antioch had been established. God had certain plans and intentions with regard to Asia, and with regard to Europe. He had conceived them they were His, and He made them known to His servants.

Our great Commander organizes every campaign, and His generals and officers do not always know the great plans. They often receive sealed orders, and they have to wait on Him for what He gives them as orders. God in heaven has wishes, and a will, in regard to any work that ought to be done, and to the way in which it has to be done. Blessed is the man who gets into God's secrets and works under God.

God has His workers and His plans clearly mapped out, and our position is to wait, that God should communicate to us as much of His will as each time is needed. We have simply to be faithful in obedience, carrying out His orders. God has a plan for His Church upon earth. But alas! we too often make our plan, and we think that we know what ought to be done. We ask God first to bless our feeble efforts, instead of absolutely refusing to go unless God goes before us. God has planned for the work and the extension of His kingdom. The Holy Ghost has had that work given in charge to Him. "The work whereunto I have called them." May God therefore help us all to be afraid of touching "the ark of God" except as we are led by the Holy Ghost.

October 28: His Separating – 2
by Andrew Murray

Then the second thought: God is willing and able to reveal to His servants what His will is. Yes, blessed be God, communications come down from Heaven still! As we read here what the Holy Ghost said, so still the Holy Ghost will speak to His Church and His people. In these later days He has often done it. He has come to individual men, and by His Divine teaching He has led them out into fields of labor that others could not at first understand or approve; into ways and methods that did not recommend themselves to the majority. But the Holy Ghost does still in our time teach His people. Thank God, in our foreign missionary societies and in our home missions, and in a thousand forms of work, the guiding of the Holy Ghost is known, but (we are all ready, I think, to confess) too little known. We have not learned enough to wait upon Him, and so we should make a solemn declaration before God: O God, we want to wait more for You to show us Your will.

That brings me to the third thought: Note the disposition to which the Spirit reveals God's will. What do we read here? There were a number of men ministering to the Lord and fasting, and the Holy Ghost came and spoke to them. Some people understand this passage very much as they would in reference to a missionary committee of our day.

We see there is an open field, and we have had our missions in other fields, and we are going to get on to that field. We have virtually settled that, and we pray about it. But the position was a very different one in those former days. I doubt whether any of them thought of Europe, for later on even Paul himself planned to go back into Asia, till the night vision called him by the will of God. Look at those men. God had done wonders. He had extended the Church to Antioch, and He had given rich and large blessing. Now, here were these men ministering to the Lord, serving Him with prayer and fasting. What a deep conviction they have. It is the hearts entirely surrendered to the Lord Jesus, in hearts separating themselves from the world, and even from ordinary religious exercises, and giving themselves to intense prayer to look to their Lord — it is in such hearts that the Heavenly will of God will be made obvious.

The fourth thought. What is now the will of God as the Holy Ghost reveals it? It is contained in one word: "Separate...The work is Mine, and I care for it, and I have chosen these men and called them, and I want you who represent the Church of Christ upon earth, to set them apart unto Me." The men were to be set apart to the Holy Ghost, and the Church was to do this separating work. The Holy Ghost could trust these men to do it in a right spirit. Here we come to the very root, to the very life of the need of Christian workers. The question is: What is needed that the power of God should rest upon us more mightily? And the answer from Heaven is: "I want men separated unto the Holy Ghost."

October 29: His Separating – 3
by Andrew Murray

Then comes my fifth thought, and it is this; This holy partnership with the Holy Spirit in His work becomes a matter of consciousness and of action. This teaches us that it is not only in the beginning of our Christian work, but all along, that we need to have our strength in prayer. We believe more in speaking to men than we believe in speaking to God. Learn from these men that the work which the Holy Ghost commands must call us to new fasting and prayer, to new separation from the spirit and the pleasures of the world, to new consecration to God and to His fellowship.

Do you understand what that means? A terrible danger in Christian work, just as in a Christian life that is begun with much prayer, begun in the Holy Spirit, is that it may be gradually shunted off on to the lines of the flesh; and the word comes: "Having begun in the Spirit, are you now made perfect by the flesh?" The Holy Spirit comes in answer to believing prayer. You know when the exalted Jesus had ascended to the throne, for ten days the footstool of the throne was the place where His waiting disciples cried to Him. And that is the law of the kingdom—the King upon the throne, the servants upon the footstool. May God find us there unceasingly!

Then comes the last thought: What a wonderful blessing comes when the Holy Ghost is allowed to lead and to direct the work, and when it is carried on in obedience to Him! You know the story of the mission on which Barnabas and Saul were sent out. You know what power there was with them. The Holy Ghost sent them, and they went on from place to place with large blessing. The Holy Ghost was their leader further on. You recollect how it was by the Spirit that Paul was hindered from going again into Asia, and was led away over to Europe. Oh, the blessing that rested upon that little company of men, and upon their ministry unto the Lord!

I pray you, let us learn to believe that God has a blessing for us. The Holy Ghost, into whose hands God has put the work, has been called "the Executive of the Holy Trinity." The Holy Ghost has not only power, but He has the Spirit of love. He is brooding over this dark world, and every sphere of work in it, and He is willing to bless. And why is there not more blessing? There can be only one answer: We have not honored the Holy Ghost as we should have done. Is there one who can say that that is not true? Is not every thoughtful heart ready to cry, "God forgive me that I have not honored the Holy Spirit as I should have done, that I have grieved Him, that I have allowed self and the flesh and my own will to work where the Holy Ghost should have been honored! May God forgive me that I have allowed self and the flesh and the will actually to have the place that God wanted the Holy Ghost to get."

Oh, the sin is greater than we know! No wonder that there is so much feebleness and failure in the Church of Christ!

October 30: His Settling
by W. B. Godbey
Excerpted from "He Will Settle You", *Work of the Holy Spirit*, published by Pickett Publishing Co., Louisville, Kentucky in 1902

And after you have suffered a little while, the God of all grace, who has called you to His eternal glory in Christ, will Himself restore, confirm, strengthen, and establish you.
1 Peter 5:10

This is the final clause of that important verse which so clearly reveals the gracious economy in its progressive development. You see here the beautiful and triumphant finale of the Spirit's work in Christian experience is our settlement in God. The very contemplation of this fact transports my soul with rapture. Long tossed upon the ocean, driven by the gales, and lashed by the storms, eventually the ship is safely anchored in the harbor. It is your glorious privilege to reach this appropriate experience of an anchored soul, settled in God till the storms will never again be able to send it away on the capricious waves of raging seas imperiled by the rolling billows. We would not be understood to teach that we can reach a state of impossible apostasy in this world, but we certainly can in the appreciation of these wonderful graces of Perfection, Establishment, Invigoration and Settlement, attain a relation to the Omnipotent Trinity in which there is no longer even the slightest probability, that we shall ever fall away.

This final and glorious Settlement in God should be the constant aspiration of every Christian. It is really a Heavenly taste, a fitting foreshadowing of impending glorification. You see from these Scriptures the great mistake in taking sanctification as the ultimatum of all progress. It is properly only the real inauguration of that glorious spiritual upheaval which is to give us a Heaven on earth and transport us on the wings of faith and hope to the realms of bliss and qualify us for citizenship among the saints in glory and companionship with angels, archangels, cherubim and seraphim.

October 31: His State - 1
by Andrew Murray
Excerpted from "Spiritual or Carnal", *The Spirit of Christ*, published by
A. D. F. Randolph & Co., New York, New York in 1888

And I, brethren, could not speak unto you as unto spiritual, but as unto carnal, as unto babes in Christ. I fed you with milk, not with meat; for you were not yet able to bear it; no, not even now are you able; for whereas there is among you jealousy and strife, are you not carnal, and walk after the manner of men?
1 Corinthians 3:1-3

If we live by the Spirit, by the Spirit let us also walk.
Galatians 5:25

The Apostle Paul tells the Corinthians that, though they have the Spirit, he cannot call them spiritual; that epithet belongs to those who have not only received the Spirit, but have yielded themselves to Him to possess and rule their whole life. Those who have not done this, in whom the power of the flesh is still more manifest than that of the Spirit, must be called not spiritual, but fleshly or carnal. There are thus three states in which a man may be found. The unregenerate is still the natural man, not having the Spirit of God. The regenerate, who is still a babe in Christ, whether because he is only lately converted, or because he has stood still and not advanced, is the carnal man, giving way to the power of the flesh. The believer in whom the Spirit has obtained full supremacy, is the spiritual man.

The whole passage is suggestive of rich instruction in regard to the life of the Spirit within us.

The young Christian is still carnal. Regeneration is a birth. The center and root of the personality, the spirit, has been renewed and taken possession of by the Spirit of God. But time is needed for its power from that center to extend through all the circumference of our being. The kingdom of God is like unto a seed; the life in Christ is a growth; and it would be against the laws of nature and grace alike if we expected from the babe in Christ the strength that can only be found in the young men, or the rich experience of the fathers. Even where in the young convert there is great singleness of heart and faith, with true love and devotion to the Savior, time is needed for a deeper knowledge of self and sin, for a spiritual insight into what God's will and grace are. With the young believer it is not unnatural that the emotions are deeply stirred, and that the mind delights in the contemplation of Divine truth; with the growth in grace, the will becomes the more important thing, and the waiting for the Spirit's power in the life and character more than the delight in those thoughts and images of the life which alone the mind could give. We need not wonder if the babe in Christ is still carnal.

November 1: His State - 2
by Andrew Murray

Many Christians remain carnal. God has not only called us to grow, but has provided all the conditions and powers needed for growth. And yet it is sadly true, that there are many Christians who, like the Corinthians, remain babes in Christ when they ought to be going on to perfection, "attaining unto a full-grown man." In some cases the blame is almost more with the Church and its teaching, than with the individuals themselves. When the preaching makes salvation chiefly to consist in pardon and peace and the hope of Heaven, or when, if a holy life is preached, the truth of Christ our Sanctification, our Sufficient Strength to be holy, and the Holy Spirit's indwelling, are not taught clearly and in the power of the Spirit, growth can hardly be expected. Ignorance, human and defective views of the gospel, as the power of God unto a present salvation in sanctification, are the cause of the evil.

In other cases the root of the evil is to be found in the unwillingness of the Christian to deny self and crucify the flesh. The call of Jesus to every disciple is," If any man will come after Me, let him deny himself." The Spirit is only given to the obedient; He can only do His work in those who are willing absolutely to give up self to the death. The sin that proved that the Corinthians were carnal was their jealousy and strife. When Christians are not willing to give up the sin of selfishness and temper; when, whether in the home relationship or in the wider circle of Church and public life, they want to retain the liberty of giving way to, or excusing evil feelings, of pronouncing their own judgments, and speaking words that are not in perfect love, then they remain carnal. With all their knowledge, and their enjoyment of religious ordinances, and their work for God's kingdom, they are carnal and not spiritual. They grieve the Holy Spirit of God; they cannot have the testimony that they are pleasing to God.

The carnal Christian cannot comprehend spiritual truth. Paul writes to these Corinthians: "I fed you with milk, and not with meat; for you were not able to bear it; no, not even now are you able." The Corinthians prided themselves on their wisdom; Paul thanked God that they were "enriched in all knowledge." There was nothing in His teaching that they would not have been able to comprehend with the understanding. But the real spiritual entering into the truth in power, so as to possess it and be possessed by it, so as to have not only the thoughts but the very thing the words speak of, this the Holy Spirit only can give. And He gives it only in the spiritually-minded man. The teaching and leading of the Spirit is given to the obedient, is preceded by the dominion of the Spirit in mortifying the deeds of the body (Romans 8:13-14). Spiritual knowledge is not deep thought but living contact, entering into and being united to the truth as it is in Jesus, a spiritual reality, a substantial existence. "The Spirit teaches, combining spiritual things with spiritual;" into a spiritual mind He works spiritual truth.

November 2: His Strengthening
by George Matheson
Excerpted from "The Spirit's Strength to a Nation", *Voices of the Spirit*, published by A. C. Armstrong & Son, New York, New York in 1892

Because the palaces shall be forsaken; the multitude of the city shall be left; the forts and towers shall be for dens forever, a joy of wild asses, a pasture of flocks; until the Spirit is poured upon us from on high.
Isaiah 32:14-15

Three things are here said to depend on the Spirit—the palace, the city, and the tower. The Spirit is the glory of royalty; to be a king in God's sense is to be the servant of all. The Spirit is the secret of citizenship; to be a citizen in God's sense is to be the brother of all. The Spirit is the root of warlike strength; to be a soldier in God's sense is to be the defender of all—the defender of that righteousness which is at last the universal interest. God's Spirit is for the nation as well as for the man, and these three are the blessings of the nation. What else can I ask for my country than this trinity of privileges—that her court shall be always pure, that her cities shall be always flourishing, and that in the cause of righteousness her towers shall be always strong.

Lord of nations, bless our native land. Let Your Divine Spirit be incarnated in His threefold life—in its rulers, in its citizens, in its soldiers. Impress its rulers with the responsibility of being great, the weightiness of being ministers to all. Impress its citizens with the multitude of their claims, the vastness of that brotherhood of which they are members. Impress its soldiers with the fearlessness that is born of duty, the courage that comes from devotion to the just and true. Purify its palaces, cleanse its streets, strengthen its bulwarks. Teach its rulers to say "Your will be done," its citizens to cry "hallowed be Your name," its soldiers to pray "Your kingdom come." Let its kings be priests unto You; let its citizens be fathers to the multitude; let its soldiers be peacemakers to the world. May Your altars not be removed from the high places; may Your Word not be silent in the homes of industrious toil; may Your banner be unfurled in the camp and on the field. Then shall our land be full of Your glory, a universal priesthood, a holy convocation. Then shall we be numbered among those nations which stand already at the right hand of Your judgment seat and receive from You the blessing of the minister, "Enter into the joy of your Lord." Your Spirit shall be poured on us from on high when You have exalted our palaces, our cities, and our towers.

November 3: His Striving - 1
by Robert P. Kerr

Excerpted from "The Striving Spirit", *Southern Presbyterian Pulpit: A Collection of Sermons*, published by The Presbyterian Committee of Publications, Richmond, Virginia in 1896

"My Spirit shall not always strive with men."
Genesis 6:3

In the sixth chapter of Genesis we have set before us the imposing spectacle of God the Holy Spirit striving with a wicked world and race of men. Sin had reached its hideous culmination. Crime of every kind was almost universal, and earth seemed to have become a province allied to the dominion of Satan. The cup of iniquity being nearly full, God was going soon to press it to the guilty lips of men, that they might drain to its dregs the last bitter drop; and the cloud of Divine wrath was soon to break with the crash of worldwide destruction upon the human race.

But though the progress of iniquity had been steady and rapid, it had not reached its culmination without Divine interference. In all their wretched criminality there had been present and active among men the august personality of the Holy Spirit. The text lifts the veil which hides the unseen, and we behold, from the Divine standpoint, a progress which had not gone on unresisted from above. God the Holy Ghost placed Himself in the way of this terrible defection of the world from truth and righteousness. The men of that day and their fathers had traveled far from all that is good, but at every step they had been confronted and opposed by a Divine barrier. Over God's most gracious influences they had trod, and in spite of a resisting omnipotence of love, they had progressed until they reached a height of crime that lifted its face into the very presence of the Majesty of Heaven.

It may be asked, How could man surpass resisting omnipotence? How could man overcome God? The answer is easy. Man is not a puppet, without power of choice; he is not a beast, without intellect, soul, conscience. He is a free moral agent originally imaged after God; and his Maker has never forced him against his will to do anything good. This would be to unmake man, to degrade him to a beast. God respects man in his freedom, nor does He seek a slavish service of the soul. In later times Christ, at the threshold of man's will, declares, "Behold I stand at the door and knock." So in the days before the flood the Holy Ghost strove with man, but did not force his will.

How great the rebelliousness of mankind was may be estimated from what it was able to overcome. For in the gigantic struggle with Divine grace they came off winners, gaining for themselves by this over-mastery the victory of black and awful success.

This could not continue forever. The Spirit would not be insulted with perpetual impunity. God's wrath is aroused, and over the heads of men fall those pregnant words, "My Spirit shall not always strive with man."

November 4: His Striving - 2
by Robert P. Kerr

The world had lived out its probation, and the hour was set on the dial of time for the destruction of the human race by a catastrophe the most stupendous that history records. The Spirit departed; grieved, He turned away, and the blow fell in swift retributive justice upon mankind, in the flood by which all perished except the family of one righteous man.

How did the Spirit strive then, and how does He strive with men today?

It was, and is, by the use of the whole apparatus of the universe; in other words, by the use of everything that is. The powers of nature show in turn the goodness and the wrath of God. Does calm sunshine mean nothing? Is there no lesson in the sunset; no invitation in the yellow harvest-fields? Have all the joys of life no Heavenly undertone of love and mercy?

Yes, and tempest, disease, fire, famine, death; is there no warning in them to listening minds? Nature tells us in unmistakable utterance that whatsoever a man sows that shall he also reap. Surely, she says, sin against law means misery, sorrow, and death. God has put a voice in everything that He has made, from glittering star to lily, rose, or wheat-sheaf; in disease, lightning flash, death, and even Hell, to tell men that sin must have its awful fruition and punishment. All this prodigious universe, thrilled with the living Presence of the eternal Spirit, throws its barrier across the path that leads away from God and truth. It was so before the flood; it is so today.

Then, also, God had living witnesses. He has never been without some to rebuke a wicked and perverse world. By example and by preached word the Spirit strove to recall the prodigal race of man. A line of preachers extends back in unbroken procession from this day to the gates of Paradise. Men have not been left to the mute testimony of nature alone, nor the foreign interference of angels, but they have had witnesses for God of their own flesh, and blood, and kindred. There have always been, under the guidance of the Holy Ghost, men to preach to men; men to strive, and pray, and weep over the iniquity of their fellows. Noah and his predecessors preached righteousness to their contemporaries, and Noah's successors have never ceased thus to preach, from the time of the flood to this hour, when by the Spirit's appointment souls are warned, by human voices, to fly from the wrath to come.

In our time the magnificent institution of a gospel Church, that touches every shore and nation, preaches from ten thousand pulpits, and from house to house, the truths of responsibility, judgment to come, and mercy through the cross. These are preached, and prayed, and sung in the hearing of millions. On the myriad pages of journals and books Christ is set forth, and civilization is but the platform for the preaching of the gospel.

November 5: His Supplicating
by George Matheson
Excerpted from "The Supplications of the Spirit", *Voices of the Spirit*, published by A. C. Armstrong & Son, New York, New York in 1892

Praying always with all prayer and supplication in the Spirit.
Ephesians 6:18

"Praying always with all prayer;" one would think the command was unqualified. Yet it is not. I am not to ask everything indiscriminately. There is a limit within which my desires are to wander. I am not to be allowed the answer to "all prayer," but to "all prayer in the Spirit." The man of science tells me that I must not ask anything that is at variance with the law of nature. The order of the Spirit is the law of God's nature, and it is an absolute law. I must not seek to change it, I dare not desire to violate it, for it is without variableness or the least shadow of turning. The order of God's Spirit is the law of love; to pray in God's Spirit is to desire conformity with love. If I ask that which is not conformable to God's nature, I am like the child that cries for the moon; I want to put asunder what God has joined together. The overture to all prayer must be "Your will be done;" no person can sing the song of supplication who has pitched their voice upon a lower key. My Father measures distance not by space but by sympathy; my voice shall He hear in the morning if I ask "in the Spirit."

Lord, teach me to pray. Teach me that form of prayer which marks the boundaries within which I may ask of You. Teach me to desire that by which Your name shall be hallowed, to seek that which shall hasten Your Kingdom, to wish that which shall be consistent with Your will. Teach me before all things to say "our Father." I sometimes forget that I have a brother, forget that he has needs common with my own. I sometimes lose the remembrance that the satisfaction of my need may mean the impoverishment of my brother; I say, "Give me this day my daily bread." Restore to me, O Divine Love, the memory of Your cross. Restore to me the fading sense of Your kingdom, Your power, Your glory. Remind me that Your kingdom is service, that Your power is sacrifice, that Your glory is humanity redeemed. Revive within me the sympathy that feels another's pain, the charity that weaves another's hope, the love that participates in another's joy. Let me cease to thank You that I am not as others; my prayer shall become Your prayer when I shall ask through Your Spirit

November 6: His Sustaining
by George Matheson
Excerpted from "The Sustenance of the Spirit", *Voices of the Spirit*, published by A. C. Armstrong & Son, New York, New York in 1892

You gave your good Spirit to instruct them and did not withhold Your manna from their mouth and gave them water for their thirst.
Nehemiah 9:20

God is said to have sustained Israel by the Spirit first and by the manna afterwards. We should have looked for the reverse order. We should have thought that the care of the Heavenly Father would have begun by strengthening the gates and then proceeded to strengthen the citadel. But the Heavenly Father knows better what is in man. He knows that no amount of manna will permanently conquer hunger as long as there is a hunger of the spirit. It is in vain to provide a couch of down if there is an unrest within the heart. It is in vain to supply strains of music if there is discord in the soul. It is in vain to spread the banquet if there is a burden on the spirit. But if the heart is already rested it will find peace everywhere, if the soul is already tuned it will find music everywhere, if the spirit is already fed, it will find a banquet everywhere. Israel's own glory was not her manna but her mind; it was her mind that sustained her in the poverty of her manna. Not without cause does the prophet thank God for this, that His first blessing to Israel was the gift of the good Spirit.

O You who have taught us to seek first Your kingdom and its righteousness, teach me to say "Your will be done" before I say "give me my daily bread." Teach me to accept Your will as the foundation of my happiness, and other things as only its superstructure. Teach me that the mandate that says to my soul "your sins are forgiven" is a more abiding miracle than the mandate which says to my body "arise and walk." I am often disappointed that You promise so much more to the spirit than to the flesh. I am more afraid of the hunger of the body than of the hunger of the spirit, more anxious for the strength of the outer man than for the health of the heart. Convince me that it would not profit a man to gain the whole world and lose his own soul. Show me that it is only the possession of my soul that makes the possession of the world any gain. Impress me with the truth that nothing can give me joy if I myself am not already joyful. Inspire me with the knowledge that the issues of life are not from without but from within. Guide me into the discovery that the pleasures at Your right hand are the only things that are "pleasures for evermore" He that tastes the earthly manna shall hunger again, but he that has received Your bread of life shall subsist even amidst its failure. In Your new creation that must be first which is spiritual, afterward that which is natural. Before You send the manna give me Your good Spirit.

November 7: His Sweetness - 1
by Charles H. Spurgeon
Excerpted from "Honey in the Mouth", *Twelve Sermons on the Holy Spirit*, published by Fleming H. Revell Company, New York, New York in 1855

"He shall glorify Me: for He shall receive of Mine, and shall show it unto you. All things that the Father has are Mine: therefore said I, that He shall take of Mine, and shall show it unto you."
John 16:14-15

Beloved friends, here you have the Trinity, and there is no salvation apart from the Trinity. It must be the Father, the Son, and the Holy Ghost. "All things that the Father hath are Mine", says Christ, and the Father has all things. They were always His; they are still His; they always will be His; and they cannot become ours till they change ownership, till Christ can say, "All things that the Father has are Mine"; for it is by virtue of the representative character of Christ standing as the surety of the covenant that the "all things" of the Father are passed over to the Son, that they might be passed over to us. "It pleased the Father that in Him should all fulness dwell; of His fulness have all we received." But yet we are so dull that, though the conduit-pipe is laid on to the great fountain, we cannot get at it. We are lame; we cannot reach it; and in comes the third Person of the Divine Unity, even the Holy Spirit, and He receives of the things of Christ, and then delivers them over to us.

So we do actually receive, through Jesus Christ, by the Spirit, what is in the Father.

Ralph Erskine, in his preface to a sermon upon the fifteenth verse, has a notable piece. He speaks of grace as honey—honey for the cheering of the saints, for the sweetening of their mouths and hearts; but he says that in the Father "the honey is in the flower, which is at such a distance from us that we could never extract it." In the Son "the honey is in the comb, prepared for us in our Immanuel, God-Man, Redeemer, the Word that was made flesh, saying, 'All things that the Father has are Mine"; and Mine for your use and advantage. It is in the comb.

But then, next, we have honey in the mouth; the Spirit taking all things, and making application thereof, by showing them unto us, and making us to eat and drink with Christ, and share of these "all things"; yes, not only eat the honey, but the honeycomb with the honey; not only His benefits, but Himself. It is a very beautiful division of the subject. There never will be any more honey than there is in the flower. There it is. But how shall you and I get at it? We do not have the wisdom to extract the sweetness. We are not as the bees that are able to find it out. It is bee-honey, but not man-honey. Yet you see in Christ it becomes the honey in the honeycomb, and hence He is sweet to our taste as honey dropping from the comb. Sometimes we are so faint that we cannot reach out a hand to grasp that honeycomb; and, alas! there was a time when our palates were so depraved that we preferred bitter things, and thought them sweet. But now the Holy Ghost has come, we have gotten the honey in the mouth, and the taste to enjoy it.

November 8: His Sweetness - 2
by Charles H. Spurgeon

Beloved friends, I scarcely need say to you, do keep the existence of the Trinity prominent in your ministry. Remember, you cannot pray without the Trinity. If the full work of salvation requires a Trinity, so does that very breath by which we live. You cannot draw near to the Father except through the Son, and by the Holy Spirit. There is a trinity in nature undoubtedly. There certainly constantly turns up the need of a Trinity in the realm of grace; and when we get to Heaven we shall understand, perhaps, more fully what is meant by the Trinity in unity. But if that is a thing never to be understood, we shall at least grasp it more lovingly; and we shall rejoice more completely as the three tones of our music shall rise up in perfect harmony unto Him who is one and indivisible, and yet is three—forever blessed, Father, Son, and Holy Ghost, one God.

Now for the point which I am to open up to you, though I cannot do it, but He must do it. We must sit here, and have the text acted out upon ourselves. "He shall glorify Me. He take of Mine, and shall show it unto you." May it be so just now!

First, what the Holy Spirit does. "He shall take of Mine, and shall show it unto you." Secondly, what the Holy

Spirit aims at and really effects: "He shall glorify Me." And then, thirdly, how in doing both these things He is the Comforter. It is the Comforter who does this; and we shall find our richest, surest comfort in this work of the Holy Spirit, who shall take of the things of Christ, and show them unto us.

It is clear, beloved friends, that the Holy Spirit deals with the things of Christ. All things that Christ had heard from His Father He made known to us. He kept to them. And now the Spirit takes of the things of Christ, and of nothing else. Do not let us strain at anything new. The Holy Ghost could deal with anything in Heaven above, or in the earth beneath — the story of the ages past, the story of the ages to come the inward secrets of the earth, the evolution of all things, if there is an evolution. He could do it all. Like the Master, He could handle any topic He chose; but He confines Himself to the things of Christ and therein finds unutterable liberty and boundless freedom.

Do you think, dear friend, that you can be wiser than the Holy Spirit? And if His choice must be a wise one, will yours be a wise one if you begin to take of the things of something or somebody else? You will have the Holy Spirit near you when you are receiving of the things of Christ; but, as the Holy Spirit is said never to receive anything else, when you are handling other things on the Sunday, you will be handling them alone; and the pulpit is a dreary solitude, even in the midst of a crowd, if the Holy Ghost is not with you there.

November 9: His Sword - 1
by John Henry Jowett
Excerpted from "The Sword of the Spirit", *The Whole Armour of God*, published by Fleming H. Revell Company, New York, New York in 1916

Take the sword of the Spirit which is the Word of God.
Ephesians 6:17

What, then, is this sword? It is "the Word of God." And what is this Word of God which we are to flash through all falsehood like the thrust of a gleaming sword? What is this Word which is to be our sword? Well, first of all, it is the word of Divine truth; God's way of thinking about things. And therefore when we are wielding the sword we are using a thought of God. We are to use God's thought about a thing in fighting all other thoughts about that thing. For instance, we are to take God's thought about life, and use it as a sword to meet and destroy all low and unworthy conceptions of life. We are to take God's thought about sin and use it in combating all the lax and deadly conceptions of sin which are so loose and rampant in our own day. We are to take God's thought about holiness, and use it in fighting all ignoble compromises which may satisfy a poor standard in the kingdom of the letter, but which have no standing in the more glorious realm of the Spirit. We are to take God's thought about worship, and fight all the little, mean, seductive ritualism which so frequently strut about in royal and gorgeous robes, but which are empty of all vital spiritual wealth and power.

And so with a thousand other relations. God's thought about a thing is to be our sword in fighting all the debasing thoughts of that thing; it may be God's thought of work, or of wealth, or of success, or of failure. Or God's thought of pleasure, or of service, or of death. What does God think about a thing? That is my sword, the thought of God which is the Word of God. And we are to take that shining, flaming, flashing thought, and use it as a sword among all the creeping, crawling things, or against all the flying and bewitching subtleties of things which abounded in Ephesus, and which are equally prolific in London or New York. And so does the Apostle Paul give us this counsel: "Take the sword of the Spirit, which is the thought or Word of God."

And now I can add a second characteristic of the sword, a characteristic which amplifies and corroborates the first. This Word of God, which is to be our sword, is not only the Word of Divine truth as laid upon the mind. It is also the Word of Divine commandment as laid upon the will. It is a word which Divinely reveals our personal duty, imposing upon us some imperative mission. Some Word of God comes to us with the mysterious suggestion of obligation, and we often receive it over against some soft and wooing temptation to an indulgent laziness; and we are to take the Divine Word of obligation, and with it fight and slay the soft seduction for ease.

November 10: His Sword - 2
by John Henry Jowett

There is still a third descriptive word about the sword, and which again corroborates and enriches the others. The Word of God, which is the sword of the Spirit, is not only the Word of Divine truth laying God's thought upon the mind; and not only the Word of Divine commandment laying God's purpose upon the will; it is also the Word of Divine promise laying God's strengthening comfort upon the heart. Just think of that fine sword, the word of promise, being handed to these young and tempted disciples in this awful, hostile city of Ephesus. I think we may easily imagine, without presumption, how they would apply Paul's counsel, and how the older men among them would train the younger men in the expert use of this shining sword. They would say, "Whenever you go out to your work, amid all the cold, bristling antagonisms of the world, carry the sword of promise! When your circumstances seem to mock you because of your unnerving loneliness, whip out the sword of promise! When you appear to be in a minority of one, and the enemy swarms in menace around you on every side, carry this sword of promise in your right hand: "I will never leave you nor forsake you." And when the enemy taunts you because of your weakness, or your lack of culture, or your lack of rank and social prestige, or your "nobody-ism" and "nothing-ism," whip out the sword and fight the taunt with this word of promise: "Neither shall any one pluck you out of My hand"!

Thus do I think these disciples would speak to one another, as, blessed be God, disciples can speak to one another today. When the devil comes to us in our loneliness, in our weakness, in our seeming abandonment, let us lay hold of the Word of grace, and fight all the enemies' taunts with the Divine promise, and pierce them through and through, turning the foe to rout, and remaining more than conquerors on the hard and finely won field. Well, such is what I think to be the sword. It is the Word of Divine truth, it is the Word of Divine commandment, and it is the Word of Divine promise. It is a superlatively excellent sword, "it is a right Jerusalem blade. Let a man have one of these blades, with a hand to wield it, and skill to use it, and he may venture upon an angel with it." Its edge will never blunt, for it is "the sword of the Spirit, which is the Word of God."

Where, then, can we find this Word of God which is to be our sword of the Spirit? Well, first of all, we can find the Word of God in the sacred Scriptures. Here is the Word which gives the revelation of truth, telling me how the great God thinks about things, and therefore, telling me how to think amid all the plausible errors of our time. And here, too, is the Word which gives the revelation of duty, telling me what the great God would have me do. And here also is the Word which gives the revelation of promise, telling me what resources are prepared for them who follow the fair gleams of truth and take the Divine road of duty and obedience. Yes, the Word of God is in the old Book, and here you can find your sword.

November 11: His Symbols - 1
by Louis Albert Banks
Excerpted from "The Symbols of the Spirit", *The Fisherman and His Friends*, published by Funk & Wagnalls Company, New York, New York in 1896

The rushing of a mighty wind...tongues of fire...
pour out My Spirit...
Acts 2:2-3, 17

You have an anointing from the Holy One...
1 John 2:20

Let us go back for a moment to Bethany, and see that little group of disciples who have just witnessed the ascension of Jesus, and whose hearts have been comforted and strengthened and aroused to high purpose by the words of the angelic messengers. They go to Jerusalem, and there for forty days they tarry in earnest prayer, waiting for the promised coming of the Holy Spirit.

We have revealed to us something of the conditions at the time of the descent of the Holy Ghost upon them. Luke says, "And when the day of Pentecost was now come, they were all together in one place." If we desire that the Holy Ghost shall come upon us with still mightier power to make us efficient witnesses for Christ, there must be in our hearts something of the same longing for the Spirit, and of the same harmony of feeling and purpose. It is not necessary that we should all believe alike about nonessentials, but it is necessary that we shall love one another as the disciples did, that we shall love Christ supremely, and that we shall be unselfishly united in our earnest prayer for the coming of the Holy Spirit upon us. Are we thus limited? Do we thus ardently desire the presence of the Spirit of God in our hearts? Is there in our hearts a sincere willingness to give up everything that stands in the way of our being used by the Holy Spirit with the greatest possible effect in the salvation of souls? Are we cherishing in our hearts or in our daily conduct anything that interferes with our being efficient ambassadors for Christ to those who have not yet come to know Him? These are very solemn and earnest questions.

A man may pray until the day of judgment for the gift of the Holy Spirit and the anointing of power for service, and if all the time he is unwilling to sacrifice certain habits or pleasures that are nullifying his Christian influence, the power from Heaven will not be given to him. Are we willing, as God gives us to see the right from day to day, to give up anything that stands in the way of our being for Jesus Christ the most influential witnesses possible? These questions are pertinent under this theme. These people who, under God, won three thousand men and women to Christ on the day of Pentecost (just one day!) were people of this spirit. To them Christ was all in all. Would it please Jesus? Would it advance the cause of the Redeemer? Would it tend to bring glory to the crucified and risen Lord? Such were the questions that were in their hearts, and such was the devotion that made it possible for God to use them as channels for Divine grace to the sinning souls who heard their message.

November 12: His Symbols - 2
by Louis Albert Banks

I desire very briefly to call your attention to four symbols of the Spirit for which we are praying. The first comparison is to the "wind." The record says, "Suddenly there came from Heaven a sound as of the rushing of a mighty wind." Jesus, in His conversation with Nicodemus concerning the new birth, said, "Marvel not that I said unto you, You must be born again. The wind blows where it wills, and you hear the sound, but cannot tell from where it comes, and where it goes: so is every one that is born of the Spirit." Wind signifies life. It is the mission of the Holy Spirit to give us life.

Again, the coming of the Holy Spirit was accompanied at Pentecost with tongues of fire. And in a spiritualized sense that has been true of every great revival of Christian life since that day. One of the certain characteristics of a genuine revival of religion in the Church is the quickening into life of the speech of those who are the followers of Jesus. Those who lead in prayer do not usually pray so long as before, but it is because their tongues are aflame and they forget to pray by rote and form, which is always the recourse of the cold heart. They speak forth earnest words of petition which come with electric thrill from the heart and flash in lightning sparks from the tongue. The testimony takes on a different type. There is about it a keener sense of gratitude to God, a tenderer feeling of love for Christ, a deeper earnestness that it may produce conviction.

Another comparison very often used is suggested by the promise, "I will pour forth of My Spirit," suggestive of cleansing, refreshing, and abundance; the water of life which shall spring up in the saved heart like an artesian well, flowing on ever in undiminished supply. But it is not obtained like an artesian well, for that is gotten by boring deep into the earth itself. The Spirit of God is something which we will never obtain by digging in our own hearts; but God is able to fulfil to us the promise which Christ made to the woman at the well in Samaria—that his Spirit bestowed shall afterward be in us a well of water, springing up unto everlasting life. How greatly we need that God shall pour out upon us streams of Divine grace, and overflow our dry and thirsty hearts with the fulness of His Spirit!

There is still another comparison to the coming of the Holy Spirit, which John describes as "an anointing from the Holy One." Under the Old Testament dispensation prophets, priests, and kings were anointed with consecrating oil as a symbol of their calling and of their fitness for their special offices. Under the new dispensation every Christian is to be a prophet. Every one of us is to be a prophet in the sense that we are to tell forth to the people the glad news of salvation. Every Christian, too, is to be a priest, in that he is to be, by pleading and persuasion and prayer, a mediator between God and men whom he would win to Christ. Oh, that God would anoint us for this purpose!

November 13: His Teaching - 1
by Fenelon
Excerpted from "On the Inward Teaching of the Spirit of God", *Christian Counsel*, published by E. Jones, Philadelphia, Pennsylvania in

It is certain from the Holy Scriptures (Romans 8; John 14) that the Spirit of God dwells within us, acts there, prays without ceasing, groans, desires, asks for us what we know not how to ask for ourselves, urges us on, animates us, speaks to us when we are silent, suggests to us all truth, and so unites us to Him that we become one spirit (1 Corinthians 6:17). This is the teaching of faith, and even those instructors who are farthest removed from the interior life, cannot avoid acknowledging so much. Still, notwithstanding these theoretical principles, they always strive to maintain that, in practice, the external law, or, at least, a certain light of learning and reason, illuminates us within, and that then our understanding acts of itself from that instruction. They do not rely sufficiently upon the interior teacher, the Holy Spirit, who does everything in us. He is the soul of our soul; we could not form a thought or a desire without Him. Alas, what blindness is ours! We reckon ourselves alone in the interior sanctuary, when God is much more intimately present there than we are ourselves.

What, then, you will say, are we all inspired? Yes, doubtless; but not as were the prophets and apostles. Without the actual inspiration of the Spirit of grace, we could neither do, nor will, nor believe any good thing. We are, then, always inspired, but we incessantly stifle the inspiration. God does not cease to speak, but the noise of the creatures without, and of our passions within, confines us and prevents our hearing. We must silence every creature, including self, that in the deep stillness of the soul we may perceive the indescribable voice of the Bridegroom. We must lend an attentive ear, for His voice is soft and still, and is only heard by those who hear nothing else.

Ah, how rare is it to find a soul still enough to hear God speak! The slightest murmur of our vain desires, or of a love fixed upon self, confounds all the words of the Spirit of God. We hear well enough that He is speaking, and that He is asking for something, but we cannot distinguish what is said, and are often glad enough that we cannot. The least reserve, the slightest self-reflective act, the most imperceptible fear of hearing too clearly what God demands, interferes with the interior voice. Need we be astonished, then, if so many people, pious indeed, but full of amusements, vain desires, false wisdom, and confidence in their own virtues, cannot hear it, and consider its existence as a dream of fanatics? Alas, what would they with their proud reasonings? Of what effectiveness would be the exterior word of pastors, or even of the Scriptures themselves, if we had not within, the word of the Holy Spirit giving to the others all their vitality? The outward word, even of the gospel, without the nourishing, life-giving, interior word, would be but an empty sound. It is the letter that alone kills (2 Corinthians 3:6), and the Spirit alone can give us life.

November 14: His Teaching - 2
by Fenelon

O! eternal and omnipotent word of the Father, it is You who speaks in the depth of our souls! The word that proceeded from the mouth of the Savior, during the days of His mortal life, has only had energy to produce such wondrous fruits, because it has been animated by that Spirit of life which is the Word itself. Hence it is that Peter says, "Lord, to whom shall we go? You have the words of eternal life" (John 6:68).

It is not, then, the outward law of the gospel alone which God shows us internally, by the light of reason and faith; it is His Spirit that speaks, touches, operates in and animates us; so that it is the Spirit which does in us and with us whatever we do that is good, as it is our soul that gives life to our body, and regulates all its movements.

It is, then, true, that we are continually inspired, and that we do not lead a gracious life, except so far as we act under this interior inspiration. But O God, how few Christians feel it! How few are they, who do not annihilate it by their voluntary distractions, or by their resistance!

Let us recognize, then, the fact that God is incessantly speaking to us. He speaks in the impenitent also, but, stunned by the noise of the world and their passions, they cannot hear Him; the interior voice is to them a fable. He speaks in awakened sinners; they are sensible of remorse of conscience, which is the voice of God reproaching them inwardly for their sins. When they are deeply moved, they have no difficulty in understanding about this interior voice, for it is that which pierces them so sharply. It is in them that two-edged sword of which Paul speaks as piercing even to the dividing asunder of soul and spirit (Hebrews 4:12). God causes Himself to be perceived, enjoyed, followed; they hear that sweet voice that buries a reproach in the bottom of the heart, and causes it to be torn in pieces. Such is true and pure contrition.

God speaks, too, in wise and enlightened persons, whose life, outwardly correct, seems adorned with many virtues; but such are often too full of themselves and their lights, to listen to God. Everything is turned into reasoning; they substitute the principles of natural wisdom and the plans of human prudence, for what would come infinitely better through the channel of simplicity and submission to the Word of God. They seem good, sometimes better than others; they are so, perhaps, up to a certain point, but it is a mixed goodness. They are still in possession of themselves, and desire always to be so according to the measure of their reason; they love to be in the hands of their own counsel, and to be strong and great in their own eyes.

November 15: His Temple - 1
by Frederic Farrar

Excerpted from "The Temple of God", *The Fall of Man and Other Sermons Preached Before the University of Cambridge, and On Various Occasions,* published by Macmillan and Co., New York, New York in 1868

Do you not know that you are the temple of God, and that the Spirit of God dwells in you?
1 Corinthians 3:16

The three different senses of this phrase, "the temple of God," mark very distinctly three different eras of God's dealings with His Church. In the Old Testament it is applied without variation to that stately sanctuary of marble and gold and cedar-wood which Solomon built in the zenith of his power. In the Gospels, on the lips of our blessed Lord, we find it used in a new sense, which filled the unaccustomed Jews with amazement: "He spoke of the temple of His body." Lastly, in the Epistles, and especially in those of Paul, the term "temple" receives a significance yet more marvelous, for it is applied, as in the text, to the mortal body of every Christian. Let us for a few moments glance at these three temples, which mark three mighty dispensations in religious history: The temple at Jerusalem, the temple of Christ's human body, the temple of every Christian's heart.

The Most High, my brethren, dwells not in temples made with hands. Lo, Heaven, and the Heaven of heavens cannot contain Him, how much less any house that man can build? If that mighty cathedral, whose dome is the body of Heaven in its clearness, whose pillars are the mountain summits, and its lamps the sun and moon and stars, are yet too small for His overwhelming magnificence, how shall any perishing structure of human toil be deemed sufficient for His abode? Yet, out of that mercy which knew and provided for the spiritual needs of man, He Himself directed the fashion of this earthly tabernacle, and deigned to place the symbol of His presence between the outstretched wings of the golden cherubim.

Through dreary ages of darkness and error that Temple stood as the visible witness against all idolatry of God's creatures; the witness that, though the great heavens continued dumb, and the world rolled on in unbroken silence, and sin, and sorrow, and unbelief, and blasphemy, and lust, rioted unrestrained among the dark places of the earth, yet God was sitting above the water-floods, a King forever; a King ruling in righteousness, although His way is in the sea, and His path in the great waters, and His footsteps are not known; not, as the Greeks imagined Him, indifferent to the sorrows and sins of men, but an infinite and merciful Father, yearning in love for the souls of His sinful who, though He is so high, yet has respect unto the lowly of heart, and who wills us to give of our best and richest to His earthly temples, as a proof alike of our love and reverence for Him, and of His everlasting presence in the midst of us to accept our thanksgivings and hear our prayers.

November 16: His Temple - 2
by Frederic Farrar

Two: But after a thousand years our Lord spoke of the Temple of God in a manner unheard before: "Destroy this temple," He said, when asked for some sign of His mission, "Destroy this temple, and in three days I will raise it up." "Forty and six years was this temple being built," answered the indignant Jews, "and You will raise it up in three days?" But He spoke of the "temple of His body." His use of the word made a deep impression: It was turned into the main charge against Him in the trial before Caiaphas; it was hurled as the bitterest taunt against Him as He hung upon the cross; it was remembered as the key to His most mysterious prophecy after He had risen from the dead. It might be well remembered, for it was full of marvelous significance. Truly hereby the veil of the material temple was torn in two, and access was given to God by a nearer and truer way.

God Himself had built His tabernacle in mortal flesh; the tent of His eternal Spirit had been made "like ours and of the same material." And though that temple of Christ's body lasted on earth, not for many centuries, but only for a few short years, let us not forget that it still lasts eternal in Heaven. Earthquakes and storms may sweep over the world; the iron rocks may be shattered, and the everlasting mountains crumble; the great gorgeous globe and all that is within it, and the universe, with all its suns and stars, may sink and perish hereafter in the surges of some fiery sea; but forever in the Heaven of heavens that living Temple shall endure; forever and forever shall the Godhead and the Manhood be truly, perfectly, distinctly, indissolubly conjoined; forever and forever, through the thunder "shall come a human voice;" forever and forever a Face like our own face looks down upon us in pity from the throne of God; and He who loved His own on earth shall love them to the end, and fold them safe, amid the universal ruin, in the bosom of His everlasting love.

Three: Nor must we forget that it was through the temple of Christ's body, as through some glorious vestibule, that the Spirit of God passed into the temple of every Christian heart. It was the promise wherewith our Lord had comforted His trembling disciples; and very soon after the temple of His mortal body had been taken up into Heaven, was the new living temple filled with the Glory of the Presence, and the brows of the assembled apostles were graced by the cloven tongues of Pentecostal flame. Since that time the mortal body of every one of us has been a temple of God—a temple of the Holy Ghost; and the Spirit of God has loved "before all temples the upright heart and pure."

There is no doctrine on which the Apostles dwell with more insistency than this, alluding to it repeatedly in their Epistles as to a main spring of spiritual life.

November 17: His Temple - 3
by Robert Burns
Excerpted from "The Spiritual Temple of Jehovah", *The Scottish Pulpit: A Series of Sermons, Vol. I*, published by George and Robert King, Aberdeen, Scotland in 1845

He shall build the temple of the Lord; and he shall bear the glory.
Zechariah 6:13

There are two points which the language of the text brings before us: First—That every true believer is a temple of God. Second—That the glory of building, and beautifying, and completing the temple belongs exclusively to the gracious Redeemer.

In the first place, a temple is the residence of Jehovah; and in this view every true believer is a temple of the living God. "You are the temples of the living God; as God has said, I will dwell in them and walk in them." We do not say that there is any real sacredness, any spiritual or moral sanctity, possessed by one building, or by one place in this world of ours more than another; but we do say that certain times, and certain places, and certain vestments are represented in the sacred Word as consecrated to the Lord—as taken out of the ordinary range of human objects, and invested with a relative sanctity; inasmuch as they are employed for sacred ends, and inasmuch as they are detached from the ordinary employment that may be made of them at other times and are invested with this specific attribute of being given up or dedicated to the Lord. It is in this way that the temple of old, and the vestments of the priests, and the vessels of the sanctuary, and the times and seasons of worship are all termed holy, and "holiness to the Lord." And although the state of things under the Christian economy is greatly changed, still we may affirm of every Christian church and place sacred to religious worship, that it is "the habitation of God's house, and the place where His honor dwells." It is indeed true, that, in one sense, God dwells everywhere, and "in Him we live, and move, and have our being," but while, in a general view, the Lord is everywhere present, and while we rejoice in this delightful truth of the omnipresence of Jehovah, there is a distinct sense in which, of every true believer, and of him alone, it is affirmed, that God "dwells in him," and "he dwells in God;" "Christ in you, the hope of glory."

Of all true believers under the New Testament economy, it is affirmed that Christ "dwells in them," that their bodies are the temples of the Holy Ghost; that they are sacred to the residence of Jehovah; that they walk with God and in God; that "Christ dwells in their hearts by faith" — and the highest, the noblest petition which apostolic fervor has addressed to the throne of grace in their behalf is "that they may be filled with all the fulness of God." In this view, every true believer is consecrated to God as a temple—the residence of Jehovah.

November 18: His Temple - 4
by Robert Burns

It is, indeed, the grand, the prominent design of that gospel of the grace of God which we preach unto you, to elevate God to the throne of the heart, to set aside all usurpers, to bring man back to his sense of allegiance, to expel from the heart the images and monuments of enmity to God, and to enthrone Jehovah in the affections, the dispositions, and the habits of men. It is in this view that Jehovah is represented as taking up His residence in every renewed man, selecting his soul, yes, even his body as His temple. Satan is compelled to retire from the supremacy; and although he may still remain in some distant corner of the field, and may still continue to carry on a kind of predatory warfare, yet he shall never be allowed to regain his hatred ascendency, for "the Lord alone shall be exalted in that day." The temple is His own residence, and chosen by Him as the place of His abode: "You are the temples of God; as God has said, I will dwell in them and walk in them."

In the second place, a temple is consecrated to the service, the worship, and the glory of God; and, in this sense, every true believer is a spiritual temple of the Lord. No man possessed of the common sensibilities of human nature can tread the ruins of a revered edifice, sacred in other times to the worship of God, without feeling the emotions of devotional melancholy. Within these goodly walls our fathers once worshipped. These aisles, now gloomy and desolate, once resounded to the voice of praise; and around that altar, now in ruins, successive generations of pious worshippers have been seen to throng, while the flame of a hallowed incense arose in silent majesty towards Heaven. "Our fathers, where are they; and the prophets, do they live forever?"

With emotions somewhat akin to these, but far more tender, far more pungent than these, does the Christian observer contemplate the ruins of that stately fabric once consecrated to God, once the residence of the Deity, and within whose domain the candle of the Lord once beamed with its brightest radiance. The soul of man, so vast in its powers, so comprehensive in its range of actions, so lofty even in its moral aspirations, is a majestic temple in ruins. And the grand design of Christianity is to set up that temple anew; while the most interesting view that we can take of the work of Christ in the gospel is this: To contemplate Him as rebuilding, renewing, and reconsecrating that temple now in ruins, but once the residence of God, once consecrated to His glory, and employed in His spiritual service. Christian believers are represented in Scripture as renewed in the spirit of their minds, as built up spiritual houses, as consecrated in their every part to the service and glory of God. All the members of their bodies, and all the powers of their minds are spoken of as instruments of righteousness, to the glory of God.

November 19: His Tongues - 1
by George D. Watson
Excerpted from "Tongues of Fire", *Love Abounding and Other Expositions on the Spiritual Life*, published by McDonald, Gill & Co., Boston, Massachusetts in 1891

And there appeared unto them cloven tongues like as of fire, and it sat upon each of them.
Acts 2:3

This tongue of fire in all its essential power is designed to be the normal state of the Church during the Spirit's dispensation, and is essential to the vital purpose of true religion. Let us notice how this tongue of fire is related to God, to our fellow men, and to ourselves.

One: The tongue of fire is related to God as the chief instrument for glorifying the work of Jesus, and proclaiming His wondrous work in the soul. It is the office of the Christian tongue to be a witness for God—a simple, straightforward, unbiased witness to the work or works that God has accomplished in the soul. This does not imply that its office is always to make a set speech or take the place of a teacher, or to attempt explaining the philosophy and processes of the work of grace, for in that case the tongue would be glorifying the mental powers of self, more than the simple power of grace; nor is it in all cases the office of the tongue of fire to formally preach or expound Scripture. Not all of the hundred and twenty became teachers, for the Holy Ghost selected those who should teach; but all were witnesses of the marvelous facts that had transpired in their consciousness. It was only the work of God which they magnified on that occasion—there was no allusion to the mere works of man. There is nothing in creation that can so glorify God as the human tongue anointed by the Holy Ghost.

The tongue of legalists, Pharisees, and backsliders, invariably glorify self in a disguised manner, and if their religious talk is accurately reported, you will find very little mention of the saving power of Jesus. But the tongue of fire reports the supernatural; it tells of conscious pardon, or regeneration, of conscious cleansing from indwelling sin, of the destruction of vicious appetites; it reports the incoming of perfect peace where all was storm and disorder; it reports the incoming of light and discernment utterly beyond the natural mind; it proclaims in one and the same breath the utter weakness of self and the imparted strength from God; it minimizes self and magnifies grace; it glorifies not only the work of God, but the highest work—that kind of work which other people fail to see or appreciate. The highest and finest work which God is carrying on is in human hearts. God's work in nature is great and marvelous, and many are the poets and philosophers who have swept their harps in praise of the wonders of external creation. God's work in judgment is sublime and terrible, and the artist has joined with the prophet in defining these judgments. But higher than all the works of external nature, higher than all the works of judgment, is the work of salvation in the soul.

November 20: His Tongues - 2
by George D. Watson

Two: The tongue of fire is related to our fellow men. It is the Divinely ordained instrument of convincing them of the reality of God's work in the soul, and of their need of it. The most essential thing in saving men is to convince them to the heart that God can work in them salvation from sin, and show them their need of it; and this is the sphere of power that is given to the witnessing believer. The witnessing tongue is God's chief method of saving the world, and nothing can be a substitute for it. The work of teaching, arguing, and the persuasive appeals to reason, however needed, can never be a substitute for the witnessing tongue of fire. There is a place for reasoning and theological instruction, but that is keeping on the level with the natural mind, and using of your human armor, and no amount of it of itself will make men feel in their hearts the Divine reality of saving grace. But a clear, truthful testimony to an inward work of God is a trumpet blast to the conscience of the hearer; it puts you on a Divine-vantage ground, and they have no weapon to counter that sword of the Spirit. When we speak from the plane of our natural faculties, we are on a level with men, and they can resist with the same implements; but when we are conscious of a Divine deliverance from guilt and sin, and we speak out of that supernatural experience, we are speaking from an elevated position, we are speaking in the Spirit, and such testimony is the Spirit's chosen weapon to pierce the heart of the unsaved and lead them to Christ.

Were it possible to live a sort of angelic life without testimony, it would be robbing God of His due, and taking all the glory to self, for everyone would credit you with making yourself angelic; and unless you report the miracle of grace worked in your soul, how would the world know where you got your virtues from? Jesus said, "We speak that we do know, and testify that we have seen." The Pentecostal baptism was preeminently designed to make witnesses: "You shall receive power...you shall be witnesses unto Me." The word "martyr" means a witness; and since the world began God's people have been persecuted and slain, not for living holy, but for testimony. The reason why Satan hates testimony with such perfect hatred, and the reason he stirs up the ungodly world and cold, carnal professors to hate it so, is because it is the greatest agency for tearing down his kingdom and spreading the salvation of Jesus. Every innuendo, every slur, every objection to Christian testimony, to relating what God has done in the heart, is either directly or indirectly from the devil. Abel was slain while he talked with Cain in the field; that is, while he testified to salvation by faith. Christ was crucified, not for living holy, but because He testified He was the Son of God.

November 21: His Trusting - 1
by Otto Stockmayer

Excerpted from "On Trusting the Spirit: Note O", *The Spirit of Christ*, written by Andrew Murray, published by A. D. F. Randolph & Co., New York, New York in 1888

[Murray] In a little book entitled *Reminiscences of the Keswick Convention, 1879*, with addresses by Pastor Otto Stockmayer, I find some most suggestive thoughts in regard to the work of the Holy Spirit, as He enables us to die to our own life, and to take Christ as our life. For the sake of preserving these, and introducing them to readers who may otherwise not have access to them, I give somewhat lengthy extracts here. The only way in which the blessing of conference and spiritual revival can become permanent, can flow ever fuller and deeper, is that each individual believer should know that what he has received in the fellowship of the saints can be secured and increased to him personally, through the blessed ministry of that Holy Spirit whom He has dwelling in Him, but whom he knows all too little.

The rest of this is written by Otto Stockmayer.

Work out your own salvation with fear and trembling, for it is God that works in you both to will and to do of His good pleasure.
Philippians 2:12-13

We shall fear to disobey, because we are not in presence of human work or human persons, but in presence of the Holy Ghost; it is not we who are working in us, it is the Holy Ghost. When Moses came before the burning bush, the Lord said to him, "Take your shoes from off your feet, for the place where you are standing is holy ground." This is holy ground, for it is God the Holy Ghost who works the willing and the doing. In all questions of sanctification or service we are in presence not of ourselves, but of our God; on holy ground, not on human ground; not on ground of human persons, but on ground of the Holy Ghost; and for that reason, because it is God that works in us to will and to do, work out your own salvation with fear and trembling. And what is it to "work out our own salvation"? The Apostle Paul tells us in the same verse: "Wherefore, my beloved, as you have always obeyed." I think that word "wherefore" brings us back to verse 8, to Christ's work. Christ had become obedient unto death. In verses 5-11 we have the work of Christ—abasement; and then, because He was abased, He was exalted so high; therefore you also obey.

In verses 12-13 we have the work of the Holy Spirit, working on the work of Jesus. Jesus has been obedient unto death; death is contrary to our nature, we do all we can to keep our own life; but as Christ, through the Eternal Spirit, offered Himself without spot to God, and by His death brought to an end His work of sacrifice, so does the work of the Holy Ghost bring us into fellowship with a dying Christ. He makes us willing to die by the power of Christ; He makes us take the position in which the death of Christ has placed us.

November 22: His Trusting - 2
by Otto Stockmayer

He died "that they which live should not from now on live unto themselves, but unto Him that died for them and rose again." Such a position as is given to us by Christ no man is willing to enter into; it is the Holy Ghost who takes us by the hand, and brings us out of our own life, and makes us willing to like and seek the fellowship of the dead and of the risen Christ. "Now also in My absence," go on yielding to the Holy Ghost, who will teach you to follow the Lamb, making you willing to die with Christ, that you may serve, and love, and walk in newness of life; and all this in fear and trembling, because it is God who works. The only fear we want, is to follow the Holy Ghost in all His operations, flying from self and yielding to Him, that He may have us in His hand, that He may be able to work for God's glory, to leave all the matter in His hands; and so soon as our fears are concentrated on that point — to not grieve the Savior — we have nothing more to fear; we can then seek first the kingdom of God and His righteousness, and all other things shall be added unto us; because as a heaven surrounds our earth on all sides, so the work of the Holy Ghost leaves nothing out of His reach in our being, brings all under His action and transforming power.

We must come back to our holy ground from which we sprang. God ought to have what is His. We came from

Him, and were made for Him; we must learn to honor the Holy Ghost, and to consider His working the most precious thing we have, fearing to lose even one hint of His, because all that He works involves infinite labor, and in loving any work of the Holy Ghost we love more infinite labor than we know. It is a matter of experience that in measure as we know more of the love of God, we learn also more to fear Him; one involves the other and regulates the other; there is no opposition.

In James 4:1 we read of "lusts which war in your members," but in the same passage (verse 5) we read of the lust of the Spirit, so you cannot put quite the same significance on the word which we generally put upon it. The word here does not mean sinful lust, the Spirit of God cannot have sinful lust; we see here two tendencies, two powers, two worlds that have nothing in common, separated as completely as Heaven from earth—the flesh and the Spirit; and we are responsible moral beings, having our responsibility through the work of the Holy Spirit; responsibility as to which of these two adversaries we will give movement and action in our interior and exterior life.

I know a position in which no rising from impure feeling can take place in the heart, or take form even as a flash in a second of time. Such a Christian has learned to let himself be kept by Christ from such risings, and they no more appear; and yet these same Christians have a consciousness of the tendency of the flesh to form such risings.

November 23: His Truth - 1
by Andrew Murray
Excerpted from "The Spirit of Truth", *The Spirit of Christ*, published by A. D. F. Randolph & Co., New York, New York in 1888

"But when the Comforter is come, whom I will send unto you from the Father, even the Spirit of Truth, who proceeds from the Father, He shall bear witness of Me."
John 15:26

"When He, the Spirit of Truth, is come, He shall guide you into all the Truth; for He shall not speak from Himself; but whatsoever things He shall hear, these shall He speak."
John 16:13

God created man in His image; to become like Himself, capable of holding fellowship with Him in His glory. In Paradise two ways were set before man for attaining to this likeness to God. These were typified by the two trees—that of life, and that of knowledge. God's way was the former—through life would come the knowledge and likeness of God; in abiding in God's will, and partaking of God's life, man would be perfected. In recommending the other, Satan assured man that knowledge was the one thing to be desired to make us like God. And when man chose the light of knowledge above the life of obedience, he entered upon the terrible path that leads to death. The desire to know became his greatest temptation; his whole nature was corrupted, and knowledge was to him more than obedience and more than life.

Under the power of this deceit, that promises happiness in knowledge, the human race is still led astray. And nowhere does it show its power more terribly than in connection with the true religion and God's own revelation of Himself. Even when the Word of God is accepted, the wisdom of the world and of the flesh ever enters in; even spiritual Truth is robbed of its power when held, not in the life of the Spirit, but in the wisdom of man. Where Truth enters into the inward parts, as God desires, there it becomes the life of the spirit. But it may also only reach the outer parts of the soul, the intellect and reason, and while it occupies and pleases there, and satisfies us with the imagination that it will thence exercise its influence, its power is nothing more than that of human argument and wisdom, that never reaches to the true life of the spirit. For there is a truth of the understanding and feelings, which is only natural, the human image or form, the shadow of Divine Truth. There is a Truth which is substance and reality, communicating to him who holds it the actual possession, the life of the things of which others only think and speak. The truth in shadow, in form, in thought, was all the law could give; and in that the religion of the Jews consisted. The truth of substance, the Truth as a Divine life, was what Jesus brought as the Only-begotten, full of grace and truth. He is Himself "the Truth."

November 24: His Truth - 2
by Andrew Murray

In promising the Holy Spirit to His disciples, our Lord speaks of Him as the Spirit of Truth. That Truth, which He Himself is, that Truth and Grace and Life which He brought from Heaven as a substantial spiritual reality to communicate to us, that Truth has its existence in the Spirit of God: He is the Spirit, the inner life of that Divine Truth. And when we receive Him, and just as far as we receive Him, and give up to Him, He makes Christ, and the Life of God, to be Truth in us Divinely real. In His teaching and guiding into the Truth, He does not give us only words and thoughts and images and impressions, coming to us from without, from a book or a teacher outside of us. He enters the secret roots of our life, and plants the Truth of God there as a seed, and dwells in it as a Divine Life. And when, in faith, and expectation, and surrender, this Hidden Life is cherished and nourished there, He quickens and strengthens it, so that it grows stronger and spreads its branches through the whole being. And so, not from without but from within, not in word but in power, in Life and Truth, the Spirit reveals Christ and all He has for us. He makes Christ, who has been to us so much only an image, a thought, a Savior outside and above us, to be Truth within us. The Spirit brings with His incoming the Truth into us; and then, having possessed us from within, guides us, as we can bear it, into all the truth. In His promise to send the Spirit of Truth from the Father, our Lord very definitely tells us what His principal work would be. "He shall bear witness of Me." He had just before said, "I am the Truth;" the Spirit of Truth can have no work but just to reveal and impart the fulness of Grace and Truth that there are in Christ Jesus. He came down from the glorified Lord in Heaven to bear witness within us, and so through us, of the reality and the power of the redemption which Christ has accomplished there. There are Christians who are afraid that to think much of the Spirit's presence within us will lead us away from the Savior above us. A looking within to ourselves may do this; we may be sure that the silent, believing, adoring recognition of the Spirit within us will only lead to a fuller, a more true and spiritual understanding that Christ alone is indeed all in all. "He shall bear witness of Me." "He shall glorify Me." He will make our knowledge of Christ Life and Truth, an experience of the Power with which He works and saves. To know what the disposition or state of mind is in which we can fully receive this guiding into all Truth, note the remarkable words our Lord uses concerning the Spirit: "He shall guide you into all the Truth, for He shall not speak from Himself; but whatsoever things He shall hear, these shall He speak." The mark of this Spirit of Truth is a wondrous Divine Teachableness. In the mystery of the Holy Trinity there is nothing more beautiful than this, that with a Divine equality on the part of the Son and the Spirit, there is also a perfect subordination. The Son could claim that men should honor Him even as they honored the Father, and yet counted it no deviation from that honor to say, "The Son can do nothing of Himself; as I hear, so I speak."

November 25: His Truth - 3
by A. B. Simpson
Excerpted from "The Spirit of Truth", *When the Comforter Came*,
published by The Alliance Press Company, New York, New York in 1911

"Another Comforter, even the Spirit of Truth."
John 14:16-17

The Holy Spirit has given us His supreme message in the Holy Scriptures. The Bible is the standard of spiritual truth, and in all His teachings and leadings, the Holy Ghost never contradicts His own Word. They who are most fully led of the Spirit will always most reverence the authority of the Scriptures, and walk in the most perfect conformity with their principles and precepts. But it is not enough to have the letter of the Word; He who gave it must also interpret it and make it spirit and life. It is His to unfold to the heart the power and reality of the written Word and to bring it to our remembrance in the opportune moment as the lamp of guidance, or the sword of defense in the hour of temptation.

A prominent member of the House of Representatives, speaking the other day about the inestimable value of the National Library of Congress, was asked how it was possible for a busy member, without much study and labor, to know how to use it effectively, and to be able always to find the right volume or page where a given subject was discussed. "Oh," he replied, "that is made perfectly easy for us by our invaluable librarian, who knows every book and subject, and all we have to do is to send a little page from our desk in the House with a note to him requesting the best authority on any subject we require, and he immediately comes back with the right book and the leaves turned down at the very spot where we need the information." Blessed be God, we have a Divine Librarian who understands the Bible better than we ever can, and who has come to be our Monitor and Guide, not only into its meaning, but also into its practical application to every need of life. It is not enough to have a good light, we must have the organs of vision or it is of no use; and we must have them in perfect condition. Now, the Holy Spirit comes to be to us sight as well as light. This is the special work of the Holy Ghost, to give to us a new spiritual vision and organ of understanding so that the soul directly perceives Divine things and realities.

Perhaps the first effect of this Divine illumination is that the things of God become intensely real, and stand out with vividness and distinctness, like figures cut in relief on the wall. The person of Christ, the light of His countenance, the distinct sweetness of His Spirit, the "peace that passes all understanding," "the joy of the Lord," the Heavenly world, all become to the heart more actual and intensely vivid than the things we see with our outward eyes, and touch with our human hands. Here we find it is not the eyes of our intellect, but the eyes of the heart that are to be illuminated, and when so quickened by the Spirit of revelation in the knowledge of Him, we shall understand what is the hope of our calling, and the glorious privileges and prospects which we are to inherit in Christ.

November 26: His Unforgiving - 1
by Horatius Bonar
Excerpted from "Sermon XXXIX: The Sin Against the Holy Spirit", *Family Sermons*, published by Robert Carter and Brothers, New York, New York in 1863

"Truly, I say to you, all sins will be forgiven the children of man, and whatever blasphemies they utter, but whoever blasphemes against the Holy Spirit never has forgiveness, but is guilty of an eternal sin" — for they were saying, "He has an unclean spirit."
Mark 3:28-30

It would serve no purpose to discuss or enumerate the various opinions that have been held respecting this sin. Let us just take the passage itself, and try to find out what the narrative really is meant to teach us.

The key to the passage is contained in the 30th verse: "Because they said" (were saying), "He has an unclean spirit." This is Mark's remark for clearing up of the statement; or rather, I should say, it is the Holy Spirit's own comment on a declaration made especially respecting Himself. In the 28th and 29th verses, the Son is speaking of the Spirit, and of the sin against Him; in the 30th, the Spirit interprets the words of the Son, and shows that the sin against Himself is in reality a sin against the Son. In reading these three verses, in this connection, as spoken successively by the Son of God and the Spirit of God, we see how jealous the one is for the honor of the other. The Holy Spirit will not put upon record this testimony of the Son regarding Himself without adding His own testimony to the Son, and showing how sin committed against Himself is committed against the Son, and dishonor cast upon Himself is dishonor cast upon the Son.

It was in Galilee that these words were spoken, for Jesus was, at this time "going through every city and village preaching, and showing the glad tidings of the kingdom of God" (Luke 8:1). He was opposed, reviled, and threatened, as He went along, teaching and healing. The opposition, however, did not come from the Galileans, but from the Scribes and Pharisees who came down from Jerusalem (Matthew 12:24; Mark 3:22). There might be among the inhabitants of that half-Gentile region, ignorance and unbelief; but they did not go so far in their malignity as the more intellectual, better educated, and (in the common acceptance of the word) more "religious" citizens of Jerusalem, as represented by their leaders, the Scribes, and Pharisees, and Priests. These, though better read in the Prophets, and professing to be waiting for Messiah, were foremost in the rejection of Christ setting themselves against Himself and His Messiahship with a persevering and desperate malignity, such as we might have reckoned impossible.

November 27: His Unforgiving - 2
by Horatius Bonar

Not only did these Jewish leaders show their unbelief, in Jerusalem and Judea; but they went everywhere, tracking the Lord's footsteps, endeavoring to provoke and entrap Him; misrepresenting all that He said and did; maligning Him as a wine-bibber and a keeper of the worst company; no, as possessed of a devil; no, more, as doing and saying all that He said and did under the influence of this possession. In the present narrative we find them in Galilee, many days' journey from Jerusalem. What were they doing there? They did not come to listen, nor to be taught, nor to be convinced, nor to admire. They had traveled all this distance out of pure malignity. Like demons from Hell, they followed the Lord in order to attack Him or plot against Him. They spared no toil, no travel, no cost, in order to carry out their hatred of Christ. They watched, with hellish eagerness, every word and motion; misconstruing all; abusing Him both for what He did and for what He did not do; and seizing every opportunity for poisoning the minds of the people against Him.

In the scene to which our narrative refers, we find Him working a miracle; a miracle of no ordinary kind. The case is a very desperate one. The man is both mute and blind — perhaps deaf too; and more than this, he is possessed with a devil. He is a monument of Satan's power. He is one of Satan's best fortified and best garrisoned fortresses. There could hardly be a clearer or more explicit exhibition of Satan's infernal enmity against man, and of his horrid character as the destroyer of God's workmanship, the inflictor of darkness and disease. Seldom had the seed of the serpent been so exhibited in his hatefulness and enmity; and seldom had he been so directly and gloriously confronted with the woman's Seed, in all His lovableness of character and His kindness to man. If ever, therefore., human unbelief were utterly inexcusable, it was here. If ever man's enmity might have been expected to give way, it was here. If ever, in the awful halting between two opinions, a better choice might have been forced upon man, and even the Pharisee made ashamed of siding against Christ, it was here. God had brought Heaven and hell face to face, before man; He had brought the Prince of light and the prince of darkness into close and direct conflict, and that in circumstances most likely to enlist man's sympathies with Heaven against hell, collision; God; with the Son of God against the devil and his demons. It might have been expected that man would, at least for once, have taken the side of Christ, and that the Scribes and Pharisees, the most enlightened and best educated of the land, would have given way in their prejudice and hatred. But it is just here that the greatness of their hostility comes out; and as afterwards the cry arose in Jerusalem, "Not this Man, but Barabbas," so here, in Galilee, a like cry is heard, from the lips of the same men, "Not the Holy Spirit, but the devil!"

November 28: His Unifying - 1
by Handley C. G. Moule
Excepted from "Christ and His Members United by the Holy Spirit",
Cathedral and University and Other Sermons, published by
Hodder and Stoughton, London, England in 1920

And I beheld, and, lo, in the midst of the throne and of the four living beings, and in the midst of the elders, stood a Lamb as though it had been slain, having seven horns and seven eyes, which are the seven Spirits of God sent forth into all the earth.
Revelation 5:6

Now, the Union of Christ with His people, and of them with Him, is a thing which may be described, in the light of the New Testament, as not only a great truth of spiritual life, but the truth of truths. It is related to all other kindred doctrines as that which combines, harmonizes, and explains them. It appears as the end where they appear as means. Here they gather and converge. Is it repentance? Is it faith? Is it regeneration? Is it justification of the person? Is it sanctification of the nature, the will, the affections, the life, the self? All stands related to this holy Union. Is the spiritual condition of the individual in question, or that of the Christian community? (And the impartial and far-reaching doctrines of the Faith never forget the community in the individual, nor the individual in the community.) Alike, the ultimate reference is to the holy Union. The eternal plan, the Divine working out of the plan in the history of the soul and of the Church, bear always in this direction—towards the consummation of this holy Union. What is "the fulness of Christ," in the Epistle to the Ephesians? It is the final and glorious realization of God's Idea of the Union of His Son and the people of His Son. Need I remind you at length of the richness of the imagery employed in Scripture to set forth this astonishing and uplifting truth? Need I speak at length of the Head and the members, of the Vine and the branches, of the Bridegroom and the bride? Need I speak of the Temple, with its living stones, and its life-giving Stone of the corner? Need I focus upon the precious truths of the Indwelling, that blessed mutuality of indescribable connection under which the Lord is said to dwell in His saints, to dwell in their hearts—and they in Him? Or of that other range and region of truth, somewhat neglected in the Church of today, but nonetheless permanent and less certain, in which Christ stands forth as the Head, and Representative, and Surety of His people, in the field of Covenant, receiving for them, that He may minister to them, all the acceptance won by His merits, as well as all the life, and power, and sanctity embodied in His Person? It is enough for my purpose thus to recount the heads and titles of this great truth of truths; only saying, as we pass on, with all the earnestness that I can command, and I humbly think with entire sincerity before Him of whom I presume to speak, that "this thing is for our life." It is no mere topic of discussion, no antiquarian curiosity of religious thought. It has to do with spiritual life and spiritual death. It discloses things which eye has not seen, nor ear heard, nor heart conceived, concerning the peace, and strength, and growth, and purification of the whole being of man; but which God has revealed by His Spirit.

November 29: His Unifying - 2
by Handley C. G. Moule

Of these things it must be blessed to be the humblest partaker. Of these things it must be woeful to fall short, even by the narrowest interval of privation. "If any man is in Christ, he is a new creation. If any man has not the Spirit of Christ, he is none of His."

That word, "the Spirit of Christ," brings me to what is special in our present theme. It reminds us of Him who is the earthward Eyes of the exalted Lamb; as it were His outflowing Presence for the Church below. It tells me, that ninth verse of the eighth chapter to the Romans, that the indwelling of the Holy Spirit in the man is for that man the presence of Christ. Read the sentences: "You are in the Spirit, if so it is that the Spirit of God dwells in you. Now if any man has not the Spirit of Christ, he is none of His. But if Christ is in you, the body is dead because of sin, but the Spirit is life because of righteousness." Wonderful equivalence and exchange! The Lord does not leave His disciple orphaned; He comes to him; He is in him; He manifests Himself to him, and abides in him. And yet it was expedient that He should go away, for otherwise the Paraclete would not come.

The Paraclete comes — and behold He mediates and makes for the Christian's soul and self a presence of the Lord which somehow is better, far better, for the man in this his pilgrimage and tabernacle than even the joy and glory, if it were granted, of his Savior's physical proximity—shall I dare to say than his Savior's personal indwelling as the Son of Man outside the vehicle of this presence of the Spirit?

This sacred mediation of the Heavenly Spirit, this conveyance through Him of every blessing of the vital Union, appears everywhere in the subject. In the parable of the Vine and branches, indeed, He is not explicitly mentioned. But the context of the whole Discourse is so full of Him that He is assuredly implied as the life-bond, the life-secret that flows and is poured from the hidden Root into the happy branches, their blossoms and their clusters. In the imagery of the Bridal it is to a life "in the newness of the Spirit" that the Spouse of Christ is called.

In the imagery of the Building it is "in the Spirit" that the saints, compacted into their Cornerstone, are "being built together to be the habitation of God." And when this figure is individualized, and the Lord Christ is seen as dwelling not now in the Church but "in the heart by faith," this is affected by the "strengthening of the inner man" by the Spirit of the Father. In the imagery of the Body, above all, it is the Spirit who is the secret of the Union, the mystery and reason of the members' life in their Head; "there is one Body and one Spirit;" "by one Spirit are we all baptized into one Body."

November 30: His Unifying - 3
by Andrew Murray
Excerpted from "The Unity of the Spirit", *The Spirit of Christ*, published by
A. D. F. Randolph & Co., New York, New York in 1888

That you walk with all lowliness and meekness, with longsuffering, forbearing one another in love; giving diligence to keep the unity of the Spirit in the bond of peace. There is one body, and one Spirit.
Ephesians 4:1-4

Now there are diversities of gifts, but the same Spirit... All these are empowered by one and the same Spirit, who apportions to each one individually as He wills... For in one Spirit were we all baptized into one body; and were all made to drink of one Spirit.
1 Corinthians 12:4, 11, 13

We know how, in the first three chapters of the Ephesians, Paul had set forth the glory of Christ Jesus as the Head of the Church, and the glory of God's grace in the Church as the Body of Christ, indwelt by the Holy Spirit, growing up into a habitation of God through the Spirit, and destined to be filled with all the fulness of God. Having thus lifted the believer to his true place in the Heaven, with his life hidden in Christ, He comes with him down to his life in the earthlies, and, in the second half of the Epistle, teaches how he is to walk worthy of his calling. And the very first lesson he has to give in regard to this life and walk on earth

(Ephesians 4:1-4) rests on the foundation-truth that the Holy Spirit has united him not only to Christ in Heaven, but to Christ's body on earth. The Spirit dwells not only in Christ in Heaven and in the believer on earth, but very especially in Christ's body, with all its members; and the full, healthy action of the Spirit can only be found where the right relation exists between the individual and the whole body, as far as he knows or comes into contact with it. His first care in his holy walk must be, therefore, to give diligence that the unity of the Spirit is maintained intact. Were this unity of the one Spirit and one body fully acknowledged, the cardinal virtue of the Christian life would be lowliness and meekness (verses 2-3), in which each would forget and give up self for others; and all would forbear one another in love amid all differences and shortcomings. So the new commandment would be kept, and the Spirit of Christ, the Spirit of Love sacrificing Himself wholly for others, would have free scope to do His blessed work.

The need of such teaching is remarkably illustrated by the first Epistle to the Corinthians. In that church there were abundant operations of the workings of the Holy Spirit. The gifts of the Spirit were strikingly manifested, but the graces of the Spirit were remarkably absent. They understood not how there are diversities of gifts, but the same Spirit; how, amid all difference, one and the same Spirit divides to each separately as He will; how all had been baptized in one Spirit into one body, and all made to drink of one Spirit. They knew not the more excellent way, and that the chief of all the gifts of the Spirit is the Love that seeks not its own, and only finds its life and its happiness in others.

December 1: His Unifying - 4
by Andrew Murray

To each believer who would fully yield himself to the leading of the Spirit, as well as to the Church as a whole, in its longings for the experience in power of all that the indwelling of the Spirit implies, the unity of the Spirit is a truth permeated with rich spiritual blessing. In previous writings I have more than once made use of the expression of Otto Stockmayer: "Have a deep reverence for the work of the Holy Spirit within you." That injunction needs as its complement a second one: Have a deep reverence for the work of the Holy Spirit in your brother. This is no easy thing. Even Christians, in other respects advanced, often fail here. The cause is not difficult to discover. In our books on education we are taught that the faculty of Discrimination, the observing of differences, is one of the earliest to be developed in children. The power of Combination, or the observing of the harmony that exists amid apparent diversity, is a higher one, and comes later; as the power of Classification, in its highest action, it is only found in true genius. The lesson finds most striking exemplification in the Christian life and Church. It needs only a little grace to know where we differ from other Christians or churches, to contend for our views, or to judge their errors in doctrine or conduct. But this indeed is grace, where, amid conduct that tries or grieves us, or teaching that appears to us unscriptural or hurtful, we always give the unity of the Spirit the first place, and have faith in the power of love to maintain the living union amid outward separation.

Keep the unity of the Spirit—such is God's command to every believer. It is the New Commandment, to love one another, in a new shape, tracing the love to the Spirit in which it has its life. If you would obey the command, note carefully that it is the unity of the Spirit. There is a unity of creed or custom, of church or choice, in which the bond is more of the flesh than of the Spirit.

There is much in you that is of self and of the flesh, and that can take part in a unity that is of this earth, but that will greatly hinder the unity of the Spirit. Confess that it is in no power or love of your own that you can love; all that is of yourself is selfish, and does not reach the true unity of the Spirit. Be very humble in the thought that it is only what is of God in you that can ever unite with what appears displeasing to yourself. Be very joyful in the thought that there is indeed that in you which can conquer self, and love even what seems unloving.

December 2: His Victory
by George Matheson
Excerpted from "The Victory of the Spirit", *Voices of the Spirit*,
published by A. C. Armstrong & Son, New York, New York in 1892

"Not by might nor by power, but by My Spirit,"
says the Lord of Hosts.
Zechariah 4:6

The Spirit of the Lord of Hosts is here distinguished from might and power, and rightly so. The Spirit of the Lord of Hosts is love — the sacrifice of might and power. The world has been made great by the gentlest of all its forces. Man had no dominion over the beast of the field until the advent of love. The animal raged within him unsubdued until Christ came. Thunder, earthquake, and fire strove in vain to quell it; it yielded only to the still small voice. The Jew proposed the terrors of the law; the philosopher advised the crucifixion of feeling; neither could suppress the passions of the soul. But when love came, it conquered the old passions by a new passion. It did not send thunder but lightning. It forbade nothing, it crucified nothing, it destroyed nothing; it simply flashed on me the light of a new presence and the old presence died. There was no mutilation of the heart, there was no destruction of the heart's ancient possessions; there was just a transcendent glory which made the ancient possessions valueless; they were destroyed "by the brightness of His coming."

O Son of Man, let my lower nature be conquered by Your Spirit. I would not have it conquered by the terrors of law; these would bind my hands, but would leave my heart at war. I would not have it conquered by the death of feeling; that would save me from stepping into evil by depriving me of the power to walk at all. But I would have it conquered by You—a larger, purer love. I would have Your beauty to extinguish all other beauties, Your light to put out all other lights, Your joy to dwarf all other joys. I do not want to be converted by mutilation but by expansion; I do not want to be made good by being narrowed but by being enlarged. Nothing but a higher love will subdue my lower love—subdue it without killing it. Might and power would reduce it to ashes in a moment, but my heart would be ashes too. You alone can preserve my heart and yet burn its sin. You alone can enlarge my nature and yet destroy its impurities. You alone can subdue my will and yet sustain its resoluteness; not by might nor by power but by Your Spirit, O Lord.

December 3: His Vision
by George Matheson
Excerpted from "The Vision of the Spirit", *Voices of the Spirit*,
published by A. C. Armstrong & Son, New York, New York in 1892

But he, being full of the Holy Ghost, looked up steadfastly into Heaven, and saw the glory of God, and Jesus standing on the right hand of God.
Acts 7:55

"He, being full of the Holy Ghost, looked up and saw." There is a vision which only comes with spiritual fulness. In the world of nature the sight is the door to the spirit, but in the world of grace the spirit is the door to the sight. In my natural life God enters from without and penetrates within; in my spiritual life God enters from within and makes His progress outward. The first thing in the life of nature is the last thing in the life of spirit—vision. I am often asking why it is that so little is revealed to me; it is because I myself am so little. If I had more spirituality I would have more sight. There are treasures lying at the door of my dwelling which seem to me simply like a dust-heap. Someday I shall awake and marvel at my own riches; I shall marvel at the wells of water which were lying in my desert; I shall marvel at the crowns that were cast at the foot of my cross; I shall marvel at the beauty which lay at the top of the mournful way. The revelation is already waiting for me; it is blazoned on the sky, it is imprinted on the air; it will be inscribed upon my heart when I have ceased to be a child. When I am full of the Holy Ghost I shall look up and see.

O Spirit of holiness, grant me Your latest gift—light. Your beginning is love, but light shall be Your ending. Your spring-time is in my heart, but Your summer shall be in my eyes. It is not a new sense I want, it is the power to interpret the old senses. I want to be led back over the old road to read its signposts in the light of later years. I want to go over the ground which I called barren and see if it had not all the time been covered with flowers. I want to see the glory of that which was once my cross, the beauty of that which was once my thorn, the triumph of that which was once my trial. I want to learn that the days which seemed to me most dark and dreary were in truth the days when Heaven was opened to my view. When You have taught me the glory of sacrifice I shall look steadfastly on the things before which I once cringed; above the very place of my martyrdom I shall see Jesus.

December 4: His Vulnerability - 1
by A. B. Simpson
Excerpted from "Sinning Against the Holy Spirit", *When the Comforter Came*, published by The Alliance Press Company, New York, New York in 1911

Do not grieve the Holy Spirit of God.
Ephesians 4:30

Perhaps it is because the Holy Spirit is the gentlest of beings that the Lord Jesus has pronounced such awful penalties against those who sin against the Holy Ghost. Everything that grieves the Holy Spirit is not necessarily to be construed as that one dreadful thing which the Scriptures call "the sin against the Holy Ghost," which never has forgiveness. But when we once begin to descend the awful incline of evil we never know where we are going to end. Therefore let us guard against the very beginnings of all that might lead to that dreadful attitude which the Apostle Paul describes when He says, "They have done contempt unto the Spirit of grace."

We may quench the Spirit. This perhaps has reference rather to His public work in the Church of God and the hearts of others than to His particular dealings with our own soul. We may discourage the work of the Spirit and the liberty of worship and testimony by our harshness and criticism. We may ourselves through timidity or disobedience fail to obey His impulses in our own hearts to testify for Him or to speak to others about their souls. The minister of Christ may quench the Spirit by worldly and sensational themes, and by discouraging the Spirit of prayer, separation and revival in the Church. The Spirit is quenched by worldliness, fashion and sinful pleasure. The Spirit is quenched by error, fanaticism and ecclesiastical pride. The cultivation of secular music and ambitious oratory, instead of humble heart-searching and soul-winning—these things quench the Holy Ghost. Nothing more quenches His reviving power than strife, controversy, evil speaking and division among the people of God. Frivolous conversation in connection with the house of God and sacred things often drives away the convicting influence of the Holy Ghost from other hearts. A wife was laughing on her way from church to her husband about some of the peculiarities of the preacher. Suddenly she felt his arm trembling and as she looked into his face the tears were falling and he said, "pray for me. I have seen myself tonight as I never have before," and she awoke to realize her dreadful sin and folly. We may quench the Spirit in our church, we may quench the Spirit in our children and have the blood of souls in our hands forever.

December 5: His Vulnerability - 2
by A. B. Simpson

Again the Scriptures speak of "grieving" the Holy Spirit. How gently this figure represents Him, not angry but pained. We may grieve Him by our doubts and fears. We may grieve Him by holding back some reserve in our consecration. We may grieve Him by disobedience and willfulness. We may grieve Him by coming short of the fulness of His blessing. We may grieve Him by a divided heart and the idolatry of earthly pleasures and affections. We may grieve Him by the neglect of His Word. We may grieve Him by our lack of love for Jesus whom He always seeks supremely to honor and for whose rights He is jealous. We may grieve Him when we cherish bitterness toward our brethren and it is of this especially that Paul says "Let all bitterness and wrath and anger and clamor and evil speaking be put away from you with all malice, and do not grieve the Holy Spirit of God whereby you are sealed unto the day of redemption." And we may grieve Him by our spiritual selfishness, by praying only for our own needs and by letting the world perish in its ignorance and sin while we heard the gospel and neglect the cry of our brother.

But there is something worse than this. To some persons God had to say in days of old, "You do always resist the Holy Ghost." The sinner resists Him when he tries to shake off religious impressions and escape conviction of sin or procrastinate a decision for Christ. He may do it very politely and intend at some "convenient season" to take up the matter again, but all the same the Holy Spirit recognizes it as rejection, refusal and insult. Therefore we read, "Today, as the Holy Ghost has said, while it is called today, if you will hear His voice do not harden your hearts."

It is possible to do this by an imperceptible process as when a piece of iron is heated and cooled again and again until it corrodes and falls to pieces, the temper has been burned out of it, and there is nothing left but dross. God says of some souls, "Reprobate silver shall men call them because the Lord has rejected them." We never can tell when for the last time we are saying "No" to God and He is giving us the final invitation. Just because the Spirit is so gentle, patient, long-suffering and forgetful of His own honor and glory, therefore God has said, "Of how much sorer punishment shall he be thought worthy who has trodden underfoot the Son of God and has counted the blood of the covenant, wherewith He was sanctified, an unholy thing, and faith has done dishonor unto the Spirit of grace."

Edward Payson [American pastor, 1783-1827] of Portland [Maine] once said to a young friend who had come to speak to him about a slight religious impression that he had begun to feel: "A little cord has dropped from Heaven and for a moment touched your shoulder. It is so fine that you can so scarcely feel it. Dear friend, grasp it quickly, for it is fastened to the throne of God and is perhaps for you the last strand of saving grace."

December 6: His Waiting - 1
by Andrew Murray
Excerpted from "Waiting for the Spirit", *The Spirit of Christ*, published by A. D. F. Randolph & Co., New York, New York in 1888

He charged them to wait for the promise of the Father, which, He said, "you heard from Me."
Acts 1:4

In the life of the Old Testament saints, waiting was one of the loved words in which they expressed the posture of their souls towards God. They waited for God, and waited upon God. Sometimes we find it in Holy Scripture as the language of an experience: "Truly my soul waited upon God." "I wait for the Lord, my soul waits." At others it is a plea in prayer: "Lead me, on You do I wait all the day." "Be gracious unto us; we have waited for You." Frequently it is an injunction, encouraging to perseverance in a work that is not without its difficulty: "Wait on the Lord; wait, I say, on the Lord." "Rest in the Lord, and wait patiently for Him." And then again there is the testimony to the blessedness of the exercise: "Blessed are they who wait upon Him." "They that wait upon the Lord shall renew their strength."

All this blessed teaching and experience of the saints who have gone before, our Lord gathers up and connects especially, in His use of the word, with the promise of the Father, the Holy Spirit. What had been so deeply woven into the very substance of the religious life and language of God's people was now to receive a new and a higher application. As they had waited for the manifestation of God, either in the light of His countenance on their own souls, or in special interposition for their deliverance, or in His coming to fulfil His promises to His people; so we too have to wait. But now that the Father has been revealed in the Son, and that the Son has perfected the great redemption, now the waiting is especially to be occupied with the fulfilment of the great Promise in which the love of the Father and the grace of the Son are revealed and made one—the Gift, the Indwelling, the Fulness of the Holy Spirit. We wait on the Father and the Son for ever-increasing of inflowing and working of the Blessed Spirit; we wait for the Blessed Spirit, His moving, and leading, and mighty strengthening, to reveal the Father and the Son within, and to work in us all the holiness and service to which the Father and the Son are calling us.

"He charged them to wait for the promise of the Father, which you have heard from Me." It may be asked whether these words have not exclusive reference to the outpouring of the Spirit on the day of Pentecost, and whether, now that the Spirit has been given to the Church, the charge still holds good. It may be objected that, for the believer who has the Holy Spirit within him, waiting for the promise of the Father is hardly consistent with the faith and joy of the consciousness that the Spirit has been received and is dwelling within.

December 7: His Waiting - 2
by Andrew Murray

The question and the objection open the way to a lesson of the deepest importance. The Holy Spirit is not given to us as a possession of which we have the charge and mastery, and which we can use at our discretion. No. The Holy Spirit is given to us to be our Master, and to have charge of us. It is not we who are to use Him; He must use us. He is indeed ours; but ours as God, and our position towards Him is that of deep and entire dependence on One who gives to everyone "even as He wills." The Father has indeed given us the Spirit; but He is still, and only works as the Spirit of the Father. Our asking for His working, that the Father would grant unto us to be strengthened with might by His Spirit, and our waiting for this, must be as real and definite as if we had to ask for Him for the first time. When God gives His Spirit, He gives His inmost Self. He gives with a Divine giving, that is, in the power of eternal life—continuous, uninterrupted, and never-ceasing. When Jesus gave to those who believe in Him the promise of an ever-springing fountain of ever-flowing streams, He did not speak of a single act of faith that was once for all to make them the independent possessors of the blessing, but of a life of faith that, in never-ceasing receptivity, would always and only possess His gifts in living union with Himself. And so this precious word wait—"He charged them to wait"—with all its blessed meaning from the experience of the past, is woven into the very web of the new Spirit dispensation. And all that the disciples did and felt during those ten days of waiting, and all that they got as its blessed fruit and reward, becomes to us the path and the pledge of the life of the Spirit in which we can live. The fulness of the Spirit, for such is the Father's Promise, and our waiting, are inseparably and forever linked together.

And do we not now have here an answer to the question why so many believers know so little of the joy and the power of the Holy Spirit? They never knew to wait for it; they never listened carefully to the Master's parting words: "He charged them to wait for the Promise of the Father, which you have heard from Me." The Promise they have heard. For its fulfilment they have longed. In earnest prayer they have pleaded for it. They have gone burdened and mourning under the felt need. They have tried to believe, and tried to lay hold, and tried to be filled with the Spirit. But they have never known what it was with it all to wait. They have never here said, or even truly heard, "Blessed are all they that wait for Him." "They that wait on the Lord shall renew their strength."

December 8: His Walking - 1
by Charles H. Parkhurst

Excerpted from "Walking in the Spirit", *The Pattern in the Mount, Sermons*, published by Anson D. F. Randolph & Company, New York, New York in 1885

But if you are led by the Spirit you are not under the law.
Galatians 5:18

In approaching the matter of the Spirit's guidance and control, there are two facts to which we shall do well to hold closely, to the end that our study may prove disciplinary to heart as well as to intellect, and to the end also that our regards may draw closely to that Lord about whom it is so essential that our thoughts should center in these days of reflection and sacramental preparation.

One of these facts is, that the Spirit, under whose leadership our text recognizes the Christian to be placed, is a Person. The personality of the Spirit is a doctrine freely confessed by us in our creed, but often denied by us in our thought, in our conversation, and in our prayers. We easily fall into the use of non-committal terms and neuter pronouns in our designation of Him. Though writing Him with a capital we are continually substituting by the pronominal "it," and He readily comes to have with us only the indefiniteness of an impulse and the impersonal quality of an influence, with none of that substantive

Being, intelligence, and will that constitutes the Holy Spirit as a true and complete personality.

The other preliminary fact to be observed is, that this Person is in some way the continuance to us, under altered conditions, of that same Jesus, who once walked among men in visible form, and in the utterance of tones that were audible. I have no ambition to dogmatize about it. The Holy Spirit came from the Father and from the Son. He in a way takes the Son's place. In a way He is the Son's messenger. "If I do not go away, the Comforter will not come unto you; but if I depart I will send Him unto you." Elsewhere the Holy Spirit is represented as the baptismal element, answering to the water with which John baptized his disciples. And still again Christ says that He is going to be with His disciples always, as though the Spirit were His own personal prolonging, in new ways and manifestations, into the weeks and years that followed on after the Ascension. We have no care to speak any exact words about it, only to urge it upon ourselves in all our efforts to come in more snugly under the dominance of the Holy Spirit, to feel that we have not broken with Christ, but rather that in letting ourselves be activated by the Spirit, we are living still under the same personal regime as did the disciples who walked abroad through Judea and Galilee in the companionship of Jesus. And that if the Holy Spirit were to take upon Himself form, we should have back with us again in some way the same holy Person who blessed His disciples out at Bethany, and was parted from them in the cloud over Mount Olivet.

December 9: His Walking - 2
by Charles H. Parkhurst

"If you are led of the Spirit you are not under the law." You perceive that the text has its affirmative and also its negative element. In neglecting the latter, and addressing ourselves (as is more satisfactory) only to its affirmative and constructive aspect, it needs to be accepted as our fundamental principle, that through whatever stages God's government passes, God's government never ceases, and that changes of dispensation are not breaks in Divine authority, but alterations simply in God's method of administering His authority. This principle is distinctly implied in our text. The Jew as such is under the law, amenable to God's authority as exercised through Moses. The Christian as a Christian is also under a kind of law, amenable to God's authority as exercised through the Son, the Holy Spirit—sovereignty, Divine sovereignty carrying its exercise through both dispensations in one uninterrupted continuity without hint of break or pause.

Now the conception we are likely to have of Christianity is of a system under which there is larger liberty enjoyed than under the system of Moses; and this conception, provided only we associate with the word "liberty" its true notion, is justified, and justified by the Scripture. Christ says, "If the Son shall make you free, you shall be free indeed." Paul says, "He that is called in the Lord, is the

Lord's freeman." Again, "Where the Spirit of the Lord is, there is liberty." He exhorts the Galatians, "Stand fast in the liberty wherewith Christ has made us free." But I question if we are all of us, or even most of us, quite careful or accurate in the notion we have of the thing called "freedom." Freedom is not an exemption from government; rather freedom is a form of government. Anarchy, lawlessness, is the opposite of government; freedom is a special variety of government. Political freedom is civil authority vested in a particular way. Christian freedom is Divine authority vested in a particular a way so that in coming out from the bondage of a Jew into the freedom of a Christian, there is no inquiry to be had respecting the reduction of authority, but only respecting the new point at which authority is vested and the new manner in which it is exercised.

Our investigation, then, it is easily enough perceived, is not being pursued at the impulse of any antagonism on our part to that element in the ten commandments that constitutes the essential ingredient of those commandments, viz., the Divine will they embody. The will of God, whether written with the finger of God on Sinai, or traced with the blood of God on Calvary — the will of God and the blessedness accruing to the man that does that will, is one of the fundamental facts of our holy faith.

December 10: His Walking - 3
by A. B. Simpson
Excerpted from "The Spirit of Truth", *When the Comforter Came*, published by The Alliance Press Company, New York, New York in 1911

If we live in the Spirit let us also walk in the Spirit.
Galatians 5:25

What is it to walk in the Spirit? Generally, it may be said, it is to maintain the habit of dependence upon the Holy Ghost for our entire life—spirit, soul and body. We know what it is at times to enjoy His conscious presence. We live in the Spirit, we have felt the touch of His quickening life, now let us walk in the Spirit. Let us abide in this fellowship. Let us lean continually upon His strength, and drink unceasingly from His life, a babe from its mother's breast.

One: To walk in the Spirit is to recognize the Spirit as present and abiding in us. How often, after we have asked for His presence, we treat Him as if He had deceived us, and cry to Him as if He were far off! Let us recognize Him as having come, and address Him as a present and indwelling Friend. He will always meet our recognition.

Two: It means to trust Him and count upon Him in the emergencies of life, to regard Him as one who has undertaken our cause and expects to be called upon in every time of need, and will unfailingly be found faithful and all-sufficient in every crisis. The very name Paraclete means one that we can always call upon and find at our side. We must trust the Holy Spirit and expect Him to respond to our need as implicitly as we expect the air to answer the opening of our lungs, and the sunrise to meet us in the morning. And yet how many treat the Holy Spirit as if He were a capricious and most unreliable friend! How many of our prayers are despairing groans or scolding reflections on His love and faithfulness!

Three: We must consult the Holy Spirit if we would walk in the Spirit. We shall often find that the things that seem most easy will fail and disappoint us when we rely upon their apparent probability and the mere promise of outward circumstances, and we shall also find where we commit our way unto Him, and acknowledge Him in all our ways, that He will so direct our paths that the things which seemed most difficult and improbable, will become the easiest and the most successful.

Four: If we would walk in the Spirit we must obey Him when He does speak, and we must remember that the first part of obedience is to listen. It is not enough to say we have done all we knew, we ought to know, and we may know, for He has said that we shall know His voice, and if we do not it must be that we are to blame, or else God is responsible for our mistake. But this cannot be.

Five: Walking in the Spirit implies that we shall keep step with the Holy Ghost, and that our obedience shall be so prompt that we shall never find ourselves a step behind Him, and following Him at a distance which we may find it hard to recover.

December 11: His Wellspring - 1
by A. B. Simpson
Excerpted from "The Wellspring and the River", *When the Comforter Came*, published by The Alliance Press Company, New York, New York in 1911

"The water that I shall give him shall be in him a wellspring of water, springing up into everlasting life."
John 14:14

"He who believes on Me, as the Scripture has said, out of His inmost being shall flow rivers of living water."
John 7:38

We miss the meaning of this first passage if we forget the difference between a well and a wellspring. The Lord is speaking of an artesian well that flows from hidden fountains and gushes up in perennial freshness and fulness. This is the Lord's own figure of ideal spiritual life and of the results of the indwelling of the Comforter. This is not trying to be good and slowly and painfully building up character by ethical culture; but this is a spontaneous life that flows from sources beyond ourselves and that works automatically, uniformly and effectually in spite of all conditions, hindrances and even natural tendencies. This is the promise of that glorious gospel in Ezekiel which so fully anticipated the advanced revelation of the New Testament, "I will put My Spirit within you and cause you to walk in My statutes, and you shall keep judgments and do them." This is the law of spiritual life in Christ Jesus, the new law of gravity which Paul says "has made me free from the law of sin and death." It is a mightier force within us overcoming the tendencies of our sinful nature and making it natural for us through a new Divine nature to do the things which once we hated, and avoid the things which once we loved.

It is impossible for us to analyze, dissect or trace by any biological and psychological process the method of this Divine mystery. This is all we can distinctly formulate — somewhere down in the depths of our subconscious being God through the Holy Spirit takes up His abode. His actual personal presence is hidden from our consciousness, just as the hidden spring of that artesian well is far out of sight in the bowels of the earth. All we are conscious of is the manifestation of His presence from time to time in various influences, operations, emotions and effects in our spirit and life. The Holy Spirit is just as truly in us when He makes no sign as when the fountains of joy are overflowing, or the waters of peace are softly refreshing our weary and troubled hearts.

The possibilities of the indwelling Spirit are limitless and infinitely varied. He may bring some new grace or gift into prominence in our life and work at different times as may seem best to His sovereign will. But we are not, therefore, to say that our old experience is void and that we have received a new baptism of the Spirit. It is the same blessed wellspring flowing in new streams and springing up in new fulness as it will continue to spring up "into everlasting life."

December 12: His Wellspring - 2
by A. B. Simpson

Beloved friend, do you know this indwelling Spirit and this Heavenly wellspring? Has God taken up His abode within your heart? And can you say:

> "He never is so distant from us,
> As even to be near?
> He dwells within the yielded spirit
> And makes our Heaven here."

But in the seventh chapter of John our Lord passes on to a much larger truth. The wellspring has now become a river, no, not one river only, but a mighty delta of many outflowing streams, for "out of his inmost being shall flow rivers of living water." The secret of this is that the direction has been changed. The river is flowing out, not in. We have been saved from the life of self and entered into the life of love, which is always the life of God.

Modern sociology calls this Altruism and tries to cultivate it on mere ethical lines of human endeavor. You can no more do this than make an artesian well by pouring water into the pump and then pumping it out as the farmers do when the well begins to run dry. No, we must be filled with the Spirit first and then the overflow will take care of itself.

But we must not fail to expect a direct overflow. This is God's test of character discipleship. "Here in is My Father glorified that you bear much fruit. So shall you be My disciples." Alas for the Christians that are always receiving and never giving, always seeking blessing and never being a blessing.

When Mr. Moody was first in England his attention was called to a lady with an illuminated face and always listening with marked attention in one of the front seats of the auditorium. Mr. Moody asked one day who she was. "Oh," said one of the committee, "we call her a bog. She has attended every religious service within her reach for years, and is always after a blessing, but no one ever knew her to do anything to help another soul, either by her hands, her testimony, or her purse. And so we call her a bog, which you know is a waterhole that never discharges its stagnant water." Beloved, are you a bog or an artesian well and a river of living water?

December 13: His Wind
by John Henry Jowett
Excerpted from "The Holy Spirit", *The Folly of Unbelief and Other Meditations for Quiet Moments*, published by Fleming H. Revell Company, New York, New York in 1900

As a...wind.
Acts 2:2

How does the Holy Spirit come to me? Like wind. How does the Holy Spirit influence the spirit of man? Like wind.

"Like a wind." Then He creates an atmosphere and a temperature for the soul. How susceptible we are to the influences of the wind! The north wind blows, and we are chilled with the diffused presence of ice and snow. The south wind blows, balmy, gentle, wooing, and its touch is like a soft caress. Yes, we are sensitive to the presence of the wind. It creates an atmosphere in which breathing becomes a luxury or an agony. The Holy Spirit comes like the wind. How does the atmosphere He creates affect and influence life?

"It is the Spirit that quickens." Then the influence He creates is like the warm, alluring, out-calling breath of the spring. How appallingly poor even a rich garden appears in the early days of March! The riches are there, but they are buried and dormant. The garden is just a graveyard, full of buried seeds and roots, waiting for the touch of some magician's wand to populate it with life and beauty. It abounds in sleeping possibilities, which will not be aroused into awakened realities until some warm breath has thawed their frozen life, and urged it in healthy and aspiring circulation. At last there comes the spring, breathing resurrection warmth into the graveyard, sending a vitalizing call into the deepest tomb, and the buried powers feel the quickening touch, and clothe themselves in the beautiful garments of light. "It is the Spirit that quickens." Why, then, is man a graveyard? Yes, many of us are just tombs in which are lying possibilities buried and un-sprung. I believe that God has planted seeds of possible power within us which only a few have realized. Spiritual organs remain undeveloped and dormant. For instance, there is the power of spiritual comprehension—the power to lay hold of God. How rarely we find it thoroughly awake and mighty! There is the power of spiritual imagination. How rarely we find it with clear eye, and strong, soaring wing! But here is another word which suggests another influence of this wind of the Spirit: "The grass withers, the flower fades, because the Spirit of the Lord blows upon it." The Lord breathes, and some things are withered. The wind of the Spirit creates an atmosphere in which some things are destroyed. That is a note of the gospel in which I rejoice. I rejoice in the withering power of the wind. I am glad that the breath that quickens also consumes. I look into my heart, the heart that I have consecrated to the King, and there is still so much there that can only be described as chaff. What shall I do with it? This is my hope: "He shall burn up the chaff with unquenchable fire." The fire of the love that saved me will burn away my chaff. That is a promise, and not a threat, to the Christian man.

December 14: His Wisdom - 1
by A. B. Simpson
Excerpted from "The Spirit of Wisdom", *When the Comforter Came*, published by The Alliance Press Company, New York, New York in 1911

"He will guide you into all truth."
John 16:13

The Holy Spirit is promised to us as our personal Guide in the path of life. "As many as are led of the Spirit they are sons of God." Some persons are so zealous for the Word of God that they deny any direct guidance of the Spirit apart from the Word, but if we truly believe the Word itself we will be forced to accept its distinct statements, that the personal presence of God is given to the humble and obedient disciple for the needed direction in every step of life. "I will instruct you in the way that you shall go; I will guide you with My eye." "The Lord shall guide you continually." "When He puts forth His own sheep He goes before them and they know His voice." "In all your ways acknowledge Him and He shall direct your paths."

We find the Apostle Paul constantly recognizing the personal direction of the Holy Spirit even in matters where there was no distinct direction in the Word. The whole course of Paul's missionary journeys was ordered by the personal direction of the Lord. "Being sent forth," we are told, "by the Holy Ghost," he and Barnabas sailed unto Cyprus. A little later the same Spirit restrained them from preaching in Bithynia and Asia, and led them from Troas to Philippi, to begin their European ministry. Still later, we are told that he "purposed in the Spirit" to go to Jerusalem and Rome, and none of the perils of the way could afterward turn him aside from that which had come to him as the voice of God.

The Spirit guides us by the Scriptures, by their general principles and teachings, and by bringing to us special passages from the Word, either through the law of mental suggestion, and impressing them upon our heart, or by various ways fitted to emphasize a passage as a Divine message to our hearts.

He also directs us by His own direct voice when necessary, and yet we must not expect the special and remarkable intimations of the Holy Ghost at all times, or when we have sufficient light from other sources. There is danger of fanaticism here. We have no right to ask God to give us a special revelation of His will where either the light of our own common sense or the teaching of Scripture have already made the matter sufficiently plain.

The Holy Spirit guides us most frequently by intuitions of our sanctified judgment, and the conclusion of our minds, to which He leads us with the quiet assurance of acting in perfect freedom and naturalness, and yet of being influenced by the presence and suggestion of His own Spirit. Under such circumstances the mind and judgment are perfectly simple and natural.

December 15: His Wisdom - 2
by A. B. Simpson

The truly consecrated spirit may expect to be thus held and influenced by the Divine wisdom; and it will often find itself restrained from things by an inward reluctance, or repulsion, which it cannot fully explain, and led to other things by a strong and distinct inclination and sense of rightness and fitness which afterwards prove, by the result, to have been the directing presence of God.

We are sometimes taught that we are guided by providences. A devout mind will, of course, always have regard to the external providences of God, and will be habitually watching to see His hand in everything that occurs; but it would be very dangerous to allow ourselves to be directed by outward events apart from the distinct leadings of God in our spirit and by His Word. Quite as frequently we shall find ourselves led to go in the face of circumstances as to follow the favoring gales of outward events. Most of the important events and accomplished purposes in the lives of God's servants, as recorded in the Scriptures, were in direct opposition to all the circumstances that were occurring around them.

Let us notice also some of the principles and conditions of Divine guidance.

The first is a surrendered spirit. Next, there must be a readiness to obey. He will not give us light unless we mean to follow it. Then we must trust His guidance. We must believe that He is with us and directing us. We must lean upon His arm with all our heart, and implicitly look up into His face and expect Him to be true to us. We must also have "our senses exercised by reason of use, to know the difference between good and evil." Sometimes our mistakes will become most instructive to us by showing us the places where we have erred, and save us from repeating the mistake afterwards with more serious consequences. We must learn to distinguish between mere impressions and the deeper convictions of the entire judgment under the light of the Spirit, and between the voice of the Shepherd and that of the spirit of error. This He will teach us, and teach us more and more perfectly through experience. We shall have to learn also to walk with Him when we cannot understand the way.

"Through waves and clouds and storms
He gently clears thy way;
Wait then His time, so shall thy night
Soon end in glorious day."

December 16: His Withering – 1
by Charles H. Spurgeon
Excerpted from "The Withering Work of the Spirit", *Twelve Sermons on the Holy Spirit*, published by Fleming H. Revell Company, New York, New York in 1855

The voice said, Cry. And he said, What shall I cry? All flesh is grass, and all the goodliness thereof is as the flower of the field: the grass withers, the flower fades: because the Spirit of the Lord blows upon it: surely this people is grass. The grass withers, the flower fades: but the Word of our God shall stand forever.
Isaiah 40:6-8

Being born again, not of corruptible seed, but of incorruptible, by the Word of God, which lives and abides forever. For all flesh is as grass, and all the glory of man as the flower of grass. The grass withers, and the flower falls away; but the Word of the Lord endures forever. And this is the Word which by the gospel is preached unto you.
1 Peter 1:23-25

The Spirit blows upon the flesh, and that which seemed vigorous becomes weak, that which was fair to look upon is smitten with decay; the true nature of the flesh is thus discovered, its deceit is laid bare, its power is destroyed, and there is space for the dispensation of the ever-abiding Word, and for the rule of the Great Shepherd, whose words are spirit and life. There is a withering accomplished by the Spirit which is in preparation for the sowing and implanting by which salvation is accomplished. The withering before the sowing was very marvelously fulfilled in the preaching of John the Baptist. Most appropriately he carried on his ministry in the desert, for a spiritual desert was all around him; he was the voice of one crying in the wilderness, to plant, but to cut down. It was not his work 'The fleshly religion of the Jews was then in its prime. Pharisaism stalked through the streets in all its pomp; complacently rested in outward ceremonies only, and spiritual religion was at the lowest conceivable ebb. Here and there might be found a Simeon and an Anna, but for the most part men knew nothing of spiritual religion, but said in their hearts, "We have Abraham to our father," and this is enough. What a stir he made when he called the lordly Pharisees a generation of vipers! How he shook the nation with the declaration, "Now also the axe is laid unto the root of the trees"! Stern as Elijah, his work was to level the mountains, and lay low every lofty imagination. That word, "Repent," was as a scorching wind to the abundance of self-righteousness, a killing blast for the confidence of ceremonialism. His food and his dress called for fasting and mourning. The outward token of his ministry declared the death amid which he preached, as he buried in the waters of Jordan those who came to him. "You must die and be buried, even as He who is to come will save by death and burial." This was the meaning of the emblem which he set before the crowd. His typical act was as thorough in its teaching as were his words; and as if that were not enough, he warned them of a yet more searching and trying baptism with the Holy Ghost and with fire, and of the coming of One whose fan was in His hand, thoroughly to purge His floor.

December 17: His Withering – 2
by Charles H. Spurgeon

The Spirit in John blew as the rough north wind, searching and withering, and made him to be a destroyer of the vain glorying of a fleshly religion, that the spiritual faith might be established.

When our Lord Himself actually appeared, He came into a withered land, whose glories had all departed. Old Jesse's stem was bare, and our Lord was the branch which grew out of his root. The scepter had departed from Judah, and the lawgiver from between his feet, when Shiloh came. An alien sat on David's throne, and the Roman called the covenant-land his own. The lamp of prophecy burned only dimly, even if it had not utterly gone out. No Isaiah had arisen of late to console them, nor even a Jeremiah to lament their apostasy. The whole economy of Judaism was as a worn-out vesture; it had grown old, and was ready to vanish away. The priesthood was disarranged. Luke tells us that Annas and Caiaphas were high priests that year — two in a year or at once, a strange setting aside of the laws of Moses. All the dispensation which gathered around the visible, or as Paul calls it, the "worldly" sanctuary, was coming to a close; and when our Lord had finished His work, the veil of the temple was torn in two, the sacrifices were abolished, the priesthood of Aaron was set aside, and carnal ordinances were rescinded, for the Spirit revealed spiritual things. When He came who was made a priest, "not after the law of a carnal commandment, but after the power of an endless life," there was "a disannulling of the commandment going before for the weakness and unprofitableness thereof." Such are the facts of history; but I am not about to expand upon them: I am coming to your own personal histories — to the experience of every child of God. In every one of us it must be fulfilled that all that is of the flesh in us, seeing it is but as grass, must be withered, and the comeliness thereof must be destroyed. The Spirit of God, like the wind, must pass over the field of our souls, and cause our beauty to be as a fading flower. He must so convince us of sin, and ourselves to ourselves, that we shall see that the flesh profits nothing; that our fallen nature is corruption itself, and that "they who are in the flesh cannot please God." There must be brought home to us the sentence of death upon our former legal and carnal life, that the incorruptible seed of the Word of God, implanted by the Holy Ghost, may be in us, and abide in us forever. Turning then to the work of the Spirit in causing the goodliness of the flesh to fade, let us, first, observe that the work of the Holy Spirit upon the soul of man in withering up that which is of the flesh, is very unexpected. You will observe in our text, that even the speaker himself, though doubtless one taught of God, when he was commanded to cry, said, "What shall I cry?" Even he did not know that in order to the comforting of God's people, there must first be experienced a preliminary visitation. Many preachers of God's gospel have Christ. They have forgotten that the law is the schoolmaster to bring men to Christ. They have sown on the unbroken fallow ground, and forgotten that the plow must break the clods.

December 18: His Witnessing – 1
by Alexander Maclaren
Excerpted from "The Witness of the Spirit", *Sermons Preached in Manchester*, published by Funk & Wagnalls Company, New York, New York in 1905

The Spirit Himself bears witness with our spirit, that we are the children of God.
Romans 8:16

This great text which I have ventured to read today — not with the idea that I can exalt it or say anything worthy of it, but simply in the hope of clearing away some misunderstandings — is one that has often and often tortured the mind of Christians. They say of themselves, I know nothing of any such evidence: I am not conscious of any Spirit bearing witness with my spirit. Instead of looking to other sources to answer the question whether they are Christians or not — and then, having answered it, thinking thus: That text asserts that all Christians have this witness, therefore certainly I have it in some shape or other. I do not feel anything that corresponds with my idea of what such a grand, supernatural voice as the witness of God's Spirit in my spirit must needs be; and therefore, I doubt whether I am a Christian at all.

I should be thankful if the attempt I make now to set before you what seems to me to be the true teaching of the passage, should be, with God's help, the means of lifting some little part of the burden from some hearts that are right, and that only long to know that they are, in order to be at rest

"The Spirit Himself bears witness with our spirit that we are the children of God." The general course of thought which I wish to leave with you may be summed up thus: Our cry "Father" is the witness that we are sons. That cry is not simply ours, but it is the voice of God's Spirit. The Divine Witness in our spirits is subject to the ordinary influences which affect our spirits. Let us take these thoughts, and dwell on them for a little while.

Our cry "Father" is the Witness that we are sons.

Mark the terms of the passage: "The Spirit Himself bears witness with our spirit." It is not so much a revelation made to my spirit, considered as the recipient of the testimony, as a revelation made in or with my spirit considered as cooperating in the testimony. It is not that my spirit says one thing, bears witness that I am a child of God; and that the Spirit of God comes in by a distinguishable process, with a separate evidence, to say Amen to my persuasion; but it is that there is one testimony which has a conjoined origin—the origin from the Spirit of God as the true source, and the origin from my own soul as recipient and partner in that testimony.

December 19: His Witnessing – 2
by Alexander Maclaren

From the teaching of this passage, or from any of the language which Scripture uses with regard to the inner witness, it is not to be inferred that there shall rise up in a Christian's heart, from some origin consciously beyond the sphere of his own nature, a voice with which he has nothing to do; which at once, by its own character, by something peculiar and distinguishable about it, by something strange in its nature, or out of the ordinary course of human thinking, shall certify itself to be not his voice at all, but God's voice. That is not the direction in which you are to look for the witness of God's Spirit. It is evidence borne, indeed, by the Spirit of God; but it is evidence borne not only to our spirit, but through it, and with it.

The testimony is one—the testimony of a man's own emotion, and own conviction, and own desire—the cry, Abba, Father! So far, then, as the form of the evidence goes, you are not to look for it in anything ecstatic, arbitrary, parted off from your own experience by a broad line of differentiation; but you are to look into the experience which at first sight you would claim most exclusively for your own, and to try and find out whether there is not working with your soul, working through it, working beneath it, distinct from it but not distinguishable from it by anything but its consequences and its fruitfulness—a deeper voice than yours—a "still small voice," no whirlwind, nor fire, nor earthquake—but the voice of God speaking in secret, taking the voice and tones of your own heart and your own consciousness, and saying to you, You are My child, in as much as, operated by My grace, and My inspiration—there rises, tremblingly but truly, in your own soul the cry, Abba, Father.

So much, then, for the form of this evidence—my own conviction. Then with regard to the substance of it: Conviction of what? The text itself does not tell us what is the evidence which the Spirit bears, and by reason of which we have a right to conclude that we are the children of God. The previous verse tells us. I have partially anticipated what I have to say on that point, but it will bear a little further expansion. "You have not received the spirit of bondage again to fear, but you have received the Spirit of adoption, whereby we cry, Abba, Father." "The Spirit Himself," by this means of our cry, Abba, Father, "bears witness with our spirit, that we are the children of God." The substance, then, of the conviction which is lodged in the human spirit by the testimony of the Spirit of God is not primarily directed to our relation or feelings for God, but to a far grander thing than that—to God's feelings and relation to us.

December 20: His Witnessing – 3
by D. L. Moody
Excerpted from "Witnessing in Power", *Secret Power*, published by F. H. Revell. Chicago, Illinois in 1881

The subject of witness-bearing in the power of the Holy Ghost is not sufficiently understood by the Church. Until we have more intelligence on this point we are laboring under great disadvantage. Now, if you will take your Bible and turn to the 15th chapter of John and the 26th verse, you will find these words: "But when the Comforter is come, whom I will send unto you from the Father, even the Spirit of Truth, who proceeds from the Father, He shall testify of Me; and you also shall bear witness, because you have been with Me from the beginning." Here we find what the Spirit is going to do, or what Christ said He would do when He came; namely, that He should testify of Him. And if you will turn over to the second chapter of Acts you will find that when Peter stood up on the day of Pentecost, and testified of what Christ had done, the Holy Spirit came down and bore witness to that fact, and men were convicted by hundreds and by thousands. So then man cannot preach effectively by himself. He must have the Spirit of God to give ability, and study God's Word, in order to testify according to the mind of the Spirit.

What is the testimony? If we keep back the gospel of Christ and do not bring Christ before the people, then the Spirit does not have the opportunity to work. But the moment

Peter stood up on the day of Pentecost and bore testimony to this one fact, that Christ died for sin, and that He had been raised again, and ascended into Heaven, the Spirit came down to bear witness to the Person and Work of Christ.

He came down to bear witness to the fact that Christ was in Heaven, and if it was not for the Holy Ghost bearing witness to the preaching of the facts the gospel, do you think that the Church would have lived during these last eighteen centuries? Do you believe that Christ's death, resurrection and ascension would not have been forgotten as soon as His birth, if it had not been for the fact that the Holy Spirit had come? Because it is very clear, that when John the Baptist made his appearance on the borders of the wilderness, they had forgotten all about the birth of Jesus Christ. Just thirty short years. It was all gone. They had forgotten the story of the Shepherds; they had forgotten the wonderful scene that took place in the temple, when the Son of God was brought into the temple and the older prophets and prophetesses were there; they had forgotten about the wise men coming to Jerusalem to inquire where He was that was born King of the Jews. That story of His birth seemed to have just faded away; they had forgotten all about it, and when John made his appearance on the borders of the wilderness it was brought back to their minds. And if it had not been for the Holy Ghost coming down to bear witness to Christ, to testify of His death and resurrection, these facts would have been forgotten as soon as His birth was forgotten.

December 21: His Witnessing – 4
by D. L. Moody

The witness of the Spirit is the witness of power. Jesus said, "The works that I do shall you shall also do, and greater works than these shall you do because I go to the Father." I used to stumble over that. I didn't understand it. I thought, what greater work could any man do than Christ had done? How could anyone raise a dead man who had been laid away in the sepulcher for days, and who had already begun to turn back to dust; how with a word could He call him forth? But the longer I live the more I am convinced it is a greater thing to influence a man's will; a man whose will is set against God; to have that will broken and brought into subjection to God's will or, in other words, it is a greater thing to have power over a living, sinning, God-hating man, than to quicken the dead. He who could create a world could speak a dead soul into life; but I think the greatest miracle this world has ever seen was the miracle at Pentecost.

Here were men who surrounded the apostles, full of prejudice, full of malice, full of bitterness, their hands, as it were, dripping with the blood of the Son of God, and yet an unlettered man, a man whom they detested, a man whom they hated, stands up there and preaches the gospel, and three thousand of them are immediately convicted and converted, and become disciples of the Lord

Jesus Christ, and are willing to lay down their lives for the Son of God. It may have been on that occasion that Stephen was converted, the first martyr, and some of the men who soon after gave up their lives for Christ. This seems to me the greatest miracle this world has ever seen. But Peter did not labor alone; the Spirit of God was with him; hence the marvelous results. The Jewish law required that there should be two witnesses, and so we find that when Peter preached there was a second witness. Peter testified of Christ, and Christ says when the Holy Spirit comes He will testify of Me. And they both bore witness to the certainties of the Lord's incarnation, ministry, death, and resurrection, and the result was that a multitude turned as with one heart unto the Lord. Our failure now is that preachers ignore the Cross, and veil Christ with sapless sermons and superfine language. They just don't present Him to the people plainly, and that is why, I believe, that the Spirit of God don't work with power in our churches. What we need is to preach Christ and present Him to a perishing world. The world can get on very well without you and me, but the world cannot get on without Christ, and therefore we must testify of Him, and the world, I believe, today is just hungering and thirsting for this Divine, satisfying portion. Thousands and thousands are sitting in darkness, not knowing about this great Light, but when we begin to preach Christ honestly, faithfully, sincerely and truthfully; holding Him up, not ourselves; exalting Christ and not our theories; presenting Christ and not our opinions; advocating Christ and not some false doctrine; then the Holy Ghost will come and bear witness. He will testify that what we say is true. When He comes He will confirm the Word with signs following. This is one of the strongest proofs that our gospel is Divine.

December 22: His Word – 1
by Andrew Murray
Excerpted from "The Spirit and the Word", *The Spirit of Christ*,
published by A. D. F. Randolph & Co., New York, New York in 1888

"It is the Spirit who quickens; the flesh profits nothing: the words that I have spoken unto you are Spirit and are life…"
"Lord, to whom shall we go? You have the words of eternal life."
John 6:63, 68

God has made us sufficient as ministers of a new covenant; not of the letter, but of the Spirit: for the letter kills but the Spirit gives life.
2 Corinthians 3:6

Our Blessed Lord had been speaking of Himself as the Bread of Life, and of His flesh and blood as the food and drink of eternal Life. To many of His disciples it was a hard saying, which they could not understand. Jesus tells them that it is only when the Holy Spirit is come, and they have Him, that His words will become clear to them. He says, "It is the Spirit that quickens; the flesh profits nothing. The words that I have spoken unto you, they are Spirit, and they are Life."

"It is the Spirit that quickens," in these words and the corresponding ones of Paul, "the Spirit gives life," we have the nearest approach to what may be called a definition of the Spirit (1 Corinthians 15:45, "a life-giving Spirit"). The Spirit always acts, in the first place, whether in nature or grace, as a Life-giving principle. It is of the deepest importance to keep a firm hold on this. His work in the believer—Sealing, Sanctifying, Enlightening, and Strengthening—is all rooted in this: It is as He is known and honored, and place given to Him, as He is waited on, as the Inner Life of the soul, that His other gracious workings can be experienced. These are just the outgrowth of the Life; it is in the power of the Life within that they can be enjoyed. "It is the Spirit that quickens." In contrast to the Spirit our Lord places the flesh. He says, "the flesh profits nothing." He is not speaking of the flesh as the fountain of sin, but in its religious aspect, as it is the power in which the natural man, or even the believer who does not fully yield to the Spirit, seeks to serve God, or to know and possess Divine things. The futile character of all its efforts our Lord indicates in the words, "profits nothing;" they are not sufficient, they avail not to reach the Spiritual reality, the Divine things themselves.

Paul means the same when he contrasts with the Spirit, the letter that kills. The whole Dispensation of the Law was just a dispensation of the letter and the flesh. Though it had a certain glory, and Israel's privileges were very great, yet, as Paul says, "Even that which was made glorious had no glory in this respect, by reason of the glory that excels." Even Christ Himself, as long as He was in the flesh, and until, in the tearing of the veil of His flesh, the dispensation of the Spirit took the place of that of the flesh, could not by His words effect in His disciples what He desired. "It is the Spirit that quickens; the flesh profits nothing."

December 23: His Word – 2
by Andrew Murray

Our Lord applies this saying now especially to the words He had just spoken, and the Spiritual truth they contained. "The words that I have spoken unto you are Spirit and are Life." He wishes to teach the disciples two things: The one is that the words are indeed a living seed with a power of germinating and springing up, asserting their own vitality, revealing their meaning, and proving their Divine Power in those who receive them and keep them abiding in the heart. He wanted them not to be discouraged if they could not at once comprehend them. His words are Spirit and Life; they are not meant for the understanding, but for the Life. Coming in the Power of the Unseen Spirit, higher and deeper than all thought, they enter into the very roots of the Life, they have themselves a Divine Life, working out effectively with a Divine energy the Truth they express into the experience of those who receive them.

As a consequence of this their spiritual character—this is the other lesson He wished His disciples to learn—these words of His need a spiritual nature to receive them. Seed needs congenial soil: There must be life in the soil as well as in the seed. Not into the mind only, nor into the feelings, nor even into the will alone must the word be taken, but through them into the life. The center of that life is man's spiritual nature, with conscience as its voice; there the authority of the Word must be acknowledged. But even this is not enough: Conscience dwells in man as a captive amid powers it cannot control. It is the Spirit that comes from God, the Spirit that Christ came to bring, becoming our life, receiving the Word and assimilating it into our life, that will make them to become the Truth and Power in us.

In our study of the work of the Blessed Spirit, we cannot be too careful to get a firm hold of this blessed truth--it will save us from many errors. It will keep us from expecting to enjoy the teaching of the Spirit without the Word, or to master the teaching of the Word without the Spirit. On the one side, we have the error of seeking the teaching of the Spirit without the Word. In the Holy Trinity, the Word and the Spirit are ever in each other, one with the Father. It is not otherwise with the God-inspired Words of Scripture. The Holy Spirit has for all ages embodied the thoughts of God in the written Word, and lives now for this very purpose in our hearts, there to reveal the power and the meaning of that Word. If you would be full of the Spirit, be full of the Word. If you would have the Divine Life of the Spirit within you grow strong, and acquire power in every part of your nature, let the Word of Christ dwell richly in you. If you would have the Spirit fulfil His office of Remembrancer, calling to mind at the right moment, and applying with Divine accuracy to your need what Jesus has spoken, have the words of Christ abiding in you. If you would have the Spirit reveal to you the will of God in each circumstance of life, choosing from apparently conflicting commands or principles with unerring precision what you must do, and suggesting it as you need, oh! have the Word living in you, ready for His use.

December 24: His Working – 1
by Robert Murray McCheyne

Excerpted from "Sermon XXXVII: The Work of the Spirit", *The Works of the Late Rev. Robert Murray McCheyne*, published by Robert Carter, New York, New York in 1847

And the Spirit of God moved upon the face of the waters.
Genesis 1:2

There is, perhaps, no subject upon which there is greater ignorance than that of the Spirit of God. Most people, in our day, if they answered truly, would say as those twelve men of Ephesus: "We have not so much as heard if there is any Holy Ghost" (Acts 19). And yet, if ever you are to be saved, you must know Him; for it is all His work to bring a poor sinner to Christ. A little boy, when dying, said, "Three persons in the Godhead. God the Father made and preserved me; God the Son came into the world and died for me; God the Holy Ghost came into my heart, and made me love God and hate sin." My dear friends, if you would die happy, you must be able to bear the same dying testimony. You know it is said in John, that "God is love." This is true of God the Father in His giving up His Son for sinners; this is true of God the Son, in His becoming man and dying for sinners; this is true of God the Holy Ghost, in His whole work in the heart of sinners. At present I wish to show you the love of the Spirit, by observing all that He has ever done for men and women in the world. Today I will show you His work at creation; at the flood; in the wilderness.

At creation. "The Spirit of God moved upon the face of the waters" (Genesis 1:2). The expression is taken from a dove brooding over its nest. "You send forth Your Spirit, they are created; and You renew the face of the earth" (Psalm 104). Here the Spirit is said to have renewed the face of the earth. "By His Spirit He has garnished the heavens" (Job 26:13). Here God does, as it were, lead us forth to look upon the midnight sky; and when we gaze upon it, He tells us that it was the loving Spirit that gave them all their brightness and their beauty. Observe, then, that whatever beauty there is in the glassy sea, in the green earth, or in the glittering sky, it is all the work of the Holy Spirit. God the Father willed all, God the Son created all, God the Holy Ghost garnished, and gave life and loveliness to all. Oh! what a lovely world that un-fallen world must have been, when God the Son walked with Adam in Paradise, when God the Holy Ghost watered and renewed the whole every moment, when God the Father looked down well pleased on all, and said that all was very good.

The love of the Spirit. He did not think it beneath His care to beautify the dwelling-place of man. He wanted our joy to be full. He did not think it enough that we had a world to live in, but He made the waters full of life and beauty. He made every green thing to spring for mankind, and made a shining canopy above, all for the joy of man. Whatever beauty still remains on earth, or sea, or sky, it is the trace of His Almighty finger. You should never look on the beauties of the world without thinking of the Holy Spirit.

December 25: His Working – 2
by Robert Murray McCheyne

The holiness of the Spirit. From the very beginning He was the Holy Spirit, of purer eyes than to behold iniquity. It was a sinless world. The sea had never been defiled by bearing wicked men upon its bosom. The green earth had never been trodden by the foot of a sinner. The star-filled sky had never been looked upon by the eye of one whose eye is full of adultery, and cannot cease from sin. It was a holy, holy, holy world, a temple of the living God, the lofty mountains were the pillars of it; the glittering heavens its canopy. The far-resounding ocean sang His praise. The hills broke forth into singing, and all the trees of the field clapped their hands. As the cloud which so filled Solomon's temple that the priests could not stand to minister by reason of the cloud, so the Holy Spirit filled this world, a holy, sinless temple to the Father's praise. When man fell into sin, and the very ground was cursed for his sake, then the Holy Spirit in great measure left His temple; He could not dwell with sin. And never do you find Him coming back, as before, till He lighted on the head of a sinless Savior; for the Holy Ghost descended upon Him like a dove, and abode upon Him.

Just so is it with the soul. As long as your soul is guilty, polluted, vile, in the sight of the Spirit, He cannot make His abode in your heart. He is a loving Spirit, full of a tender desire to make you holy. But as long as you are guilty in His sight, it is contrary to His nature that He should dwell in you. But come to the blood of Jesus, sinner; come to the blood that makes you white as snow, then will the Spirit see no iniquity in you, and He will come and dwell in your heart, as He dwelt at first in the sinless world. As He moved on the face of the waters, like a dove over its nest, so will He make His nest in your heart, and brood there. As He renewed the face of the ground, so will He renew your heart. As He garnished the heavens, so will He beautify your soul, till He makes you shine as the stars forever and ever.

At the flood. "My Spirit shall not always strive with man. for that he also is flesh (fading): yet his days shall be a hundred and twenty years" (Genesis 6:3). The few children of God that remained were hated and persecuted, hunted like the partridge on the mountains. The Lord was sorry that He had made man, and it grieved Him in His heart. How is the Holy Spirit engaged? He does not dwell with sinful men. He cannot dwell with unpardoned sinners; for He is the Holy Spirit. But still He strives with men, and strives to the very end. The men were giants in sin. Every imagination of their heart was only evil continually. But this is the very reason He strives. He sees the flood that is coming, He sees the Hell that is beneath them; therefore does He strive. In the preaching of Noah He pleaded with them; He pricked their hearts, made them think of their danger, their sin, their misery. In preparing the ark He pleaded with them, showed them the way of safety, and said, "Yet there is room." He made every stroke of the hammer go to their hearts. "The Spirit and the Bride said, Come."

December 26 His Working – 3
by William Nixon

Excerpted from "Work of the Spirit of Christ", *All and In All: The Relations of Christ as God: Creator and Redeemer*, published by Johnstone, Hunter & Co., Edinburgh, Scotland in 1882

"But this is that which was spoken by the prophet Joel, 'And it shall come to pass in the last days, says God, I will pour out of My Spirit upon all flesh…'"
Acts Chapter 2

Having died for the redemption of all that were given to Him in the everlasting covenant, He had risen again; and having shown Himself alive by many infallible proofs, He had ascended to Heaven. His followers were to see Him no more in this world, in His bodily presence, until He comes at last in glory, to raise the dead, and judge mankind. Formally clothed with all power in Heaven and earth, He had begun to establish His kingdom among men, and had left His disciples behind Him to take care of its interests, and to labor for its advancement. The disciples themselves were eventually and effectively beginning to forsake their carnal notions, desires, and hopes of an outward and temporal reign of the Messiah, and to have their eyes opened on the spirituality of the dispensation which Jesus had introduced, and would employ them to establish. Left behind Him in the world with such a charge, and surrounded with difficulties and dangers, they were now feeling more deeply than before that nothing but special guidance and strength from on high could direct their minds, support their hearts, and establish the work of their hands. Yet they were not so comfortless as might have been expected from their former state of mind. They rather had begun to feel that they were not forsaken by their Lord, and to look for such tokens of His presence and power, as would prove that in a very effective manner He was still with them.

Various circumstances were leading them to expect, and to prepare for, a special visitation from their ascended Lord. He had again and again promised, that as the result of His bodily departure from among them, He would send the Comforter, the Spirit of truth, to dwell in them, and to abide with them forever. For the fulfillment of this promise, they were now waiting with prayerful expectation. Further, they were now beginning more adequately to understand and realize the glory of Christ, as Head over all things to the Church, and as still truly with them, though unseen, as still with them in respect of His Divine presence and almighty power, and of His all-sufficiency and faithfulness, as their Redeemer and their Lord. They felt strong in Him, and in the power of His might. They also had their minds filled with altogether new views, both of this world and of the next; of the shadowy nature of things seen and temporal, and of the greatness of the things that are unseen and eternal; of the vanishing nature of the heaviest earthly trials before them, and of the enduring glory to which they now felt destined. In a special manner they were manifestly filled from above with anticipation of the coming of the Spirit, and with a readiness to receive Him.

December 27: His Working – 4
by William Nixon

In fact, the Spirit was already in them, secretly and silently, yet strongly and irresistibly, drawing out their desires, and enlarging their expectations, and enlivening their hopes of His remarkable descent. Carnal lusts were now repressed. Earthly ambition was gone. Pride and jealousy had vanished. Guilty fear had fled. The spirit of unholy rivalry had left them. Deep humility clothed them as with a garment. Holy love for God and for one another filled their hearts, and breathed in all their conduct. Living faith and hope carried them near to God, conveyed them within the curtain, brought them near to the eternal throne, and bound and held them fast to Christ, as one in Him, yes, one with Him, and as ready, waiting, and expecting to be filled out of His fulness.

This was the state of preparation into which the disciples were brought for the reception of the richest blessings from on high. And these blessings were not withheld. For while they were with one accord in one place, "suddenly there came a sound from Heaven as of a rushing, mighty wind, and it filled all the house where they were sitting. And there appeared unto them cloven tongues as of fire, and it sat upon each of them. And they were all filled with the Holy Ghost, and began to speak with other tongues as the Spirit gave them utterance." From that hour, the apostles clearly perceived, and boldly proclaimed, the true glory of Christ, and the spiritual nature of the salvation to be found in Him. The views of Christ and of His salvation, however, that now and from then on filled their minds, as this chapter shows, were owing, in reality, not to the miraculous gifts of the Spirit, but to the inwardly illuminating power with which He accompanied His gifts. At the same time, so remarkably did the Holy Spirit of Christ then work in their minds, and in the minds of those who crowded to hear them, that multitudes trembled and cried out under conviction of their sin and danger, and as many as three thousand were actually and savingly converted to Christ.

The Holy Spirit came with "a sound" that captured every ear and riveted every heart. He came as "a wind" denoting the spiritual life and strength with which He fills the soul. He came "suddenly" to mark His sovereignty in working when and where He pleases. He came as "a rushing, mighty wind," that "filled the house," to mark the resistless force with which He acts in and upon the subjects of His grace. And more impressively still, He rested on the disciples in the form of "cloven tongues of fire."

The recorded effects of the word preached that day show the nature of the Spirit's saving work. If the three thousand then brought to salvation felt their lost condition and their need of redemption, it was because the Spirit convinced them of sin, and righteousness, and judgment. If they were truly enlightened, it was because the Spirit guided them into the truth. If they were savingly changed, it was by the washing of regeneration, and the renewing of the Holy Ghost.

December 28: His Working – 5
by David James Burrell
Excerpted from "The Work of the Comforter", *The Morning Cometh: Talks for the Times*, published by American Tract Society, New York, New York in 1893

"Nevertheless I tell you the truth: it is expedient for you that I go away: for if I go not away, the Comforter will not come unto but if I depart, I will send Him unto you. And when He is come He will reprove the world of sin and of righteousness and of judgment: of sin, because they believed not on Me; of righteousness, because I go to My Father and you see Me no more; of judgment, because the prince of this world is judged."
John 16:7-11

In the days of man's innocency he held communion with God as one friend with another. They walked together in the garden "in the cool of the day." There were strange confidences, wonderful trysts. We cannot understand it.

Then came the fall, and with it alienation: The two friends parted. Manifestations of God thereafter were mere glimpses, an occasional theophany, the Angel of the Covenant or a shadowy Presence known only by the rustling of His garments. The time came, however, when God bowed the heavens and came down and dwelt among men. He took flesh upon Himself and walked along the common thoroughfares of life. We can understand that. Men saw Him, clasped hands with Him, ate with Him. He was their fellow. Was it not a glorious privilege to look upon this Incarnate God and talk with Him by the way? I am not sure, however, that ours is not a far more blessed privilege. He has indeed vanished out of our sight; His face is a sweet memory, a blissful hope; but His spiritual presence is with us.

"It is expedient," He said, " that I go away from you; for if I go not away, the Comforter will not come; but if I depart, I will send Him unto you." This Jesus had been with them as child and man for thirty years. They had heard His words and were prepared to say, "Never man spoke like this Man." They had seen His works and could testify, "No man could do these things except God were with Him." And what was the result? A little group of fishermen and other humble folk had gathered about Him. That was all. To outward seeming His work was a fiasco. His announced purpose was to revolutionize the spiritual structure of the world; but what an insignificant outcome. Where was the trouble? It lay in the limitations of the flesh. All bodily presence is weak. No man in the flesh has ever attained to universal conquest or ever will. Caesar?

> "Imperial Caesar, dead and turned to clay,
> May stop a hole to keep the wind away."

Alexander? When all was told he lay dead under his supper table. Napoleon? In lonely, friendless exile he wore away his life. If a man is going to lift the world, the fulcrum of his lever must be set outside of it.

So long as Jesus dwelt among His disciples they were wholly dependent upon His bodily presence.

December 29: His Working – 6
by David James Burrell

One night, while rowing across the Sea of Galilee, the storm fell upon them and they were overwhelmed with fear. What at that moment was their Master's power to them? Yet He was only three miles away. Their faith was so tangibly-based that it reached only to their finger-tips. He must therefore vanish out of their sight; for their sake, for the world's sake, He must leave them.

Lycurgus who, about 900 B. C, prepared a code of laws for Sparta, believing that his personal presence was a hindrance to the just observance of that code, mysteriously disappeared and was never seen or heard of. In like manner, to secure the legitimate fruits of His ministry Christ must go away.

But when He vanished He left behind Him a bequest which was to be a manifold equivalent for every loss. The Holy Ghost, His last and unspeakable Gift, was not hemmed in by any environment of time or space. To this Omnipresent Power the work was now to be transferred, and He was to carry it on unto "the restitution of all things." The followers of Jesus would indeed know Him no more after the flesh, but they would know Him far more gloriously and effectively in the power of this Spirit of God.

So He went His way. He bowed His weary shoulders, burdened with the world's sorrows, and passed through the narrow gate. And what then? For a season His followers felt that all was over. "I go fishing," said Peter; and the others said, "We also go with you."

Then, after His resurrection, Christ reappeared and remained among His disciples forty days—long enough to convince them that whereas He had died He was now alive forevermore—long enough to mark out for them the plan of the campaign. Then, having emphasized their Great Commission, "Go everywhere and preach the gospel," He breathed on them, saying, "Receive the Holy Ghost;" and the clouds received Him out of their sight.

The gift of the Holy Ghost thus conferred was only an earnest of what was to come. Ten days passed by then, while they were praying in the open court, all of a sudden the sound of a rushing mighty wind was heard, the flame, parting asunder into tongues of fire, sat upon each one of them, and they began to speak with various tongues. This advent of the Holy Ghost was evidenced by the conversion of three thousand in a single day. His power is abroad today.

We are living in this Dispensation of the Spirit. It is the golden age of privilege and opportunity. Anyone who desires may have part in it. The measure of power is willingness. The harvest is plenteous, the fields are ripe. Go, thrust in a sickle and reap!

December 30: His Worship – 1
by Andrew Murray
Excerpted from "Worship in the Spirit", *The Spirit of Christ*, published by A. D. F. Randolph & Co., New York, New York in 1888

"The hour comes, and now is, when the true worshippers shall worship the Father in Spirit and in truth; for such does the Father seek to be His worshippers. God is a Spirit, and they that worship Him must worship Him in Spirit and in truth."
John 4:23-24

We are the circumcision, who worship by the Spirit of God and glory in Christ Jesus, and have no confidence in the flesh.
Philippians 3:3

To worship is man's highest glory. He was created for fellowship with God. Of that fellowship worship is the loftiest expression. All the exercises of the religious life — meditation and prayer, love and faith, surrender and obedience — all culminate in worship. Recognizing what God is in His holiness, His glory, and His love, realizing what I am as a sinful creature, and as the Father's redeemed child, in worship I gather up my whole being and present myself to my God, to offer Him the adoration and the glory which is His due. The truest and fullest and nearest approach to God is worship. Every sentiment and every service of the religious life is included in it. To worship is man's highest destiny, because in it God is all.

Jesus tells us that with His coming a new worship would commence. All that heathen or Samaritans had called worship, all even that the Jews had known of worship in accordance with the provisional revelation of God's law, would make way for something entirely and distinctively new—the worship in Spirit and in Truth. This is the worship He was to inaugurate by the giving of the Holy Spirit. This is the worship which now alone is well-pleasing to the Father. It is for this worship especially that we have received the Holy Spirit. Let us, at the very commencement of our study of the work of the Spirit, take in the blessed thought that the great object for which the Holy Spirit is within us is that we worship in spirit and in truth. "Such does the Father seek to be His worshippers"—for this He sent forth His Son and His Spirit.

In Spirit. When God created man a living soul, that soul, as the seat and organ of his personality and consciousness, was linked, on the one side, through the body, with the outer visible world, on the other side, through the spirit, with the unseen and the Divine. The soul had to decide whether it would yield itself to the spirit, by it to be linked with God and His will, or to the body and the solicitations of the visible. In the fall, the soul refused the rule of the spirit, and became the slave of the body with its appetites. Man became flesh; the spirit lost its destined place of rule, and became little more than a dormant power; it was now no longer the ruling principle, but a struggling captive. And the spirit now stands in opposition to the flesh, the name for the life of soul and body together, in their subjection to sin.

December 31: His Worship – 2
by Andrew Murray

When speaking of the unregenerate man in contrast with the spiritual (1 Corinthians 2:14), Paul calls him physical, soulish, or animal, having only the natural life. The life of the soul comprehends all our moral and intellectual faculties, as they may even be directed towards the things of God, apart from the renewal of the Divine Spirit. Because the soul is under the power of the flesh, man is spoken of as having become flesh, as being flesh. As the body consists of flesh and bone, and the flesh is that part of it which is especially endowed with sensitiveness, and through which we receive our sensations from the outer world, the flesh denotes human nature, as it has become subject to the world of sense. And because the whole soul has thus come under the power of the flesh, the Scripture speaks of all the attributes of the soul as belonging to the flesh, and being under its power.

So it contrasts, in reference to religion and worship, the two principles from which they may proceed. There is a fleshly wisdom and a spiritual wisdom (1 Corinthians 2:12; Colossians 1:9). There is a service for God trusting in the flesh and glorying in the flesh, and a service for God by the spirit (Philippians 3:3-4; Galatians 6:13). There is a fleshly mind and a spiritual mind (Colossians 1:9; 2:18). There is a will of the flesh, and a will which is of God working by His Spirit (John 1:13; Philippians 2:13). There is a worship which is a satisfying of the flesh, because it is in the power of what flesh can do (Colossians 2:18, 23), and a worship of God which is in the Spirit. It is this worship Jesus came to make possible, and to realize in us, by giving a new spirit in our inmost part, and then, within that, God's Holy Spirit. In Spirit and in Truth! Such a worship in Spirit is worship in Truth. Just as the words "in Spirit" do not mean internal as contrasted with external observances, but Spiritual, worked within by God's Spirit, as opposed to what man's natural power can effect, so the words "in Truth" do not mean hearty, sincere, upright. In all the worship of the Old Testament saints, they knew that God sought Truth in the inward parts; they sought Him with their whole hearts, and most uprightly — and yet they attained not to that worship in Spirit and Truth, which Jesus brought us when He tore the veil of the flesh. Truth here means the substance, the reality, the actual possession of all that the worship of God implies, both in what it demands and what it promises. If we take truth as opposed to falsehood, the law of Moses was just as true as the gospel of Jesus; they both came from God. But if we understand what it means, that the law gave only a shadow of "good things to come," and that Christ brought us the things themselves, their very substance, we see how He was full of truth, because He was Himself the Truth, the reality, the very Life and Love and Power of God imparting itself to us. We then also see how it is only a worship in Spirit that can be a worship in Truth, in the actual enjoyment of that Divine Power, which is Christ's own life and fellowship with the Father, revealed and maintained within us by the Holy Spirit.

Scripture Index

1 Corinthians 2; 3:1-3, 16	85
1 Corinthians 2:9-10	206
1 Corinthians 2:10	40, 230
1 Corinthians 2:11	53
1 Corinthians 2:12	368
1 Corinthians 2:13	77
1 Corinthians 2:14	53, 368
1 Corinthians 3:1-3	246
1 Corinthians 3:1-3	86
1 Corinthians 3:16	276
1 Corinthians 6:17	272
1 Corinthians 6:19-20	192
1 Corinthians 10:4	216
1 Corinthians 12:3	176
1 Corinthians 12:4, 11, 13	306
1 Corinthians 12:11	40
1 Corinthians 14:32-33	22
1 Corinthians 15:45	351
1 John 2:20	268
1 Peter 1:12	57
1 Peter 1:23-25	338
1 Peter 5:10	244
1 Samuel 13:13	97
1 Samuel 17:37	101
1 Samuel 18:7	101
2 Chronicles 15:1-2	158

2 Corinthians 1:22; 5:5	150
2 Corinthians 3	85
2 Corinthians 3:6	350
2 Corinthians 3:8	28
2 Corinthians 3:12-16	77
2 Corinthians 4:2	168
2 Corinthians 4:17	64
2 Corinthians 5:11	149
2 Kings 4:2	88
2 Peter 1:21	77
2 Timothy 1:7	22
Acts 1:4	318
Acts 1:8	122, 132
Acts 1:24-26	25
Acts 2	358
Acts 2:1-4	79, 92
Acts 2:2	332
Acts 2:2-3, 17	268
Acts 2:3	284
Acts 2:33	193
Acts 7:55	312
Acts 8:29	18
Acts 10:38	73
Acts 13:1-4	238
Acts 16:6-7	18
Acts 16:7	152
Acts 16:9-10	24
Acts 16:10	23
Acts 16:14	202
Acts 19	354
Acts 19:2	56
Acts 20:28	10
Acts 27:25	149

Acts 28:1 184
Colossians 1:8 2
Colossians 1:9 368
Colossians 1:9; 2:18 368
Colossians 2:18, 23 369
Daniel 6:22 101
Ephesians 1:13 ....12, 226
Ephesians 1:13; 4:30; 150
Ephesians 2:1 182
Ephesians 3:16 232
Ephesians 4:1-4 ....306, 307
Ephesians 4:30 314
Ephesians 6:17 264
Ephesians 6:18 256
Ezekiel 3:12 204
Ezekiel 36:26 86
Ezekiel 36:27 154
Galatians 3:19 43
Galatians 5:16 70
Galatians 5:18 ....84, 322
Galatians 5:25 ....63, 86, 246, 326
Galatians 6:13 368
Genesis 1:2 ....76, 146, 354, 355
Genesis 2:7 76
Genesis 3:15 72
Genesis 6:3 ....252, 357
Genesis 11:38 136
Genesis 13:14-17 96
Hebrews 4:12 275
Hebrews 9:14 220
Hebrews 10:28-29 110
Hebrews 11:13 64
Isaiah 6:9-10 185

Isaiah 8:20	15
Isaiah 11:2	40, 106
Isaiah 28:10	69
Isaiah 32:14-15	250
Isaiah 40:6-8	338
Isaiah 40:7	180
Isaiah 44:3	160, 212
Isaiah 44:5	213, 214
Isaiah 55:13	186
Isaiah 60:21; 61:2	186
Isaiah 66:13	68
James 4:1	291
Jeremiah 9:24	i
Jeremiah 23:28	15
Job 26:13	80, 355
Job 34:14-15	82
John 1:13	369
John 1:18	73
John 3:8	76
John 3:34	73
John 4:23-24	366
John 6:63, 68	350
John 6:68	274
John 7:38	328
John 7:38-39	192
John 14:12	79
John 14:14	328
John 14:16	74
John 14:16-17	296
John 14:17	77
John 14:21	44
John 14:26	39
John 15:26	39, 292

John 16:7	46, 55
John 16:7-11	36, 362
John 16:8	46, 112
John 16:8-11	75
John 16:12-14	77
John 16:13	i, 292, 334
John 16:14	78
John 16:14-15	260
John 16:15	41
John 16:25	49
John 17:17	78
John 20:22	108, 174
Jonah 1:3	26
Luke 4:1	73
Luke 4:14	73
Luke 4:18	73
Luke 8:1	299
Luke 17:20	104
Luke 21:15	75
Mark 3:22	299
Mark 3:28-30	298
Mark 13:11	75
Matthew 3:16-17	74
Matthew 4:6	17
Matthew 10:19-20	79
Matthew 12:24	299
Matthew 12:28	73
Matthew 16:24	26
Matthew 25:34-40	148
Matthew 26:41	87
Nehemiah 9:20	258
Numbers 11:25	234
Philippians 2:12-13	288

Reference	Page
Philippians 2:13	369
Philippians 3:3	366
Philippians 3:3-4	368
Psalm 27:14	100
Psalm 27:3	101
Psalm 37:5	100
Psalm 40:1	94
Psalm 42:11	103
Psalm 51:10	188
Psalm 51:12	8
Psalm 73:23-24	14
Psalm 104	355
Psalm 119:105	14
Revelation 1:10	196
Revelation 1:9	64
Revelation 2:4-5	224
Revelation 2:17	54
Revelation 5:6	302
Revelation 13:14	66
Revelation 14:13	198
Revelation 21:10	170
Revelation 22:1	193
Revelation 22:17	67
Revelation 22:20	67
Romans 1:17	85
Romans 6:13	191
Romans 7:6	84
Romans 7:11	166
Romans 7:14, 18	86
Romans 7:15-21	87
Romans 8:2	222
Romans 8:13-14	249
Romans 8:16	342

Romans 8:23	150, 178
Romans 8:26-27	138, 142
Romans 12:1	190, 191
Romans 12:2	58
Romans 15:30	4
Zechariah 4:6	310
Zechariah 6:13	280

Printed in Great Britain
by Amazon